TRUSTS AND TAX PLANNING

TRUSTS AND TAX PLANNING

PATRICK C SOARES

LLB LLM *Solicitor*

OYEZ PUBLISHING LIMITED

Oyez Publishing Limited
Norwich House, 11/13 Norwich Street,
London EC4A 1AB

ISBN 0 85120 379 5

First published 1979

Printed in Great Britain by
Redwood Burn Limited, Trowbridge & Esher

PREFACE

Since the introduction of capital transfer tax, with effect after 26 March 1974, the taxation of trusts has become largely a question of classification. If one satisfies the requirements of a maintenance and accumulation trust, or a protective trust, or a mentally disabled person's trust, then certain capital transfer tax consequences will flow; some classification of trusts is required for income tax and capital gains tax but the main classification is required for capital transfer tax purposes.

Gone are the days when one could set up a wide discretionary trust to cater for future situations. The new trust draftsman will have to draft technical documents satisfying specific requirements set out in the legislation.

I have attempted to examine the planning opportunities for trusts from the point of view of classifying the various trusts and identifying those which are useful. The book is therefore divided into a number of chapters dealing with the different types of trust. Certain trusts, not being of very wide application, have not been dealt with in this book, although they can, in appropriate circumstances, offer useful tax advantages; the main ones are Maintenance Funds for historic houses, Newspaper Trusts and Compensation Funds. Unit Trusts and Investment Trusts are not dealt with in this book.

For each of the various types of trust examined in this book I have generally looked at their taxation position from the point of view of capital transfer tax, capital gains tax, income tax, development land tax and stamp duty. These taxes do not integrate well and the taxation of trusts is an area which is in need of comprehensive reform.

Although the setting up of discretionary trusts is probably no longer to be advised—unless the capitalization of income is important—particular types of trust can be most useful. In particular, the maintenance and accumulation trust stands out as offering extremely important tax advantages, not only of capital transfer tax but also income tax and capital gains tax.

The employees' trust is most attractive, especially as a funding process for the ultimate acquisition of company shares. The profit-sharing trust is one which all companies should consider setting up if they wish to provide genuine incentives to employees and give them shares tax free. Charitable trusts continue to be 'tax havens' within the United Kingdom. The trading trust is under-used in this country and people setting up businesses should consider setting one up even if they might ultimately decide in favour of trading in their own name or through a company; a tax adviser has not, in the author's view, completed his list of possible trading entities unless the trading trust is on the list.

A degree of uncertainty in the law has been created by the recent High Court decision of *Pearson* v *IRC* (discussed at p51 et seq), and this uncertainty is likely to continue until the case is finally decided upon by the House of Lords. The case has raised doubts as to the precise meaning of the term 'interest in possession', which is a term which is fundamental to the taxation of trusts for capital transfer tax purposes. It is still possible to set up trusts which are clearly either ones with interests in possession or ones without, but there is a middle area where the law is uncertain—where beneficiaries are entitled to income but there are powers, such as the power to accumulate, which can deprive them of it. This uncertainty can only be cleared up when *Pearson's* case is finally decided.

The position of overseas trusts is also unclear as far as income tax is concerned because of the two recent cases of *Vestey* v *IRC* (discussed at p164 et seq). Once again, the matter will only be settled when the House of Lords has decided on the case.

Finally, the Capital Gains Tax (Consolidation) Act, became law from 5 April 1979; being a consolidation measure, the law is only consolidated and not altered.

The law is otherwise stated as at 1 March 1979.

Patrick C Soares

CONTENTS

Page

TABLE OF CASES

TABLE OF STATUTES

Finance Act 1975—*continued* Page

ABBREVIATIONS

Acts of Parliament	
Taxes Act or TA	Income and Corporation Taxes Act 1970
FA	Finance Act
LPA	Law of Property Act
DLTA	Development Land Tax Act
Law Reports	
AC	Appeal Cases
All ER	All England Law Reports
Beav	Beavan's Reports, Rolls Court
Ch or Ch D	Chancery Division
Cr and Ph	Craig and Phillips's Reports, Chancery
Giff	Giffard's Reports, Vice-Chancellor's Court
My and K	Mylne and Keen's Reports, Chancery
Sel Cas t King	Select Cases, temp King
STC	Simon's Tax Cases
STI	Simon's Tax Intelligence
TC	Tax Cases
Vern	Verney's
WLR	Weekly Law Reports
WN	Weekly Notes
Journals	
LSG	Law Society Gazette
BTR	British Tax Review
CBR	Canadian Bar Review
LQR	Law Quarterly Review

'Another difference between
death and taxes is that death
is frequently painless'

Anon

CHAPTER 1

THE TRUST

What is a trust?

A *trust* is a relationship between persons and property under which property is vested in persons known as *trustees*, who hold the property for the benefit of other persons known as *beneficiaries*. A trustee may also be a beneficiary, in which case benefits from the trust property can accrue in his favour to the extent of his beneficial position under the trust. The *settlor* is the person who provides the property to be held on trust.

The interests of the beneficiaries can be laid down in the instrument creating the trust or can be implied or imposed by law.

The beneficiaries will usually be free to deal with their interests which arise under the trust; that is, they can sell them, exchange them, surrender them, mortgage them, or give them away. The trust funds themselves will be vested in the trustees and these funds are separate from the interests which arise under the trust. It is the trustees, and not the beneficiaries, who will deal with the trust funds. The trustees will have a general obligation to deal with the trust property for the benefit of the beneficiaries, and the beneficiaries have certain rights to ensure that this is done.

Thus, if 10,000 shares are held by trustees to pay the income to A for life and then to B absolutely, the trustees can deal with the shares in accordance with the terms of the trust deed. Both A and B also have separate and independent interests under the trust which they can deal with, A having a right to income and B having a right to the capital on A's death.

This distinction between the trust property and the interests under the trust can be of vital importance for tax purposes. For instance, for capital gains tax purposes the disposal of trust property will generally give rise to a charge to capital gains tax, whereas the disposal of interests under trusts are generally exempt from that tax (FA 1965, Sched 7, para 13). It was held in *Baker* v *Archer-Shee* [1927] AC 844, however, that where securities were held on trust for A for life, the securities, and not the beneficial interest under the trust instrument, were the source of A's income for income tax purposes.

Modern uses of trusts

Trusts are used today for a multitude of purposes. In *Scott on Trusts*, Vol I

(3rd edn, Little, Brown & Co, Boston 1967), at p3, A W Scott wrote:

> ... the trust is available for all kinds of purposes. A trust can be created for any purpose which is not illegal, which is not against public policy. The duties of the trustees are such as the creator of the trust may choose to impose; the interests of the beneficiaries are such as he may choose to confer upon them. The purposes for which trusts can be created are as unlimited as the imagination of lawyers.

Some of the more important of these are as follows:

(1) to enable property to be held for people who cannot hold it themselves, for example, mentally handicapped persons and minors;

(2) to enable the beneficial ownership of property to be kept private and secret, for example, nomineeship holdings;

(3) to provide scholarships by setting up educational trusts;

(4) to tie up property in succession by way of fixed trusts, for example, a trust of property for the settlor's son and then the son's children; the settlor would otherwise have to rely on his son to use the settled property for the benefit of his children;

(5) to protect the trust property from spendthrifts, for example, by setting up a protective trust;

(6) to make gifts now which can be effective to deal flexibly with future circumstances, for example, a discretionary trust;

(7) to benefit non-human objects such as a trust for the benefit of a pet;

(8) to enable land to be held by two or more persons; if this is to be done it is necessary for a trust to be created;

(9) to provide for employees and their dependants, for example, with pension schemes, profit-sharing trusts and employees' trusts;

(10) to facilitate investment through the creation of unit trusts;

(11) to carry out trading ventures through trading trusts;

(12) to benefit charitable objects; and

(13) to minimize the incidence of taxation.

Classification of trusts for tax purposes

Trusts can take many forms and there are numerous methods of classifying them (see, for example, G W Keeton and L A Sheridan, *Law of Trusts*, 10th edn, Chapter III). None of the usual classifications have any particular significance for tax purposes. The most helpful classification of trusts, in the author's view, for tax purposes, is between trusts where property is held beneficially in succession and those where the property is not so held.

Trusts where Property is Held in Succession

The most important of these are set out below. They are all trusts in which the beneficial interest is held upon some sort of contingency or in succession.

The term 'settlement', generally speaking, can be said to connote a trust where the beneficial interest is held in succession. Not all trusts involve the beneficial interest being held in succession. Thus it can be said that all settlements, as the author generally understands the term, are trusts but that not all trusts are settlements.

Unless a Settled Land Act settlement is involved, trustees will usually hold trust land upon trust for sale (LPA 1925, s205(1)(xxix)). In the case of chattels, the trust instrument will usually give the trustees the power to sell them and reinvest; in the absence of such power the trustees cannot generally sell the chattels.

Fixed Trusts—These trusts will normally involve an express declaration that the property is held by the trustees upon trust for sale for the benefit of persons who are entitled to a determined share of the trust property. For example, if the trust fund is held to pay the income to A for life and then to B absolutely when he shall attain the age of twenty-one years, this is a fixed trust. A will normally have what is known as an interest in possession and B will have a reversionary interest.

Discretionary Trusts—Under these trusts the trustees holding the property upon trust for sale will usually have a discretion as to which of the beneficiaries will receive any benefit from the income or capital of the fund and the extent of their benefit. The beneficiaries are said to have a mere 'spes' or hope of receiving a benefit under the trust. These trusts were very popular under the Estate Duty regime but now suffer certain disadvantages under Capital Transfer Tax.

Settled Land Act Settlements—These are trusts where a series of interests are created in land and the land is not held upon trust for sale (Settled Land Act 1925, s1(7), added by the Law of Property (Amendment) Act 1926). For example, if land is conveyed to A for life and then to B this will be a Settled Land Act settlement. However, if it is conveyed to A upon trust to sell the land and hold the proceeds upon trust for A for life, and then to B absolutely, this will not be a Settled Land Act settlement.

There are elaborate rules governing these trusts set out in the Settled Land Act 1925. One of the chief effects of creating a Settled Land Act settlement is that the legal estate is vested not in the trustees of the settlement (whose main function is to receive and hold capital money when, for example, land is sold) but in the person who for the time being is beneficially entitled in possession to the settled property. This will usually be the tenant for life who thus has a dual capacity; he is the legal owner and he has a beneficial ownership, and as far as his legal ownership is concerned he is a trustee of the land for all the persons interested under the settlement. He, and not the trustees of the settlement, will be the person who conveys the land to a purchaser. It would be a fatal flaw in the purchaser's title if he took a conveyance from the trustees purporting to sell as trustees for sale if it turns out to be settled land, so that the only person competent to dispose of the land is the tenant for life. Because of the elaborate rules governing these settlements it is very uncommon for such settlements to be set up nowadays except perhaps inadvertently.

Trusts where Property is not Held in Succession

The most important of these are set out below. They are trusts in which all the beneficial interests are held for all the beneficiaries for the time being immediately, without involving any element of succession (except, perhaps, it might be argued that one joint tenant has the hope of succeeding to the other joint tenant's interest if the other dies first). The references to tenants (ie, tenants in common and joint tenants) mean simply forms of ownership, and have nothing to do with leases.

Tenants in Common—Section 34 of the LPA 1925 provides that whenever land is conveyed to persons in undivided shares it will vest in the first four named persons on a statutory trust for sale for all the transferees as beneficial tenants in common. This is the usual way of holding property by two or more persons in commercial deals. Each has a separate interest. When a tenant in common dies his interest passes under his will or intestacy and not to the other tenants in common.

Joint Tenants—Under the LPA 1925, s36, where land is conveyed to joint tenants, it vests in the first four named transferees on trust for sale for all the transferees beneficially as joint tenants. On the death of a joint tenant his interest automatically accrues to the other joint tenant or joint tenants, even if he leaves his interest elsewhere under his will. A joint tenant can, however, convert during his lifetime a joint tenancy into a tenancy in common. This is known as severing the beneficial joint tenancy. Joint tenancy is the usual way of holding land by a husband and wife.

Implied and Resulting Trusts—These are trusts which arise from the presumed intention of the owner of the property. For example, where an individual buys assets in the name of his wife, the presumption is that he intends to transfer the assets to her (*Silver* v *Silver* [1958] 1 WLR 259; *Kingdon* v *Bridges* (1688), 2 Vern 67; *Smith* v *Smith* [1945] 1 All ER 584). If he buys them in the name of a stranger, the stranger is presumed to hold them on trust for him. The beneficial interest in the latter case comes back to him, or 'results back' to him, and this is said to be a resulting trust, which is a type of implied trust.

Constructive Trusts—These are trusts imposed by the Courts of Equity regardless of the intention of the parties. They normally arise where there has been a breach of confidence, for example, where a trustee obtains a renewal in his own name of a lease held by him as a trustee (see *Keech* v *Sandford* (1726) Sel Cas t King 61 and *Re Knowles' Will Trusts* [1948] 1 All ER 866).

Nomineeship—Where property is held by a trustee absolutely for the benefit of the beneficiary then this is a bare trusteeship situation and the trustee is ignored for all tax purposes. This is often used for shareholdings if the true beneficial owner does not wish to reveal his identity; certain provisions of the company law legislation may force the nominee, however, to reveal the identity of the beneficial owner (see Chapter 7).

Importance of the classification

The importance of the classification of trusts set out above is as follows:

(1) Where property is held in trust beneficially in succession, it can amount to a settlement for the purposes of capital transfer tax (FA 1975, Sched 5, para 1); capital gains tax (FA 1965, s45(1); *Kidson* v *MacDonald and Another* (1973) 49 TC 503; *Stephenson* v *Barclays Bank Trust Co Ltd* [1975] 1 WLR 882 and *Booth* v *Ellard* [1978] STC rep 487, income tax (TA 1970, ss444(2) and 454(3)); and development land tax (DLTA 1976, s30).

(2) Where property is not held in succession it cannot usually amount to a settlement for the purposes of any tax, except for certain income tax purposes where the definition of settlement is exceedingly wide and can even in some cases include an asset not held upon any trusts (see TA 1970, Pt XVI).

Although the classification is generally of importance to the taxation of trusts, this book is concerned primarily with trusts where property is held beneficially in succession, especially discretionary trusts and fixed trusts. It is also only a very broad classification which permits of exceptions, because of the wide variety of trusts which can be created. The only safe way, therefore, is to look at the different definitions of settlement for each of the taxes, to ascertain whether the particular trust which has been created falls within the appropriate definition. The problem is that the term is not defined for all the different taxes, and where it is defined this differs from tax to tax. This is dealt with in the next chapter.

How long can a trust last?

The trust fund must vest in a beneficiary or beneficiaries within the perpetuity period or the trust could be void.

Property is vested in a beneficiary if the beneficiary is alive, the size of his gift is ascertained, and the conditions attached to the gift are satisfied. The simplest case of property vesting is where a beneficiary becomes absolutely entitled to the property.

The perpetuity period can be:

(1) the period of lives or a life in being plus twenty-one years, for example, A for life then B for life (both being alive at the time of the settlement), plus twenty-one years; or

(2) if there is no life in being, a period of twenty-one years; or

(3) in the case of post-1964 gifts, a period, not exceeding eighty years, which is specified in the instrument creating the gift as the perpetuity period (Perpetuities and Accumulations Act 1964, s1).

The period in (3) could be shorter than the period in (1), but (3) has the advantage of simplicity and certainty—the eighty year period, expressly stated in the trust deed, is one of the most popular periods. It is common in (1) to have a 'royal lives clause', that is, a clause which selects the lives of the descendants, for example, of His late Majesty King George V in being at the date of the gift.

Section 3(1) of the Perpetuities and Accumulations Act 1964 introduced the 'wait and see' rule. This rule provides that a trust shall be treated as valid until such time that it is clear that the interest cannot vest in the perpetuity period; the mere possibility, in itself, that the interest might vest outside the perpetuity period will not cause the disposition to be invalid.

Certain trusts are exempt from the perpetuity period and the most important of these is the charitable trust, which can, in theory, last for ever.

How long can the income of a trust be accumulated?

Trusts can accumulate income for the accumulation period applicable to the particular trust. The following are the accumulation periods specified under the LPA 1925, s164(1):

(*a*) the life of the settlor (this period is adopted in lifetime settlements where no other period is specified);

(*b*) twenty-one years from the death of the testator or settlor (this period is adopted in the case of gifts by will where no other period is specified);

(*c*) the duration of the minority or minorities of any persons living at the death of the testator or settlor (this period begins from the death of the settlor or testator); and

(*d*) the duration of the minority or minorities of any persons entitled under the settlement (this period clearly contemplates the minorities of persons who are not necessarily in existence at the settlor's death).

Section 13 of the Perpetuities and Accumulations Act 1964 added, in respect of instruments coming into operation after 15 July 1964, the following periods:

(*e*) twenty-one years from the date of making the disposition; and

(*f*) the duration of the minority or minorities of any persons in being at the date of the making of a lifetime transfer.

A popular period in modern trust deeds is a period of twenty-one years from when the trust was set up. However, since the abolition of the Estate

Duty penalties suffered by trusts which used the lifetime of the settlor as the accumulation period (FA 1894, s2(1)(*b*)(iv), as substituted by FA 1969, s36), settlors should consider using their own lives as the accumulation periods.

The accumulation period which has been adopted in a particular trust is a question of interpretation of the document (*Jagger* v *Jagger* [1883], 25 Ch D 729).

There are no statutory restrictions on the accumulation of income in the following cases:

(1) for payment of the debts of any grantor, settlor, testator or other person;

(2) for raising portions for—

(i) any child, children or remoter issue of any grantor, settlor or testator; or

(ii) any child, children or remoter issue of a person taking any interest under any settlement or other disposition directing the accumulations or to whom any interest is thereby limited;

(3) respecting the accumulation of the produce of timber or wood (LPA 1925, s164(2)).

The special rules that apply to minors

If minors are beneficiaries under the trust special rules will apply.

The Trustee Act 1925, s31

Where a beneficiary under a trust is a minor, then, whether his interest is vested or contingent, the trustees may, in their absolute discretion, pay or apply any part of the income towards his maintenance education or benefit as may, in all the circumstances, be reasonable (Trustee Act 1925, s31(1)(i)). This power is exercisable even if there is a fund applicable for the same purpose, or there is a person bound by law to provide for the minor's maintenance or education. In exercising the power the trustees must have regard to the age of the minor, his requirements, the circumstances of the case and in particular to what other income is available for the same purpose (proviso to Trustee Act 1925, s31(1).

Where the minor has a contingent interest the trustees can only exercise the power of maintenance if the gift or trust 'carries the intermediate income', ie, broadly, where the income from the fund goes along with the capital which is held contingently for the beneficiary and does not go elsewhere to other beneficiaries. A vested interest always carries the intermediate income. A contingent interest arising from a settlement carries the intermediate income, provided the contingency is attaining the age of majority or the happening of some event before that age is attained. In general, and subject to important exceptions, a pecuniary legacy will not carry the intermediate income and nor will deferred gifts of residue.

The above rules are subject to any express directions of the settlor or testator. Thus, if the trust instrument directs that the income shall be accumulated, that direction will prevent the income from being used for maintenance (*Re Turner's Will Trusts* [1937] Ch 15; *Re Ransome* [1957] Ch 348; *Re Reade-Revell* [1930] 1 Ch 52).

The section is usually widened in modern trust deeds in two respects: the words 'may in all the circumstances, be reasonable' are deleted in s31(1)(i) and replaced by 'the trustees may in their absolute discretion think fit', and the proviso to 31(1) is usually omitted.

The Trustee Act 1925, s32

The trustee may apply capital for the advancement or benefit of any person entitled to the whole or part of such capital of the trust fund, whether his interest is vested or contingent and whether or not his interest can be defeated by the exercise of a power of appointment, or diminished by an increase in the class of which he is a member, provided that—

(*a*) the amount advanced must not exceed one-half of the vested or presumptive share of that beneficiary;

(*b*) the holder of a prior interest must be alive, be of full age and must consent in writing to such advance; and

(*c*) the amount advanced must be brought into account on the beneficiary becoming absolutely entitled (if the beneficiary dies before becoming absolutely entitled there is no liability to account).

The provision is not confined to minor beneficiaries although it will often be used where there are minors.

The section only applies where the trust property consists of money, securities and property held on trust for sale. It does not apply to capital money under the Settled Land Act 1925 nor to property which is, by statute or in equity, considered to be land (Trustee Act 1925, s32(2)). The section may be excluded or widened by the settlor or testator. It is often widened to enable the whole of the presumptive or vested share or interest of a person to be advanced to him.

Valid Receipts

Unless a minor is married the trustees will not be able to obtain a valid receipt for any part of the trust funds transferred to him, be it income, accumulated income or capital.

However, the Trustee Act 1925, s31 provides that if the gift to the minor carries the intermediate income the trustees are able to apply the income for his maintenance, education and benefit. This is a further reason why it is vital to ascertain whether a gift carries the intermediate income.

Section 21 of the LPA 1925 provides that where the beneficiary is a married minor, a valid receipt can be given by him or her for income and accumulated income but not capital.

Application to Court

In some cases where the powers of maintenance and advancement are not sufficient for the beneficiary's needs, an application to court can be made to have the trusts varied under the Variation of Trusts Act 1958, or under the Trustee Act 1925, s23 (vesting order in relation to infant's beneficial interests), or in reliance on the court's inherent jurisdiction to deal with such matters.

Formalities

In general there are no particular formalities which must be gone through in order to create a trust. There are however specific statutory requirements.

Law of Property Act 1925, s53(1)(b)

By the Law of Property Act 1925, s53(1)(*b*) 'a declaration of trust respecting any land or any interest therein must be manifested and proved by some writing signed by some person who is able to declare such trust or by his will'. This provision only deals with the creation of express trusts of land; it does not affect trusts of personalty, such as shares, which may still be declared orally (*Benbow* v *Townsend* (1833) 1 MY and K 506).

The section does not affect the creation or operation of resulting, implied or constructive trusts (LPA 1925, s53(2)). It is not essential that the trust is declared in writing; it is only necessary that it is proved to have been made by some writing signed by the person who declared the trust.

LPA 1925, s53(1)(c)

By the LPA 1925, s53(1)(*c*) 'a disposition of an equitable interest or trust subsisting at the time of the disposition, must be in writing signed by the person disposing of the same, or by his agent thereunto lawfully authorised in writing or by will.'

Under this provision the disposition must actually be in writing, and merely to evidence it in writing is not sufficient. The provision is wider in scope than s53(1)(*b*), as it applies to all property and not just land.

The ability to assign an interest under a trust has important tax planning consequences and the requirements of this provision must be borne in mind.

The duties of a trustee

The main duties are as follows:

(1) The trustee must act in accordance with the terms of the trust deed with which he should be fully acquainted. If he is taking over from retiring trustees he should check to make sure there have been no breaches of trust. He should have the trust property vested in his name and the names of the other trustees.

(2) In dealing with trust investments the trustee is bound to use such due diligence and care as an ordinary man of business would use in the management of his affairs (*Re Whiteley* [1886] 33 Ch D 347, at p355, per Lindley LJ).

(3) The trustee should keep accurate records of the trust capital and income.

(4) The trustee should actively consider any discretions which have been given to him by the settlor.

(5) Finally, the trustee should not put himself into a position where there is a conflict between his personal interests and the interests of the trust.

The three certainties

When drafting trust documents the three certainties must be satisfied. These are:

(1) The words used to create the trust should make it clear that it is an imperative trust and not just a request or desire expressed by the settlor for the trustee to act in a particular way.

(2) The trust fund should be clearly set out.

(3) The objects or persons intended to benefit under the trust must be certain.

These three certainties were laid down by Lord Langdale MR in *Knight* v *Knight* (1840) 3 Beav 148, at p173.

A flexible tax planning instrument

It is often said that the trust is a flexible instrument of tax planning and this is generally correct, especially with regard to dealings with the interests under the trust. However, there are important limitations on this flexibility, and these should now be examined.

(1) There are certain areas where the rules are inflexible. These include the requirement for the trust fund to actually vest within the perpetuity period, the accumulation period requirements, the satisfaction of the three certainties, and the requirement that all beneficiaries be sui juris before the rule in *Saunders* v *Vautier* (1841) Cr and Ph 240 can apply. The duties of a trustee are strict and they must act with care and diligence in order to escape personal liability for any loss caused to the trust estate. If a mistake is made in drafting

the document, such as the insertion of 'and' instead of 'or', it can be almost impossible to get the document rectified even if application is made to court.

(2) If particular powers are not included in the trust document (unless implied by general trust law), the trustees cannot exercise any such powers unless an application is made to court.

Also, if there are powers given to the trustees as such (and there is no additional power to release them) the trustees must take due note of them unless they go to court (*Re Wills' Trust Deeds* [1964] Ch 219).

(3) Devious methods cannot be employed to circumvent trust rules, because equity looks to the substance and not the form.

> Courts of Equity make a distinction in all cases between that which is matter of substance and that which is a matter of form; and if it finds that by insisting on the form the substance will be defeated it holds it to be inequitable to allow a person to insist on such form, and thereby defeat the substance (*Parkin* v *Thorold* (1852) 16 Beav 59, at p66, per Romilly MR).

The very flexibility of the trust may therefore be a cause of its rigidity. This is unlike tax legislation where the form still takes precedence, in general, over the substance of transactions.

> If the person sought to be taxed comes within the letter of the law he must be taxed, however great the hardship may appear to the judicial mind to be. On the other hand, if the Crown, seeking to recover the tax, cannot bring the subject within the letter of the law, the subject is free, however apparently within the spirit of the law the case might otherwise appear to be. In other words, if there be admissable, in any statute, what is called an equitable construction certainly such a construction is not admissable in a taxing statute, where you can simply adhere to the words of the statute (*Partington* v *A-G* (1869) LRHL 100, at p122, per Lord Cairns).

CHAPTER 2

AN OUTLINE OF HOW TRUSTS ARE TAXED

This chapter deals, in outline, with the provisions which tax trusts in the United Kingdom.

Trusts are subject to stamp duty, income tax, capital gains tax, capital transfer tax and development land tax. The rates of these taxes, as they apply to trusts, are set out in Appendix 1. Estate duty, development gains tax, and the first letting charge under the Finance Act 1974 have been abolished but they can still be exigible, in certain circumstances, under various transitional provisions. If a trust carries on a business, it can also be chargeable to value added tax in the same way as any other trader.

Trustees, for Revenue purposes, are generally regarded as a separate, single and continuing body of persons. Because they are 'separate', transactions between the settlor and the trustees, or the trustees and the beneficiary, can have tax consequences. Because they are looked upon as being a 'single' body, they are taxed as one taxable entity regardless of the number of trustees, while a 'continuing' body of persons means that the death or retirement of a trustee has little or no tax consequences.

Subject to these general rules, each of the taxes mentioned above seeks to tax trusts under its own separate rules and provisions, with very little attempt being made to co-ordinate these provisions.

Stamp duty

Setting up Trusts

When property is settled inter vivos it attracts ad valorem duty as a voluntary disposition (Finance (1909–10) Act 1910, s74(1)). The document declaring the trust will, in this event, only be liable to a 50*p* duty (Stamp Act 1891, Sched 1).

It is not possible to mitigate the duty by selling the property to the trust at a nominal consideration, or for a substantial but clearly inadequate consideration, because the Finance (1909–10) Act 1910, s74(5) provides that where, in the opinion of the Commissioners, the consideration for sale is less than the value of the property transferred, so that the purchaser derives a benefit, there is a liability to ad valorem stamp duty in respect of the gift element. There would thus be a full liability to duty—as to part being a conveyance on sale and as to the other part being a voluntary disposition.

Whether there is any scope for the mitigation of this duty will depend on the type of property being settled. If it is proposed to settle shares this could be effected perhaps by using a share reconstruction scheme coupled with a bonus issue. If cash or bearer securities are to be settled, then, if they are settled orally, there will be no stamp duty. If the trusts in connection with the cash and bearer securities are declared prior to the transfer there will be a 50*p* declaration of trust duty payable. If, however, the trusts are declared after the property is vested in the trustees then there could be a charge to ad valorem duty, as there is a transfer of the beneficial interest (*Grey* v *IRC* [1960] AC 1). Clearly the delaration of trust relating to the cash and bearer securities should be made prior to the transfer itself.

Vesting Property in a Beneficiary

When trustees vest property in a beneficiary no stamp duty is payable (Finance 1909–10) Act 1910, s74(6)), except perhaps a 50*p* charge under the miscellaneous conveyance or transfer provisions (Stamp Act 1891, Sched 1). Thus, if the trustees vest property in a discretionary beneficiary or a life tenant or advance property to a remainderman under the terms of the trust there will only be a 50*p* duty payable on that document of transfer.

Dealings by Beneficiaries

Dealings by beneficiaries with their interests under the trust, such as a life interest or a reversionary interest, are subject to ad valorem stamp duty. These dealings by the beneficiaries are separate from transfers of property by the trustees to the beneficiaries. In the latter case there will be no ad valorem duty.

Transfers by beneficiaries of their interests could be liable as voluntary dispositions (*Platt Trustees* v *IRC* [1953] 34 ATC 292—a case involving a release by a life tenant of his interest under the trust in order to accelerate the remainder; such a transfer was chargeable to ad valorem duty), or they could be chargeable, if sold, as a conveyance or transfer on sale (Stamp Act 1891, Sched 1) (*Oughtred* v *IRC* [1960] AC 206, which involved the release of a reversionary interest under a trust).

Example—S executes a settlement and subsequently settles £100,000 worth of shares upon T, the trustee, to hold the same for A for life and then to B absolutely. A subsequently sells his life interest to B thereupon making B the absolute owner of the trust fund. T transfers the shares to B. Ad valorem duty of 2 per cent would be payable on the £100,000 worth of shares settled by S (Finance (1909–10) Act 1910, s74(1)). There would be a further charge to ad valorem duty on the value of the life interest which A sells to B (Stamp Act 1891, Sched 1—conveyance or transfer on sale duty). As B is the total beneficial owner, the transfer of the shares into his name will not result in any beneficial interest passing. That transaction, therefore, is exempt from ad valorem duty under the Finance (1909–10) Act 1910, s74(6), but there could be a 50*p* fixed duty under the Stamp Act 1891, Sched 1, as a miscellaneous conveyance or transfer or possibly as an appointment of a new trustee. The settlement deed will bear stamp duty of 50*p* (Stamp Act 1891, Sched 1).

Change of Trustees

The appointment of a new trustee by any instrument not being a will is liable to 50*p* duty (Stamp Act 1891, Sched 1—appointment of new trustee provision). This provision does not apply to the appointment of the original trustees but only to new trustees (*Re Potter* 1889, [WN] 69).

When the trust property is vested in the new trustees the stamp duty will then be 50*p* on the instrument, being a miscellaneous conveyance or transfer within the Stamp Act 1891, Sched 1. The 50*p* duty is also payable on any conveyance or transfer for effectuating the reirement of a trustee, although no new trustee is appointed (Finance Act 1902, s9).

Any conveyance or transfer of properties to the new trustees or from a retiring trustee is not treated as a voluntary disposition for the purposes of charging ad valorem duty (Finance (1909–10) Act 1910, s74(6)).

Even if a single deed is used to deal with the retirement of a trustee and the appointement of a replacement, the 50*p* duty will be payable twice.

Relief for Charities

The general doubling of stamp duties in the FA 1974 was expressly made not to apply to a body of persons established for charitable purposes only or to the trustees of a trust so established. Thus, in the case of a conveyance or transfer made to such a body or trust, the duty is 1 per cent (FA 1974, s49(2)).

Husband and Wife

There are no particular reliefs or exemptions from stamp duty for dealings between husband and wife.

Certificates of Value

Conveyances or transfers on sale or by way of gift of property, other than transfers of stock, marketable securities or unit trusts, or a lease where the rent exceeds £150 per annum, where the amount or value of the consideration or the value of the property transferred does not exceed the amount shown below, and the instrument is so certified, will be entitled to the reduced rates of stamp duty as follows:

not exceeding £15,000	—Nil
not exceeding £20,000	—½%
not exceeding £25,000	—1%
not exceeding £30,000	—1½%
in all other cases	—2%

(FA 1963, s55; FA 1972, s125(2); FA 1974, Sched 11, para 4.) Thus, in appropriate circumstances, transfers to trustees and transfers of trust interests by beneficiaries can have a nil charge to stamp duty or be subject to the above reduced rates.

The certification procedure applies to charities. The effect is that the duty on a transfer to a charity need never exceed 1 per cent, but the charge may be eliminated or reduced if the instrument is certified at £15,000 or £20,000 or charged at the same rate (ie, 1 per cent) without the need for adjudication in the case of an instrument certified at £25,000.

Adjudication

Adjudication is the process whereby the Revenue ascertain whether duty is chargeable on a particular instrument and the amount of that duty (Stamp Act 1891, s12).

Any voluntary conveyance or transfer inter vivos shall not be deemed to be duly stamped unless it has been adjudicated (Finance (1909–10) Act 1910, s74(2)). Thus, a gift in settlement or gifts of interests under trusts should be adjudicated.

It is also necessary for charities, if they are to obtain the 1 per cent reduction in ad valorem duty on conveyances and transfers, to have the instrument adjudicated (FA 1974, s49(2) proviso).

Rate of Duty

Subject to the above mentioned reliefs and exemptions and a sliding scale of duty where the consideration is less than £300 (FA 1974, Sched 11, para 3), the rate of stamp duty on voluntary dispositions and conveyances or transfers on sale is 2 per cent of the value of the property disposed of, or the amount or value of the consideration, as the case may be.

Income Tax

The detailed rules governing the imposition of income tax upon trustees and beneficiaries have, in general, been developed by the courts over the years. For this reason this area of the law has been referred to as a 'common law' area of taxation.

'Trust' or 'settlement', for the purposes of income tax, can include many types of trust and is not limited to those trusts where property is held beneficially in succession. In some cases wholly non-trust situations can amount to 'settlements' for income tax purposes. This is so for the purposes of the TA 1970, s444, for example, where 'settlement' is defined to include a transfer of assets to a person.

How the Trustees are Taxed

The trust income is liable to tax at the basic rate by direct assessment upon the trustees, unless it has already suffered basic rate tax by deduction at source. Thus, dividends will have suffered deduction at source while bank interest will suffer tax by direct assessment upon the trustees.

Trust income is assessable under the appropriate schedule. Thus, if the trustees carry on a trade they will be assessable under Case 1 of Schedule D and if they receive rents they will be assessed under Schedule A. They will be entitled to deduct from their taxable receipts all deductions appropriate to the schedule in question.

The personal circumstances of the trustees are not relevant to the treatment of the trust income. They are 'persons' and not 'individuals', so that their personal income tax reliefs are not available for offset against trust income.

No deduction is permitted against the charge to basic rate tax for the trustees' expenses of managing the trust (*Aikein* v *MacDonald's Trustees* (1894) 3 TC 306).

Trustees are not liable to the higher rates of tax although they can be liable to the additional rate of tax which is currently 15 per cent. The additional rate only applies to income arising to trustees in any year of assessment so far as it—

(1) is income which is to be accumulated or which is payble at the discretion of the trustees or any other person (whether or not the trustees have power to accumulate it); and

(2) is neither (before being distributed) the income of any person other than the trustees nor treated for any of the purposes of the Income Tax Acts as the income of a settlor; and

(3) is not income arising under a trust established for charitable purposes only, or income from investments, deposits or other property held for the purpose of a fund or scheme established for the sole purpose of providing relevant benefits within the meaning of the FA 1970, s26; and

(4) exceeds the income applied in defraying the expenses of the trustees in that year which are properly chargeable to income (or would be so chargeable but for any express provisions of the trust) (FA 1973, s16(2)).

Prior to the High Court decision of *Pearson* v *IRC* (see p51 below) it was felt that interest in possession trusts would not suffer the 15 per cent charge, because there would be no power to accumulate and there would be beneficiaries entitled to the income as it arose. Assuming the High Court decision is not upset on appeal, if there are persons entitled to the trust income, even though there is a power to accumulate, those persons will have interests in possession. The reference in s16(2)(*a*) to 'income which is to be accumulated' is a reference to trusts where there is an obligation to accumulate, or where there is no obligation to accumulate but as a matter of fact it is to be accumulated as the trustees have so decided. In this latter case if the income is not accumulated it may not be subject to the 15 per cent charge; if the trustees do decide to accumulate, however, it will be so chargeable. The fact that the trustees had the power to accumulate the income but did not exercise it, may not mean that the income 'is payable at the discretion of the trustees'; the beneficiaries are entitled to that income and the trustees have no discretion over it if they do not exercise their power to accumulate. Against this, it could be argued that the power to accumulate means that the income is payable to the beneficiaries at the discretion of the trustees, since they might decide to exercise that power, even though as a matter of fact, they do not exercise it. The position is not clear but the author feels that the latter interpretation is probably the correct one so that the 15 per cent charge would be payable by such a trust whether the income is accumulated or paid out.

Where, in any year of assessment, trustees make a payment, in the exercise of a discretion exercisable by themselves or by other persons, to a beneficiary, the payment is treated as a net amount from which tax at the basic and additional rates has been deducted at the rates in force for that year of assessment, ie, the year of assessment in which the payment is made. The trustees are assessable at these rates but may set off any tax already paid (FA 1973, s17(2)). This means that there is no further assessment if the rates have not been increased between the year of receipt and the year of payment.

Income which trustees had received but not distributed on or before 5 April 1973 is assessable in the same way if subsequently distributed as income. They can set off against the assessment in this case, however, an amount of tax, in respect of income available to them for distribution at the end of the year 1972/73, which shall be taken to be two thirds of the net amount of that income (FA 1973, s17(3)(*d*)). Such income is thus treated as having suffered a rate of tax of about 40 per cent.

How the Beneficiaries are Taxed

If the beneficiary is entitled to the trust income it will form part of his total income for tax purposes whether he receives it or not (*Baker* v *Archer-Shee* [1927] AC 844 and *Stern* v *IRC* (1930) 15 TC 160). If there is a discretionary trust and income is paid to a beneficiary the payments will form part of the beneficiary's total income (*Drummond* v *Collins* [1915] AC 1011).

Income which a beneficiary is not entitled to call for, and which is validly accumulated by the trustees, will suffer tax at the basic rate and at the additional rate in the hands of the trustees (FA 1973, s16). If the income is paid out to a beneficiary as income he can claim back the tax imposed upon the trustees if his tax rate is less than that suffered by the trustees. If his tax rate is higher the trustees should try to capitalize the income and pay it out to the beneficiary free of any further income tax. This power to convert trust income into capital is dealt with more fully in Chapter 3.

How the Settlor is Taxed

Generally, once the settlor has put property into a trust, he will have alienated the income for tax purposes for the period that it is held in trust. There are, however, a number of provisions contained in Part XVI of the TA 1970 (ss434–458) which seek to tax the income arising from trust property upon the settlor, even though he might have attempted to alienate that income for tax purposes.

The aim behind the sections is to prevent a settlor alienating income to trustees, and therefore perhaps paying a lower rate of income tax than he would otherwise pay, when at the end of the day he might be able to get that accumulated income back. The effect of the provisions is to deem the income to be that of the settlor, usually for the purposes of income tax and the higher rates of tax, but sometimes only for the higher rates of tax. These provisions do not take the income away from the beneficiary, they merely alter the amount of tax payable on that income.

These provisions only apply to 'settlements', but the term has a wide meaning. It includes 'any disposition, trust, covenant, agreement or arrangement' (ss454(3) and 459(1)). In the case of settlements by virtue of which income is paid to or for the benefit of an infant unmarried child of the settlor, the definition is extended to include 'transfers of assets' (s444(2)). It is therefore virtually impossible to prevent the creation of a settlement, although a bona fide commercial transaction will not be a settlement for these purposes (*Bulmer* v *IRC* [1967] Ch 145, and *IRC* v *Plummer* [1978] STC p517).

This chapter deals only with the provisions contained in Part XVI which relate to the creation of settlements by transferring capital sums to trustees (mainly ss437 to 459), and not with the provisions which relate exclusively to covenants to pay income or 'income settlements', as they are often called. The main sections which relate to 'income settlements' (ss434 to 436) are set out in Appendix IV, pp193 to 195.

The settlor must, when creating a settlement, make certain that he does not come within any of these provisions to be discussed; it is not sufficient that he avoids one or two of the provisions—he must avoid all of them. There is no substitute, in the author's view, when drafting a settlement, for going through the provisions one by one to make certain that the settlement is not caught by one or more of them.

References to the settlor's wife in these provisions include any wife whom he may marry but do not include his widow (*Vestey's Executors* v *IRC* (1949) 31 TC 1).

The general rule with regard to these provisions might be said to be that the settlor will not avoid tax on the income which arises from the capital which he has settled, unless he and his wife are excluded from all possible benefit. In addition, the settlor's infant unmarried children must not receive any benefit from the settlement.

Infant Unmarried Children of Settlor—Section 437 provides that where there is a settlement, and during the life of the settlor any income is paid to or for the benefit of a child of the settlor in any year of assessment, the income shall, if at the time of payment the child is unmarried and below the age of eighteen, be treated as the settlor's income and not the income of any other person.

A settlement for this provision would include a transfer of assets to an infant child absolutely so that any income which arises from that property transferred will be treated as the settlor's (*Thomas* v *Marshall* [1953] AC 543). The income becomes the highest part of the settlor's income (s441(3)), although the settlor has a right to recover the tax from the trust (s441(1) as amended by FA 1971, Sched 6, para 61 and Sched 14, Pt II).

In *d'Abreu* (*Arthur*) v *IRC* [1978] STC p538 it was held that where a parent released and assigned a right to income, which she had under a trust, for the benefit of her children, there was a sufficient disposition to come within the TA 1970, s437.

If that income is lawfully accumulated in an irrevocable settlement it cannot be taxed on the settlor. However, if there is then an advancement to the unnamed minor out of capital, that capital is treated as income paid to the child to the extent of the accumulated income.

For these purposes a settlement shall not be deemed to be irrevocable if its terms provide, under the TA 1970, s439(1):

> (*a*) for the payment to the settlor or, during the life of the settlor, to the wife or husband of the settlor for his or her benefit, or for the application for the benefit of the settlor or, during the life of the settlor, of the wife or husband of the settlor, of any income or assets in any circumstances whatsoever during the life of any child of the settlor to or for the benefit of whom any income, or assets representing it, is or are or may be payable or applicable by virtue or in consequence of the settlement; or
>
> (*b*) for the determination of the settlement by the act or on the default of any person; or
>
> (*c*) for the payment of any penalty by the settlor in the event of his failing to comply with the provisions of the settlement:
>
> Provided that a settlement shall not be deemed to be revocable by reason only—
>
> (i) that it contains a provision under which any income or assets will or may become payable to or applicable for the benefit of the settlor, or the wife or husband of the settlor, on the bankruptcy of any such child as is mentioned in paragraph (*a*) of this subsection or in the event of an assignment of or charge on that income or those assets being executed by such child; or
>
> (ii) that it provides for the determination of the settlement as aforesaid in such

a manner that the determination will not, during the lifetime of any such child as aforesaid, benefit the settlor or the wife or husband of the settlor; or

(iii) in the case of a settlement to which s33 of the Trustee Act 1925 applies, that it directs income to be held for the benefit of such a child as aforesaid on protective trusts, unless the trust period is a period less than the life of the child or the settlement specifies some event on the happening of which the child would, if the income were payable during the trust period to him absolutely during that period, be deprived of the right to receive the income or part thereof.

As well as the statutory requirements the settlement must be irrevocable within the ordinary meaning of the word (*IRC* v *Delamere* [1939] 2 KB 667). If a settlement is not stated to be irrevocable, this is implied (*Boughton v Boughton* (1739) 1 ATK 625).

When examining the settlement to ascertain whether it is irrevocable one must look only to the trust deed and not to other factors such as the ability of the settlor to wind up a company, the shares of which are the only asset of the trust (*Jenkins* v *IRC* (1944) 26 TC 265, overruled on another point by *IRC* v *Jamieson* [1964] AC 1445; [1962] 41 TC 46).

If one can satisfy the conditions for effectively alienating income in a settlement for one's children, ie, making certain that no income, or capital which could represent that income, is paid to an unmarried infant child of the settlor, and making certain that the trust is irrevocable under the general meaning of the word and as set down by statute, the benefits can be considerable. The income can be accumulated, paying tax at only 48 per cent, and can ultimately be transferred out to the child, when he actually marries or attains the age of eighteen, free of income tax.

Also, if a grandparent were to set up such an accumulation trust for the benefit of grandchildren, then income can be paid out to a grandchild when a minor and unmarried, without the income being aggregated with the income of the grandparent or the parents of the beneficiary. The child allowance of the parent may be affected by such payment (see TA 1970, s10).

Despite a mention of this in Parliament, there are no general provisions which provide for the aggregation of investment income of an unmarried minor with that of his parents. Only in one circumstance can this aggregation take place: where the parent sets up a settlement for the benefit of that child and the income arises from that settlement and is paid to the child.

Revocable Settlements—Section 446 of the TA 1970 applies where any person has power to revoke or otherwise determine a settlement or any provision thereof, and the settlor or his spouse may become beneficially entitled to all or any part of the settled property or income thereof as the result of such revocation or determination. A settlement for these purposes does not include a transfer of assets. If caught by s446 the income of the settlement will be treated as the income of the settlor for all purposes.

In *Kenmare* v *IRC* [1958] AC 267 it was held that a power of appointment over the entire trust fund was a power to revoke or otherwise detemine the settlement. As these powers could be exercised in favour of the settlor and his wife the whole of the fund was taxable upon the settlor.

Any tax charged under s446 is assessed under Case VI of Schedule D, and the settlor is entitled to any deduction or relief against it as if it has been received by him as income (TA 1970, s449(1) and (2), as amended by FA 1971, Sched 6, para 63 and Sched 14, Pt II). The settlor is able to recover the tax paid by him from any trustee or person to whom the income arises under the settlement, subject to crediting any allowance or relief so obtained by the settlor. Where any power to revoke or determine cannot be exercised within six years from the time when any particular property first becomes comprised in the settlement, the subsection does not apply to income arising under the settlement from that property, or from property representing that property, so long as the power cannot be exercised.

In setting up a settlement, whether for the benefit of his children or other persons, it is vital, if the settlor wishes to alienate the income effectively, that there is no power to revoke the settlement and upon such revocation trust property or income will go to the settlor or the spouse.

Settlor must not Retain an Interest in the Trust Property or Income—If the settlor retains an interest in any income arising under the settlement or in any of the property comprised in the settlement, then any income which arises from the settled property, to the extent that it is not distributed, will be treated as the income of the settlor (TA 1970, s447). In general terms this means that if one sets up a trust to accumulate income, and the settlor has not completely divested himself of the trust property, he will be chargeable to income tax on the trust income. The mere possibility that the settlor or his spouse might benefit from the trust assets is sufficient to bring this section into operation.

The provisions are very wide. There is, however, dicta in the House of Lords decision in *Vestey's Executors* v *IRC* (1949) 31 TC 1 that transactions on commercial terms between the settlor and the trustee are not caught by the section. It is possible that the settlor may benefit under a beneficiary's will. This possibility is not a sufficiently retained interest under the settlement to enable the section to come into operation (*Walker's Trustees* v *IRC* [1955] 34 ATC 135).

In the case of *Wachtel* v*IRC* (1970) 46 TC 543, the settlor deposited money with a bank interest free and the bank lent money to the trust at 1 per cent. It was agreed that the trust would repay the bank out of accumulated income, and the bank enabled the settlor to reduce his deposit to the extent of such repayment. It was held that the settlor had retained an interest in the accumulated income because the payments of income gave him the benefit of being able to withdraw his capital deposited at the bank.

The settlor and his spouse should thus effectively be excluded from all possible benefit under the trust. A clause along the following lines could be inserted in the trust deed if it is intended that the same be effective for income tax purposes:

> 'No part of the capital, capitalized income, or income shall in any circumstances whatsoever be paid or lent to or applied for the benefit of the settlor or any spouse of the settlor.'

It should be noted that there are circumstances, set out in the proviso to s447(2), where the settlor can retain an interest in the trust and not contravene the alienation of income provision. These exceptions are important and consideration should be given to inserting them in trust documents. The proviso to s447(2) states that the settlor shall not be deemed to have an interest in any income arising under, or property comprised in, the settlement:

> (*a*) if and so long as that income or property cannot become payable or applicable as aforesaid except in the event of—
>
> (i) the bankruptcy of some person who is or may become beneficially entitled to that income or property; or
>
> (ii) any assignment of or charge on that income or property being made or given by some such person; or
>
> (iii) in the case of a marriage settlement, the death of both the parties to the marriage and of all or any of the children of the marriage; or
>
> (iv) the death under the age of twenty-five or some lower age of some person who would be beneficially entitled to that income or property on attaining that age; or
>
> (*b*) if and so long as some person is alive and under the age of twenty-five during whose life that income or property cannot become payable or applicable as aforesaid except in the event of that person becoming bankrupt or assigning or charging his interest in that income or property.

There should be no Discretionary Powers in the Settlement which could be Exercised for the Benefit of the Settlor or his Spouse—If and so long as the terms of any settlement are such that any person has power to pay or apply income or capital to or for the benefit of the settlor or his spouse, all income arising under the settlement shall be treated for all the purposes of the Income Tax Acts as the income of the settlor for that year and not the income of any other person (TA 1970, s448 and see also *Blausten* v *IRC* (1971) 47 TC 542, CA).

Thus all discretionary powers to benefit persons should be clear that there is no inclusion of the settlor or his spouse amongst the discretionary class. Subsection (2), however, suspends the operation of the section where the power cannot be exercised within six years, and also the section does not apply if the discretionary power is exercisable only in the events, such as bankruptcy, specified in the proviso to s447(2) (TA 1970, s448(3)).

Sums Paid to the Settlor in a Capital Form—If a settlement has accumulated income, where any capital sums are paid out to the settlor or his spouse, those capital sums are treated as income to the extent that the trust has accumulated income (TA 1970, s451)).

'Capital sum' means any sum paid by way of loan or repayment of loan, and any other sum paid otherwise than as income being a sum which is not paid for full consideration in money or money's worth. It does not include, however, any sum which could not have become payable to the settlor or his spouse except in one of the events specified in the proviso to s447(2).

For the purposes of this section any capital sum, paid to the settlor or his spouse in any year of assessment by any body corporate connected with the settlement in that year, shall be treated as having been made by the trustees of the settlement. A body corporate shall be deemed to be connected with the settlement in any year of assessment if it is at any time in the year a close company and the participators include the trustees of or a beneficiary under the settlement.

It should be noted that a capital sum includes a repayment of a loan, so that if a settlor lends money interest free to a settlement, and income accrues in the settlement, it will not be possible to repay that loan without coming within these provisions.

Where the trust owns shares in a close company and the close company makes loans, the situation should be watched very carefully, since loans to the settlor or his spouse could come within these provisions. Also, if the settlor makes a loan to such a close company, the provisions could apply on the repayment of the loan. Any payments of capital by trustees, or loans or repayments of loans by trustees or close companies connected with the trust, should thus be carefully watched if there is any accumulated income.

These provisions have no relevance if the trust is a 'dry trust', ie, a trust which has no income.

In *IRC* v *De Vigier* (1964) 42 TC 25, the wife of the settlor advanced £7,000 to the trustees and this advance was repaid in two amounts within twelve months. It was held that the repayments were capital sums and the settlor was correctly assessed to surtax. The case of *Pott's Executors* v *IRC* [1951] AC 443 revealed a surprising loophole in this otherwise harsh section. It was held that a payment to a third party to discharge a liability of the settlor to the third party was not a sum paid to the settlor. However, if a sum is paid to the settlor to discharge a liability of his to his bank, the payment will be within the section *IRC* v *Bates* (1966) 44 TC 225).

Income from Property of which the Settlor has not Divested himself of Absolutely—Section 457 (1) of the TA 1970 provides as far as it affects capital as opposed to income settlements such as covenants as follows:

Where, during the life of the settlor, income arising under a settlement made on or

> after 7 April 1965 is, under the settlement and in the events that occur, payable to or applicable for the benefit of any person other than the settlor [eg, trustees], then, unless, under the settlement and in the said events the income . . . is income from property of which the settlor has divested himself absolutely by the settlement . . . the income shall be treated for the purposes of [excess liability] as the income of the settlor and not as the income of any other person.

'Excess liability' means the excess of liability to income tax over what it would be if all the income were charged at the basic rate, to the exclusion of any other rate.

Section 457(6) provides that:

> The settlor shall not be deemed . . . to have divested himself absolutely of any property if that property or any income therefrom or any property directly or indirectly representing proceeds of, or income from, that property or any income therefrom is, or will or may become, payable to or applicable for the benefit of the settlor or the wife or husband of the settlor in any circumstances whatsoever.

The proviso to subs (6) sets out four exceptions relating to bankruptcy, assignments or charges, marriage settlements and deaths under the age of twenty-five years or some lower age.

Capital transfer tax

Capital transfer tax was introduced by the FA 1975, effective from 26 March 1974. It is a sophisticated piece of legislation which has learnt much from the mistakes of the old estate duty law which it replaced.

It is chargeable on the reduction in the value of an individual's estate as a result of gratuitous transfers. The liability to pay the tax arises when the transfers are made, and the tax is charged on a cumulative basis, ie, the more transfers that are made the higher the rate of tax will be, since each gift is added to earlier gifts to find the appropriate tax rates. It is the total loss to the donor which is chargeable and this will include the tax which is to be paid by the donor. Thus, gifts have to be 'grossed up' to find the loss to the estate of the donor and the tax charge is based on this total loss. Finally, on the death of the individual, all his lifetime gifts will be added to his estate as at the date of death and this will determine the charge to capital transfer tax on his death. There is, however, no 'grossing up' on death.

The rates of capital transfer tax are contained in Appendix 1. The death rates apply to a transfer made on or at any time within three years of the death of the transferor and the lifetime rates apply on any other transfer (FA 1975, s37(2)). The basic capital transfer tax structure has been adapted to incorporate settlements and the principal provisions are contained in the FA 1975, Sched 5.

'Settlement', for the purposes of capital transfer tax, is defined in the FA 1975, Sched 5, para 1(2), as being any—

> disposition or dispositions of property, whether effected by instrument, by parole or by operation of law, or partly in one way and partly in another, where the property is for the time being—
>
> (*a*) held in trust for persons in succession or for any person subject to a contingency; or
>
> (*b*) held by trustees on trust to accumulate the whole or part of any income of the property or with power to make payments out of that property at the discretion of the trustees or some other person, with or without power to accumulate surplus income; or
>
> (*c*) charged or burdened (otherwise than for full consideration in money or money's worth paid for his own use or benefit to the person making the disposition), with the payment of any annuity or other periodical payment payable for a life or any other limited or terminable period;
>
> or would be so held or charged or burdened if the disposition or dispositions were regulated by the law of any part of the United Kingdom; or whereby, under the law of any other country, the administration of the property is for the time being governed by provisions equivalent in effect to those which would apply if the property were so held, charged or burdened.

It will thus be seen that 'Settlement' for the purposes of capital transfer tax is narrower than the definition for income tax and it involves some element of succession to the beneficial interest of the property.

It is provided by the FA 1975, Sched 5, para 1(3), that a lease of property which is for life or lives, or for a period ascertainable only by reference to a death, or which is terminable on, or at a date ascertainable only by reference to, a death, shall be treated as a settlement and the property as settled property, unless the lease was granted for consideration in money or money's worth, and where a lease not granted as a lease at a rack-rent is at any time to become a lease at an increased rent it shall be treated as terminable at that time.

'Settlor' includes any person by whom a settlement was made, directly or indirectly, and in particular (but without prejudice to the generality of the preceding words) includes any person who has provided funds directly or indirectly for the purpose of or in connection with the settlement, or who has made with any other person a reciprocal arrangement for that other person to make the settlement (FA 1975, Sched 5, para 1(6)).

'Trustee' means any person in whom settled property or its management is vested for the time being (FA 1975, Sched 5, para 1(7)).

Types of Settlement

The capital transfer tax rules entail first a classification of trusts into those where there is an interest in possession and those where there is no such interest (the general classification); and secondly, a classification of all trusts to see whether they fall within certain requirements set down by the legislation, so that particular reliefs and exemptions might apply to those particular trusts (the specific classification).

The General Classification—The major division of all trusts is between those which create an interest in possession and those which do not.

Very broadly an 'interest in possession' means that, in the view of the Inland Revenue, the beneficiary is entitled for the time being to all the benefit and income which arises from the trust property. The decision in *Pearson* v *IRC* [1978] STC 627 has caused uncertainty in this area and the term is discussed in much greater detail in Chapter 5. The capital transfer tax legislation treats a person who has an interest in possession as owning the trust property itself (FA 1975, Sched 5, para 3(1)). The corollary of this is that any reversionary interests are generally excluded from capital transfer tax.

Trusts under which there are no interests in possession (usually called discretionary trusts) have to be divided into two categories. With regard to pre-27 March 1974 discretionary trusts, the trustees are treated as separate individuals with their own cumulative totals and with the £25,000 exemption. Transfers to beneficiaries are chargeable to capital transfer tax. Such trusts are also subject to periodic charges equalling 30 per cent of the normal rate on every tenth anniversary of the date of the settlement, except that there is to be no charge before 1 April 1980.

With regard to post-26 March 1974 discretionary settlements, the charge to capital transfer tax is based on the position of the settlor when he put the property into the settlement (see Chapter 6). These trusts are also subject to the periodic charge to tax.

Non-resident discretionary trusts can be liable to a 3 per cent annual charge under the FA 1975, Sched 5, para 12(2) (see Chapter 19, at p169).

The Specific Classification—As well as classifying trusts generally, it is necessary to classify them to see whether they satisfy certain conditions which give relief or exemption from the usual charges to capital transfer tax as referred to above.

The following types of trusts enjoy certain reliefs:

(1) accumulation of maintenance settlements (see Chapter 8);

(2) superannuation schemes (FA 1975, Sched 5, para 16, and Chapter 17);

(3) trusts for the benefit of employees (see Chapter 15);

(4) protective trusts (see Chapter 9);

(5) trusts for the benefit of mentally disabled persons or persons in receipt of an attendance allowance (see Chapter 10);

(6) charitable trusts (see Chapter 18);

(7) compensation funds (FA 1975, Sched 5, para 21);

(8) administration period trusts (FA 1975, Sched 5, para 22);

(9) trustee annuities (FA 1975, Sched 5, para 19A, inserted by FA 1976, s10);

(10) survivorship clauses (FA 1975, Sched 5, para 22A, inserted by FA 1976, s105(1); and

(11) marriage trusts (at least with regard to putting property into a trust (see Chapter 11)).

Certain of the above trusts are dealt with in the appropriate chapters of this book as indicated above.

If trust property does not satisfy the requirements of a specific classification it will fall within the general classification, so that it is either held upon trusts which create an interest in possession in the property or not.

Capital gains tax

Settled property for the purposes of capital gains tax is defined in the FA 1965, s45(1) as meaning any property held in trust, other than property to which the FA 1965, s22(5) applies. This means that property is settled property unless it is held by a person (*a*) as nominee for another person, (*b*) as a trustee for another person absolutely entitled as against the trustee, or (*c*) for any person who would be so entitled but for being an infant or other person under disability. The definition is very wide; it is in fact the widest definition to be applied to any tax, apart from income tax.

The term 'settlement' is not defined in the legislation, and the definition of settled property is the only indication there is of the meaning of the term settlement.

Property held by persons as tenants in common is not settled property (*Kidson* v *MacDonald* [1974] Ch 339). However, property held in common subject to the payment of an annuity is settled property (*Stephenson* v *Barclays Bank Trust Co Ltd* [1975] STC 151). In *Booth* v *Ellard* [1978] 1 WLR 927 the Revenue contended that a shareholders' agreement created a settlement by virtue of a requirement that the shares be vested in trustees. The shareholders contended that the trustees were bare-trustees for the shareholders, and this was held, on the facts, to be the case.

Where property is held for a minor it is only settled property if there is some further contingency, and not just the minority, which prevents the property vesting absolutely in the beneficiary.

In *Tomlinson* v *Glyns Executor and Trustee Co Ltd and Another* (1970) 45 TC 600 (CA) property was held for a minor contingently on his attaining his majority. It was held by the Court of Appeal to be settled property because the minority was not in itself the only bar to the beneficiary being absolutely entitled; there was also the requirement that the beneficiary survive to his majority. If the beneficiary had a vested interest, so that the minority was the sole bar to giving the trustees a valid receipt, it would not have been settled property.

References in the capital gains tax legislation to any asset held by a person as trustee for another person absolutely entitled as against the trustee are references to a case where the other person has the exclusive right (subject only to satisfying any outstanding charge, lien or other right of the trustee to resort to the asset for payment of duty, taxes, costs or other outgoings) to direct how the asset shall be dealt with (FA 1969, Sched 19, para 9).

Putting Property into a Settlement

A gift of chargeable assets to the settlement, whether the settlement is revocable or irrevocable, is a disposal of the entire property of the settlor which is settled, despite the fact that the settlor has some interest as a beneficiary under the settlement and despite the fact that he might also be the trustee or one of the trustees of the settlement (FA 1965, s25(2).

For the purposes of capital gains tax the trustees of the settlement and the settlor are connected with each other (FA 1965, Sched 7, para 21(3). Thus, if on the disposal by the settlor, a loss accrues to the settlor, it shall not be deductible from any chargeable gains except from those accruing to the settlor on some other disposal to the trustees. This provision, however, does not apply to a disposal after 5 April 1969 if the assets settled, and the income from them, are wholly or primarily applicable for educational, cultural or recreational purposes, and the persons benefiting from the application for those purposes are confined to members of an association of persons for whose benefit the gift was made, not being persons all or most of whom are connected persons. Thus the settlor will not have his capital gains tax losses restricted in this way if he genuinely sets up a trust for public purposes (FA 1965, Sched 7, para 17(3), with the proviso being added by FA 1969, Sched 19, para 12).

Disposals by Trustees

The disposal of assets by trustees, if the trustees sell assets or switch investments, will be liable to capital gains tax in the usual way (FA 1965, s20(1).

Beneficiary Becoming Absolutely Entitled

When a beneficiary becomes absolutely entitled to any settled property as against a trustee, the assets to which he becomes so entitled shall be deemed to have been disposed of by the trustee and immediately reacquired by him in his capacity as a trustee for a consideration equal to the market value of the assets. A liability to capital gains tax will therefore accrue. If an allowable loss shall accrue on this notional disposal, or if there shall be any allowable losses in the trust carried forward from earlier years of the trust, and that loss cannot be deducted from chargeable gains accruing to the trustees in the year of the disposal (but the loss occurs before the notional disposal), the loss shall be treated as if it were an allowable loss accruing at that time to the person becoming so entitled, instead of to the trustees. Thus, if trust assets are standing at a loss and they are appointed out absolutely to a beneficiary, those losses will be, in effect, handed over to the beneficiary to use against his future gains (FA 1965, s25(8)).

The charge to capital gains tax on the termination of a trust, or on the appointment out of trust assets, causes a 'locked-in' effect to arise with regard to assets held by trusts and which have large inherent gains. These assets could be 'released', however, without charge on the death of a life tenant, where the gain would be eliminated by the notional disposal on death or under the provisions of the FA 1978, Sched 8, if the trust fund consists of business assets.

Paragraph 2(1) of Sched 8 provides as follows:

> If, after 11th April 1978, a trustee is deemed, by virtue of subsection (3) or subsection (4) of section 25 of the Finance Act 1965 (settled property) to have disposed of, and immediately reacquired—
>
> (*a*) an asset which is, or is an interest in, an asset used for the purposes of a trade, profession or vocation carried on by the trustee or by a relevant beneficiary; or
>
> (*b*) shares or securities of a trading company as to which not less than 25% of the voting rights are exercisable by the trustee at the time of the disposal and reacquisition,
>
> subsection (3) of the principal section shall apply in relation to the disposal if a claim for relief under that section is made by the trustee.

The principal section is s46 (FA 1978), and subs (3) enables a claim to be made to 'roll over'—or 'hold over' as the section calls it—the chargeable gain made on the notional disposals under subs (3) and (4) of s25 to the FA 1965. The beneficiary will take over the trustee's base value.

'Relevant beneficiary' means—

(1) where the disposal is deemed to occur by virtue of the FA 1965, s25(3), a beneficiary who had an interest in possession in the settled property immediately before the disposal; and

(2) where the disposal is deemed to occur by virtue of s25(4) on the termination of a life interest in possession, the beneficiary whose interest it was (FA 1978, Sched 8, para 2(3)).

'Trading Company' has the same meaning as in the FA 1965, s34.

Section 46 and Schedule of the FA 1978 are very important. They will enable trusts to be broken up where previously, because of the charge to capital gains tax, they had to be left in being often serving no particular purpose.

The trustees have the right to pay the tax on deemed disposals by instalments, in certain instances without interest, over eight years in the case of certain assets. These assets are as follows (FA 1965, Sched 10, para 4, replaced by FA 1972, s117 amended by F (No 2) A 1975, s57):

(1) land;

(2) shares or securities of a company which, immediately before the disposal, gave control of the company to the person by whom the disposal was deemed to be made;

(3) any shares or securities of a company not falling within (2) above and not quoted on a recognized stock exchange in the United Kingdom or elsewhere; and

(4) any assets used exclusively for the purposes of a trade, profession or vocation which, immediately before the disposal, was carried on (whether alone or in partnership) by the person by whom the disposal was deemed to be made.

If the assets are subsequently sold, the right to pay by instalments will cease.

Termination of a Life Interest

When a person entitled to a life interest in possession dies and another person consequently becomes entitled to the trust property absolutely, there will be no charge to capital gains tax on the life tenant's death but there will be deemed disposal and reacquisition of the trust assets; the gain up to death is therefore eliminated and not just postponed (FA 1965, s25(3) and FA 1971, Sched 12, para 6).

Thus, if assets are held on trust for A for life and then for B absolutely, there will be an uplift in the base for capital gains tax purposes as at A's death. There will be no charge to capital gains tax at A's death.

On the termination of a life interest in possession in all or any part of the settled property there will be a deemed disposal and reacquisition of the whole or a corresponding part of the trust assets where the property does not cease at that time to be settled property (FA 1965, s25(4)). However, where the life interest terminates on the death of the person entitled to it, no chargeable gain shall accrue on the deemed disposal and reacquisition (FA 1965, s25(4) and FA 1971, Sched 12, para 9).

Thus, if property is held on trust for A for life, B for life and then to C absolutely there will be a charge to capital gains tax if A's life interest terminates otherwise than on A's death.

Special provisions apply, to prevent tax being avoided, if the death of the life tenant results in a reversion to the disposer (FA 1971, Sched 12, para 6).

A 'life interest' in relation to a settlement is defined in the FA 1965, s25(10), as amended by the FA 1966, Sched 10, para 1(3) (see below, p59). If there is a life interest in a part of the settled property, and, where this is a life interest in income, there is no right of recourse to, or to the income of, the remainder of the settled property, the part of the settled property in which the life interest subsists shall, while it subsists, be treated for the purposes of these provisions as being settled under a separate settlement (FA 1965, s25(12), as amended by FA 1971, Sched 12, Pt V).

Disposals of Interests under Trusts

Disposals of interests under trusts are, in general, exempt from capital gains tax (FA 1965, Sched 7, para 13(1)). This exemption is vitally important in the tax planning context and is dealt with more fully in Chapter 4.

Exemptions and Reliefs for Small Gains

Trustees shall not be chargeable to capital gains tax for a year of assessment if the taxable amount for the year does not exceed £500 (FA 1978, s44(1) and Sched 7, para 6(2)). If the trustees' taxable gain for a year of assessment exceeds £500, the amount of capital gains tax to which they are chargeable for that year shall not exceed one-half of the excess. These provisions apply where the settlement was made before 7 June 1978 and apply for the year 1977–78 and subsequent years of assessment (FA 1978, s44(9) and Sched 7, para 6(5)).

Special provisions apply where capital losses are available to the trustees (FA 1978, s44(4) and Sched 7, para 6(2)), while extended reliefs apply to trusts for the mentally disabled and trusts for persons in receipt of an attendance allowance (FA 1978, Sched 7, para 5, and see p93 below). Further special exemptions and reliefs apply to sales of tangible movable property (FA 1965, s30, and FA 1978, s45).

Development land tax

Settled property, for the purposes of development land tax, means an interest in land held on trust for any person or persons in such circumstances that it is not held on a bare trust (DLTA 1976, s30(1)). The tax is a charge on the increase in the value of land due to an actual or potential planning permission which can result in material development being carried out (DLTA 1976, s4). Where development value has accrued the tax becomes chargeable, broadly, when land is sold or let, or when a project on material development commences; there must thus be a realization of the development value (DLTA 1976, s1(1)). The tax replaces Development Gains Tax which was introduced by the FA 1974 and it also replaces the First Letting Charge (DLTA 1976, ss35–38).

Development land tax is chargeable at a flat rate of 80 per cent, except for the first £10,000 per financial year which is exempt and the next £150,000 per financial year which will be taxed at the reduced rate of 66⅔ per cent until 31 March 1980 (see DLTA 1976, ss12 and 13, as amended by FA 1978, s76). It is anticipated that the 80 per cent rate will gradually be increased, over the years, to virtually 100 per cent.

The liability to the tax in respect of trustees will arise when they dispose of land in the normal way. The trust will be entitled to the annual exemption of £10,000, and the reduced rate will be available to the trustees.

On the termination of a life interest or on the occasion when a beneficiary becomes absolutely entitled to the settled property no development land tax will be payable. This is because it is not a sale but a gift. It may be necessary for the beneficiary to retain the property for at least twelve months (DLTA 1976, ss5(6), 12 and 13).

Section 10 of the DLTA 1976 will apply so that on any subsequent disposal of the interest the beneficiary's acquisition costs, for example, will be taken to be those of the trustees.

The interest of a beneficiary in settled land is not an interest in land for the purposes of development land tax (DLTA 1976, s46(2)(*c*)). Thus, the disposal by a beneficiary of his beneficial interest cannot give rise to a charge. The price paid by a person for the interest of a beneficiary in settled property is not allowable as part of the acquisition cost of land by that person, even though, through that acquisition of the interest, he ultimately becomes entitled to the entire interest (DLTA 1976, Sched 2, para 25).

If in fact the trustees hold the property as bare trustees for the beneficiary the situation is different, since the general tax maxim that 'a bare trusteeship is no trusteeship' is applied; any disposal by the beneficiary will give rise to a charge to development land tax in the usual way (DLTA 1976, s28(1)).

Value added tax

Value added tax is charged on any supply of goods or services made in the United Kingdom, where it is a taxable supply made by a taxable person in the course of or furtherance of any business carried on by him (FA 1972, s2 (as amended)). A person who makes or intends to make taxable supplies is a taxable person while he is or is required to be registered under the FA 1972, Pt 1. A taxable supply is a supply of goods or services made in the United Kingdom, other than an exempt supply (FA 1972, s3 (as amended)).

A supplier may not be liable to register for VAT if, broadly, the size of his taxable supplies in a year does not exceed £10,000 (FA 1972, Sched 1 (as amended)).

Trustees are 'persons', and if they therefore carry on a business they must register for VAT as appropriate.

Development gains tax and the first letting charge

This imposition, which charged not only trustees but also beneficiaries if they disposed of certain interests under trusts (FA 1974, s42), has now been abolished. Nevertheless it might still be applicable under certain transitional provisions. Thus, if material development was commenced before 1 August 1976, but after 17 December 1973, on a subsequent disposal, whenever it takes place, development gains tax (not development land tax) will be chargeable.

With regard to the first letting charge, which can give rise to a charge to capital gains tax as well as development gains tax, no interest shall be deemed to be sold and reacquired for the purposes of that charge after 31 July 1976 unless the relevant development relating to the chargeable building in question was begun before 18 May 1976 (DLTA 1976, s38(1)).

Estate duty

Estate duty, which was first imposed by the FA 1894, has been replaced by capital transfer tax. This replacement, however, took place in four stages and the estate duty rules can still be relevant in certain, but now diminishing, circumstances.

(1) Up to 12 November 1974 estate duty applies with regard to all deaths.

(2) After 26 March 1974, capital transfer tax applies to all lifetime transfers.

(3) After 12 November 1974, but before 13 March 1975, a modified estate duty applies to deaths.

(4) After 12 March 1975 capital transfer tax applies to all deaths.

Section 22(5) of the FA 1975 provides that if a person had made a gift inter vivos (including a gift in settlement) before 27 March 1974, he must survive the old seven-year estate duty period to avoid an estate duty charge at capital transfer rates. Business relief, agricultural land relief and tapering relief, where appropriate, can be obtained.

There is a similar carry-over of liability where a person had before 27 March 1974, but not at any time after that date, a beneficial interest in possession in any settled property which could be chargeable under the FA 1894, s2(1)(*b*)(i).

CHAPTER 3

TAX ALCHEMY

Parliament and the courts have always found it difficult to know how to tax income which accumulates in a trust. Should it be taxed as if it is the settlor's income, or the beneficiary's income or the trustee's income? The matter has never been properly resolved. The present position is that income which has been validly accumulated in a trust under which no beneficiary has a vested interest in the income can be capitalized and paid out to the beneficiary in the form of capital (*IRC* v *Blackwell Minor's Trustees* [1924] 2 KB 351; 10 TC 235). The higher rates of income tax are thus avoided (see also *Stanley* v *IRC* [1944] KB 255; 26 TC 12 (CA); *IRC* v *Countess of Longford* [1928] AC 252; and *Reid's Trustees* v *IRC* (1929) 14 TC 512.

Thus, if a trust is set up which has the power to accumulate income, that income can be converted into capital by the trustees exercising the power to accumulate. This could apply to a discretionary trust or a trust which qualifies as an 'accumulation and maintenance settlement' (see FA 1975, Sched 5, para 15 (as amended).

These provisions cannot apply to a trust where there is an interest in possession, since the trustees cannot then accumulate the income (see, however, the decision in *Pearson* v *IRC* (1978) STC p627, discussed at pp51–53 below). 'Tax Alchemy' therefore involves using trusts which may suffer capital transfer tax disadvantages. If there is no interest in possession the trust will normally suffer the ten year charge to capital transfer tax; in addition there will be cumulation with the settlor's estate as at the time of transfer. However, there is still scope for the use of discretionary trusts especially if income tax savings are important.

It is with regard to the 'accumulation and maintenance settlement', however, that this power to capitalize is particularly important. This power, when taken with the capital transfer tax advantages of an 'accumulation and maintenance settlement', makes such settlements very beneficial.

It is to be noted that accumulation settlements (whether discretionary trusts or 'accumulation and maintenance settlements'), as well as suffering the basic rate of tax at present 33 per cent, will also be liable to the additional rate of tax at the full 15 per cent under the provisions of the FA 1973, ss16 and 17. The settlor must not be a beneficiary under the settlement or be able to benefit under the settlement, otherwise all the income of the trust could be taxed upon him (see, for example, TA 1970, s477).

Converting income into capital

Once income has been validly accumulated by the trustees it becomes capital of the trust fund. If it is paid to a beneficiary in later years he will receive it as capital and cannot be charged to income tax on it, except in some of the situations mentioned at p38 below ('When income cannot be capitalized').

On the other hand if the trustees do not exercise their power of accumulation, but merely leave the income in suspense, a sum paid to a beneficiary in a later year may be received by him as income. The trustees have a reasonable time in which to decide whether to accumulate or distribute. They should therefore make a firm decision as to whether to accumulate or not, record their decision in the minutes, and draw up the trust accounts accordingly.

Converting capital into income

A payment to a beneficiary out of capital and accumulated income which has been capitalized can be taxable as income upon the beneficiary if the payment has the quality of income about it when it reaches the beneficiary. In *Michelham's Trustees* v *IRC* (1930) 15 TC 737, 745; CA, Rowlatt J said: 'If a person receives a payment which, so far as the payer is concerned, is paid out of capital, and the receiver receives it as income on his part, of course he has to pay income tax on it.' In the leading case of *Brodie's Will Trustees* v *IRC* (1933) 17 TC 432, the trustees were directed to pay part of the trust income to the testator's widow and there was a further provision that should the income not reach a certain amount there should be payments out of capital to make up the difference. It was held that the sums paid out of capital in seven successive years were annual payments under Case III of Schedule D, and therefore formed part of the beneficiary's total income. There would now be an assessment on the trustees under the TA 1970, s53, or under the FA 1973, s17(1), as appropriate. The position would be the same if the beneficiaries had no right to demand that their income be augmented, but had to rely on the discretion of the trustees (*Lindus and Hortin* v *IRC* (1933) 17 TC 442).

This conversion of capital into income can take place regardless of what the parties describe the payment as (*Jackson's Trustees* v *IRC* (1942) 25 TC 13). Thus, in the case of a discretionary trust or an Accumulation and Maintenance Settlement there should not normally be any express provisions which can convert capital into income, and it will then be a question of the trustees exercising their discretion properly to make sure that the capital does not take on the form of income. The basic criteria for ascertaining whether the payment is income is that it must possess the quality of recurrence which it may do even though the amount may be variable.

The safest way therefore of avoiding these provisions is to make irregular payments, preferably of irregular amounts, and also it will help if the documentation refers to the payments as being capital.

Example 1—A trust makes six annual payments of the same amount from the capital of the trust. It is felt that this would amount to income in the hands of the beneficiary.

Example 2—A trust makes one payment out of accumulated income or out of capital at the end of the sixth year of its existence. Providing subsequent payments do not in any way prejudice this, this will clearly come out as capital.

This power to reconvert capitalized income back into income could be worked to the advantage of the taxpayer if it is desired that the beneficiary, because of his low tax rate, should be receiving income rather than capital. It should be noted that if trustees do pay out capital, in the exercise of a discretion, in the form of income, they can be assessed to tax at a rate equal to the sum of the basic rate and the additional rate in force for the year in which the payment is made (FA 1973, s17(2)(*b*)). If it is pure capital (ie, not capitalized income) they will have no amount to set off against that assessment (s17(3)) since the capital will not have previously suffered any income tax. If the trustees make payments to the beneficiary out of capitalized income they will have amounts to offset against their tax liability, because that income will have suffered tax at the basic and additional rates in the years it was received by the trustees, or suffered tax at the appropriate rates in respect of income available for distribution at the end of the year 1972–73. In the latter case there shall be set against the amount assessable on the trustees on amount of tax (in respect of income found on a claim made by the trustees to have been available to them for distribution at the end of the year 1972–73), which shall be taken to be two-thirds of the net amount of that income.

Thus, if the tax rate of the beneficiary is less than the tax rate suffered on that income by the trust, consideration should be given to deliberately giving capitalized income the nature of income again so that a tax reclaim can be made.

One situation where the trustees might want to convert pure capital (ie, not capitalized income) into income arises where a very wealthy discretionary trust suffers on transfers a rate of capital transfer tax higher than the rate of income tax which would be chargeable on the payment of income to a beneficiary. The payment of 'income' would not be a distribution payment for capital transfer tax purposes because of the FA 1975, Sched 5, para 11(7)(*a*).

When income cannot be capitalized

In the following instances the capitalization of income will not affect the nature of the capitalized income for tax purposes and the income will retain its nature as income. The list is not exhaustive.

(1) If there is a payment to an employee from an employees' trust, the payment will still be income chargeable under Sched E whether it comes out of capital, income or accumulated income (see below, p129).

(2) Where the settlor sets up a trust for his infant unmarried children and a payment is made from the trust to any such child, whether made out of accumulated income or income or out of capital, the payment will be treated as income to the extent that there is income or accumulated income in the trust (TA 1970, ss437, 438). The parent should thus, wherever possible, particularly in trusts where a small sum is to be settled and invested in an enterprise which could show substantial income in the future, arrange for the grandparents to settle the initial fund for the benefit of their grandchildren. This will solve the problem since payments to the minors, in this case, will not be aggregated with their parents' income.

(3) If the payments from the trust out of accumulated income or capital have the nature of income about them they retain this nature (*Brodie's Will Trustees* v *IRC* (1933) 17 TC 432).

(4) If the settlor has retained some benefit or interest in his trust, the income will be treated as the income of the settlor (eg, see TA 1970, s447).

(5) If the settlor obtains a loan or capital sum from his trust, any accumulated income will be treated as income in the hands of the settlor (TA 1970, s451).

(6) If the provisions of the TA 1970, s478 apply to tax income upon persons ordinarily resident in the United Kingdom who have power to enjoy that income, it will retain its nature as income.

(7) If payments are made to certain employees' children out of educational trusts set up by the employers, such payments will be treated as income (see Chapter 14).

(8) If the trustee is a bare trustee, the source of the income is not relevant—all income of the trust is the beneficiary's income and all capital of the trust will be the beneficiary's capital (*Brodie's Will Trustees* v *IRC* (1933) 17 TC 432, per Finlay J at p438).

(9) If a beneficiary is entitled to the income, for example, if he is a tenant for life with an interest in possession in the fund, he will be taxable upon it as income whether or not it is accumulated (but see *Pearson*, at p51 below).

Tax planning

Income arising in trusts where there is a power to accumulate should be capitalized or left as income, or reconverted from capitalized income into income according to the tax position of the beneficiaries.

In the summary this means:

(1) making payments from the trust at the right times and for the right amounts;

(2) keeping proper records of trustee meetings;

(3) keeping proper accounts; and

(4) knowing the tax position of the beneficiaries, in particular what other income they have, their personal reliefs, and what child allowances are available to their parents.

If a taxpayer is going to receive dividends on his shares he could waive those dividends to enable the accumulation trust to receive a higher dividend than would otherwise have been payable on its shares. This works provided the dividend has not already been declared. A deed is required and 50*p* stamp duty is payable on it. A person who waives a dividend within twelve months before any right to the dividend has accrued is exempt from capital transfer tax on the waiver (FA 1976, s92). The nature of the company (it should be a trading company), its shortfall position, and the effect upon the value of the shares of the company should be taken into consideration before such transaction is entered into.

CHAPTER 4

INTERESTS UNDER TRUSTS

This chapter deals with interests under trusts from the point of view of the beneficiary. This area of trust law has traditionally been one which the Parliament has been reluctant to get involved with. This is because the types of interests can be of extreme complexity and of almost infinite variety.

These interests have generally been left outside the scope of capital gains tax. The drafters of the development land tax legislation have made no attempt to charge such interests to that tax, perhaps learning from the complicated, yet easily avoided, rules imposed on such interests under the development gains tax legislation (FA 1974, s42). Even with capital transfer tax, where the legislator has attempted to get to grips with the problem, having almost a century of estate duty law to learn from, there is substantial area—reversionary interests—which are largely excluded from the charging provisions.

Oddly enough, stamp duty, which has often been branded 'the voluntary tax', is the only fiscal imposition which appears to deal effectively with most disposals of interests under trusts.

What is an interest under a trust?

Interests under a trust might be defined as the present or future rights of the beneficiaries under the trust to the benefit and enjoyment of the trust income and capital held by the trustees. The beneficiaries might have a right to the income for the time being (an interest in possession), or they might have the right to the income from the trust assets for life (an interest in possession for life or a life interest), or they might have a right to the assets absolutely on the death of a person who has a prior right under the trust or on the remarriage of such a person. All such persons have an interest under the trust.

For most of the taxes to be mentioned hereafter, the type of interest under the trust is not generally relevant. There are minor exceptions with regard to capital gains tax but the major exception relates to capital transfer tax, where the distinction between an interest in possession and a reversionary interest is critical.

Interests under trust should be distinguished from a 'mere spes' or 'hope'. A discretionary beneficiary who has no right to income or capital does not, in the author's view, have an interest under the trust (see *Gartside* v *IRC* [1968] All ER, at p121, and *Sainsbury* v *IRC*[1969] 3 All ER 919). He might perhaps be able to assign his hope by, for instance, declaring himself a bare trustee of it for the transferee, giving effect to the transfer if he should receive something from the trust. However, it would be quite unusual to sell or give away mere hopes even if it could be done in law or equity.

An interest under a trust can itself be put into another trust by the beneficiary entitled to it, so that the trust consists of an interest under another trust. It was clearly decided in *Shafto* v *Adams* (1864) 4 Giff 492 that a reversion can be settled.

Disposals must be in writing

Section 53(1)(*c*) of the LPA 1925 states as follows:

> A disposition of an equitable interest or trust subsisting at the time of the disposition, must be in writing signed by the person disposing of the same, or by his agent thereunto lawfully authorised in writing or by will.

The provision actually requires the transfer of the interest under the trust to be in writing, and merely evidencing it in writing is not sufficient. It applies to all types of property and there is no exception for interests under resulting, implied or constructive trusts. An 'equitable interest' would include an interest under a trust.

The four ways of disposing of interests under trusts

The position was stated by Romer L J in *Timpson's Executors* v *Yerbury* [1936] 1 All ER 186, at p194—

> Now the equitable interest in property in the hands of a trustee can be disposed of by the person entitled to it in favour of a third party in any one of four different ways. The person entitled to it—
>
> (i) can assign it to the third person directly;
>
> (ii) can direct the trustees to hold the property in trust for the third person (see per Sargant J in *Re Chrimes* [1917] 1 Ch 30, 36);
>
> (iii) can contract for valuable consideration to assign the equitable interest to him; or
>
> (iv) can declare himself to be a trustee for him of such interest.

The consequences of all four methods will be more or less the same, ie, the assignee will become the beneficial owner of the interest under the trust.

Restrictions on disposal

There are, in general, no restrictions on the disposal of interests under trusts, so that the beneficiary is free to deal with his interest as he pleases. An interest under a protective trust, however, will come to an end if the principal beneficiary tries to deal with it (Trustee Act 1925, s33). A participant in a profit-sharing trust under the FA 1978 will also have restrictions attaching to his beneficial interest under the trust (FA 1978, s54(1)(*b*)). There are also restrictions on the assignment of pensions, which is a type of trust interest (see FA 1970, s19(2A)(*d*)).

Capital gains tax

The disposal of interests under trusts are generally exempt from capital gains tax. The governing provision is the FA 1965, Sched 7, para 13(1), which reads as follows:

> No chargeable gain shall accrue on the disposal of an interest created by or arising under a settlement (including, in particular, an annuity or life interest, and the reversion to an annuity or life interest) by the person for whose benefit the interest was created by the terms of the settlement or by any other person except one who acquired, or derives his title from one who acquired, the interest for a consideration in money or money's worth, other than consideration consisting of another interest under the settlement.

Subject to that general rule where a person who has acquired an interest in settled property (including in particular the reversion to an annuity or life interest) becomes, as the holder of that interest, absolutely entitled as against the trustees to any settled property, he is treated as disposing of the interest in consideration of obtaining that settled property, but without prejudice to any gain accruing to the trustee on the disposal of that property deemed to be effected by him under s25(3) (the charge when a beneficiary becomes absolutely entitled to trust assets as against the trustee). Thus, if a person with an interest under a trust (which he did not buy), sells it, he will pay no capital gains tax. However, the person who acquires the same for money or money's worth could be chargeable to capital gains tax when he disposes of the interest.

Provided the interest never comes into the hands of somebody who has acquired it for a consideration in money or money's worth, each transfer will be completely free of capital gains tax. This applies where an interest under a trust itself is settled by the beneficiary upon new trusts and the trustee of the new trust then transfers it out to another beneficiary. Also, it is clear from the provision that if the beneficiary disposes of his interest under the trust in return for another interest under the trust, that is not treated as being a disposal for consideration in money or money's worth.

The recent case of *Berry* v *Warnett* ([1978] STC, p504), before Goulding J, illustrates that the creation and disposal of interests under trusts can provide an effective means of avoiding capital gains tax. In that case the taxpayer disposed of a reversion on a right he retained to receive the income from the asset in question. That disposal gave rise to a charge to capital gains tax, being a part disposal of the asset within the FA 1965, s22(2)(*b*), and not a complete disposal of the asset under the FA 1965, s25(2). Subsequent to that disposal the taxpayer disposed of his very valuable right to receive the income from the asset, and this was held to be clearly exempt from capital gains tax under the FA 1965, Sched 7, para 13. Both interests in the assets were ultimately sold to a single purchaser as part of the tax-avoidance scheme. This is an effective way of avoiding capital gains tax, although now the basic arrangement, which was carried out in 1972, will have to be altered in order that no adverse capital transfer tax consequences will arise.

In another recent case of *Eilbeck* v *Rawling* [1979] STC p16, the taxpayer intended to cause a reversionary interest to be a 'chargeable asset' by purchasing the reversionary interest for full value and then selling it at a loss. The loss was artificially manufactured, so that an equivalent gain arose in another settlement under which the taxpayer had another reversionary interest. Slade, J, in the Chancery Division, held that the loss was not allowable for capital gains tax purposes, because on the facts of the case the acquisition price of the reversion was not paid wholly and exclusively for the reversion, but as part of the consideration for the implementation of the tax avoidance scheme of which the purchase and sale of the reversion formed part.

Income tax

If a beneficiary disposes of his interest in possession under a trust he could be, in effect, capitalizing his future income especially as the income would be investment income in his hands. This capitalization of future income will be highly beneficial to a high-rate taxpayer.

If the beneficiary disposing of the interest makes a gain on the disposal, he will not be subject to income tax unless he is a trader in interests under trusts and therefore chargeable to income tax under Sched D, Case 1.

Development land tax

Unlike development gains tax, there are no provisions to charge a beneficiary to development land tax if he gives away or sells the interest under a trust, unless the trustees are merely his nominees (DLTA 1976, s28(1)).

Stamp duty

On the voluntary assignment of an interest under a trust inter vivos, stamp duty at 2 per cent is payable on the value of the property transferred (Finance (1909–10) Act 1910, s74(1)).

If the interest is sold, the stamp duty charge is made under the conveyance or transfer on sale provisions (Stamp Act 1891, Sched 1). If the interest is sold at an under value then the gratuitous part is chargeable to stamp duty as a voluntary assignment and the part sold is chargeable as a conveyance or transfer on sale. Clearly, stamp duty cannot be saved by selling at an under value.

A Certificate for Value, if appropriate, will reduce or eliminate the charge to duty (see above, p15).

Capital transfer tax

If the beneficiary is entitled to an interest in possession, on the disposal of that interest he is treated as if he had disposed of the part of the capital of the fund supporting that interest. Thus, if a life tenant has a life interest in half the fund he would be treated as having given away one half of the fund and would be chargeable to capital transfer tax accordingly. Even if he sells the life interest for full actuarial value he will be liable to capital transfer tax on the difference between the sale price and the value of the trust fund supporting his life interest.

A purchaser of an interest in possession could be liable for capital transfer tax if he buys the interest in possession at an inflated price, eg, he buys a three months interest in possession for a price equal to the full capital value of the fund (see FA 1978, s69(7)).

In order to prevent a double charge to capital transfer tax, the legislation generally treats the reversionary interest as excluded property and therefore not chargeable to capital transfer tax. A reversionary interest is defined in the FA 1975, s51(1), as a future interest under a settlement, whether it is vested or contingent (including an interest expectant on the termination of an interest in possession). Thus, a reversionary interest is basically a future interest, such as a right to take the settled property at the time when the settlement comes to an end or the right to a life interest some time in the future.

Under s24(3) of the FA 1975 a reversionary interest is excluded property unless—

(1) it has at any time been acquired (whether by the person entitled to it or by a person previously entitled to it) for a consideration in money or money's worth; or

(2) it is one to which either the settlor or his spouse is beneficially entitled

(this was added by FA 1976, s120(1); under s120(2) it is deemed to come into force on 16 April 1976, but it does not apply to a reversionary interest under a settlement made before that date); or

(3) it is an interest expectant on the determination of, eg, a lease for life, treated as a settlement under Sched 5, para 1(3) of the Act.

Thus it will be seen that, rather like the capital gains tax rules, the general rule is that provided no consideration in money or money's worth has passed as a result of transfers of reversionary interests, the interests will be outside the scope of capital transfer tax.

If a reversionary interest is not excluded property because consideration has passed, or for one of the other reasons mentioned above, it might still be excluded property if it can come within the foreign property exclusion. FA 1975, Sched 5, para 2 states the following:

> (1) Where property comprised in a settlement is situated outside the United Kingdom—
>
> (*a*) the property (but not a reversionary interest in the property) is excluded property unless the settlor was domiciled in the United Kingdom at the time the settlement was made; and
>
> (*b*) section 24(2) of this Act applies to a reversionary interest in the property but does not otherwise apply in relation to the property.
>
> (2) In determining whether property comprised in a settlement which became so comprised before 10th December 1974 is excluded property section 45 [extended meaning of domicile] of this Act shall be disregarded.

Section 24(2) of the Act states that property situated outside the United Kingdom is excluded property if the person beneficially entitled to it is an individual domiciled outside the United Kingdom.

There has been a considerable amount of difficulty in interpreting s24(3) and Sched 5, para 2, and reconciling the provisions. The author is of the view that s24(3) takes precedence over Sched 5, para 2, so that, if the conditions stated in that sub-section are satisfied, wherever the property is situated, it will be excluded property. Only if it fails to satisfy those conditions need one then see whether the property is excluded property under the foreign property provisions (Sched 5, para 2).

If a reversionary interest is sold, the purchaser may be treated as having made a gift of the sale proceeds to the vendor. This is because the vendor is treated as having not transferred anything for capital transfer tax purposes in return for the cash.

Tax planning

The main scope for tax planning and trust interests is as follows:

(1) If a fairly wealthy individual has a reversionary interest he should

consider disposing of it either on further trusts, or for the benefit of less wealthy individuals, before the interest falls in. It will then not form part of his estate. The transfer will be free of all tax apart from stamp duty. Even then, if a Certificate for Value can be put in the document of transfer the exemptions and reduced rates for stamp duty might be available, depending on the value of the interest.

If the reversionary interest relates to a trust which comes within the FA 1975, s22(4) (relief on death of surviving spouse) there will be, in addition, no charge to capital transfer tax on the death of the life tenant.

(2) If a wealthy person has an interest in possession which is producing substantial income, he should consider selling the interest or giving it away so that he, in effect, capitalizes the future income rights. If he gave it to another trust which had power to accumulate the income tax on the income could be made not to exceed 48 per cent by the trustees accumulating and capitalizing it. He could be liable, however, to capital transfer tax.

(3) Wherever assets pregnant with capital gains are held on trust, the beneficiaries should consider selling their trust interests rather than the trustees selling the trust assets and becoming liable to capital gains tax.

(4) In appropriate cases beneficiaries should consider holding on to life interests, because on their deaths any capital gains in the trust will be eliminated up to the date of death. Against this, they should take into account the charge to capital transfer tax which will arise.

CHAPTER 5

SETTLEMENTS WITH INTERESTS IN POSSESSION (FIXED INTEREST TRUSTS)

There are not many tax advantages to be obtained from the setting-up of trusts where there are interests in possession.

The general rule is that on the death of a person with an interest in possession the entire trust fund supporting that interest will be chargeable to capital transfer tax and, because the income belongs to the beneficiary, the income cannot be accumulated and capitalized; the decision of *Pearson* v *IRC* (1978) STC 627 has, however, caused some difficulty in this area. The case is discussed at pp51 to 53 below. Any gifts of interests in possession by the beneficiaries will be chargeable to capital transfer tax on the full value of the fund supporting the interest and not just on the actuarial value of the interest in possession.

What is a trust with an interest in possession?

These are trusts under which a beneficiary is immediately entitled to the benefit or income of the trust property, although the trustees might have the power to take this entitlement away and benefit other persons or accumulate the income of the trust.

Example—Property is held on trust to pay the income to A for his life and then to B, as to income and capital, absolutely: A has an interest in possession.

Example—Property is held on trust to pay the income to X until she remarries or dies and then to Y for life and then to Z absolutely. X has an interest in possession which will terminate on her remarriage or death whereupon Y will get an interest in possession for his life. Until X remarries or dies Y will not have an interest in possession.

The concept of the interest in possession lies at the heart of the taxation of trusts (see *Interest in Possession; the nature of the beast*, C McCall and N R D Powell (LSG 17 December 1975, p1259); and *The Meaning of Interest in Possession in the Finance Act 1975*, Robert Walker (BTR 1976, p49); and *Capital Taxes Encyclopaedia*, C 1.04). It is critical from the outset to ascertain whether a trust, which is in existence or which is to be set up, is one which creates an interest in possession in the trust property. If an interest in possession exists in part of a settled fund that part has to be dealt with according to the interest in possession rules and the rest of the trust fund in accordance with the provisions which deal with trusts without an interest in possession.

Paragraph 11(10) of Sched 5 to the FA 1975 defines an interest in possession as an interest in possession to which an individual is beneficially entitled or, if the following conditions are satisfied, an interest in possession to which a company is beneficially entitled. The conditions are:

(1) that the business of the company consists wholly or mainly in the acquisition of interests in settled property; and

(2) that the company has acquired the interest for full consideration in money or money's worth from an individual who is beneficially entitled to the interest.

Where the acquisition in (2) took place before 14 March 1975 the condition in (1) is deemed to have been satisfied if the business of the company at the time of the acquisition was such as described in that paragraph, and that condition need not be satisfied if the company is authorized to carry on long-term business under Pt I of the Insurance Companies Act 1974 (FA 1975, Sched 5, para 11(10A), inserted by FA 1977, s50). In the case of a company which is close this qualification appears to be subject to the provision which treats the participators in such a company as entitled to any interest in possession in settled property to which the company is entitled (FA 1975, Sched 5, para 24(5)).

The Revenue have given guidance as to the meaning of the term in a Press Notice issued on 12 February 1976. This reads as follows:

> The Board of Inland Revenue are aware that doubts have been expressed in the legal press and elsewhere concerning the precise scope of the term 'interest in possession' as used in Part III of the Finance Act 1975 and in particular about its application where an interest in settled property is subject to a discretion or power, to accumulate the income of the property or to divert it elsewhere.
>
> The Board therefore feel it appropriate, in view of the importance of the expression in Schedule 5, Finance Act 1975, to make known their understanding of the meaning of the expression. This is that an interest in possession in settled property exists where the person having the interest has the immediate entitlement (subject to any prior claim by the trustees for expenses or other outgoings properly payable out of income) to any income produced by that property as the income arises; but that a discretion or power, in whatever form, which can be exercised after income arises so as to withhold it from that person negatives the existence of an interest in possession. For this purpose a power to accumulate income is regarded as a power to withhold it, unless any accumulation must be held solely for the person having the interest or his personal representatives.

On the other hand the existence of a mere power of revocation or appointment, the exercise of which would determine the interest wholly or in part (but which, so long as it remains unexercised, does not affect the beneficiary's immediate entitlement to income) does not in the Board's view prevent the interest from being an interest in possession.

The Inland Revenue's view, as expressed in that Press Notice, so far as it affects powers to accumulate income and take away income from a beneficiary after it has arisen, was rejected by Fox J in *Pearson* v *IRC* (1978) STC 627. This is a case of far-reaching effect and of fundamental importance, since it has raised doubts as to the nature of an interest in possession.

A settlement was created in 1964. The settled fund was held upon trust for such one or more of the settlor's children and their issue as the trustees should appoint during the trust period. Until and subject to such appointment, during a period of twenty-one years from the settlement date, the trustees were to accumulate as much income as they thought fit. Subject to this the fund was held, as to both capital and income, upon trust for such of the settlor's children as should attain the age of twenty-one years in equal shares absolutely. The settlor had three children and all of them had attained the age of twenty-one years by February 1974. In March 1976 the trustees created an indisputable 'interest in possession' in part of the fund for one of the children. The Inland Revenue contended that the power of accumulation prevented any of the children from obtaining an interest in possession under the settlement, and the appointment did create such an interest thus causing a capital transfer tax charge to arise. The trustees held that the power to accumulate did not prevent interests in possession arising since the children had attained the age of twenty-one years. Fox J held that the children had interests in possession since they had an immediate entitlement to the income; the fact that this was subject to a power to accumulate did not derogate from the interest in possession. They had a present right to whatever income was not accumulated pursuant to the power. Thus, at the time of the appointment the child in question had an interest in possession so that no charge to capital transfer tax could arise.

'Interest in possession' generally in English Law is used to connote a present enjoyment of the trust property as opposed to an interest in that property in remainder or reversion. Fox, J felt that an entitlement to income, subject only to a power in the trustees to accumulate income, was a present interest as opposed to an interest in reversion or in remainder.

The three children would be entitled to the income from their shares if the trustees decided not to accumulate, or they failed to agree to accumulate, or a reasonable time elapsed from the receipt of the income so that the power became inoperative. They would receive it not because the trustees decided to give it to them but in accordance with the terms of their trust interests. The cases of *A-G* v *Power* (1906) 1 IR 272 and *Gartside* v *IRC* (1968) 1 All ER 121, (1968) AC 553 were distinguished because the beneficiaries in those cases would have received nothing unless the trustees had decided to give it to them.

In *Pearson* v *IRC* the children were absolutely entitled to the net income unless the trustees decided to accumulate it.

The Crown made a wider submission: for the purposes of capital transfer tax there is an interest in possession if the holder of the interest is entitled to the net income (if any) of the property as it arises but not if the income is subject to a discretion or power which can be exercised so as to withhold it from him after it arises. Because the trustees have a reasonable time in which to decide whether to accumulate or not the power operates over income which will have been received by the beneficiary already.

After referring to the difficulties to which the Crown's contention could give rise, Fox, J stated at pp638 and 639—

> All these considerations lead me to doubt whether the test based on a distinction between cases where the beneficiary is entitled to income as it arises and cases where the trustees have power to withhold income after it has arisen is satisfactory. The fact is that an income beneficiary's right to income is always a right to receive what remains after the trustees have exercised the powers which by the general law or by the settlement are conferred on them in respect of the income. The trustees are always entitled to a reasonable time in which to exercise the powers. They can thus retain income as it arises and, depending on the mode of exercise of the power, divert it from the beneficiary altogether . . .
>
> And if one asks, 'What is the subject-matter of the daughters' interest?' the answer, I think, is that it is the whole income of the trust fund but as diminished by any exercise of the trustees' powers thereover . . .
>
> The fundamental question, I think, is whether his entitlement, whatever, if anything, it may turn out to be in terms of quantum, is a present entitlement in right of an interest in the trust property subject only to the proper exercise of the trustees' powers. And, an entitlement is a present entitlement notwithstanding that the trustees have, as they must have, a reasonable time in which to consider what course to adopt as to exercise of powers.

What the judge appeared to be saying in this case was that if a beneficiary were entitled to the income from the trust fund, but subject only to the proper exercise of trustees' powers, the beneficiary would have an interest in possession. Such a power may be a power to accumulate but that makes no difference. The entitlement to the income must, however, exist, and if income can only be paid to a beneficiary at the discretion of the trustees, that beneficiary will not have an interest in possession.

It was common ground between the parties that it made no difference to the issue whether the power of accumulation had been exercised or not. It thus seems possible to set up a trust for the benefit of persons over the age of twenty-five years who are entitled to the trust income subject only to the power of accumulation for twenty-one years. If the decision is not overturned on appeal, or the law is not changed, it seems possible to have an interest in possession trust (so that the capital transfer tax disadvantages of discretionary trusts are not suffered) under which income can be accumulated and capitalized suffering income tax at only 48 per cent (see Chapter 3). From the tax point of view these would be very attractive trusts. The disadvantage is that there will be a charge to capital transfer tax on the death of the beneficiary with the interest in possession, even though he may receive no income because it has been accumulated.

The difficulty with this case is that it is being appealed, and until the outcome trustees may not know whether or not their trust is one with an interest in possession. The answer might not be known until after the transitional reliefs for discretionary trusts (trusts without interests in possession), under FA 1975, Sched 5, para 14(5), have expired in March 1980 (see below, p67). If trustees feel that certain beneficiaries have interests in possession within Fox's judgment they could appoint funds absolutely to those beneficiaries or indisputably create interests in possession by deed. If the final judgment on the case comes after March 1980 and Fox's judgment is overturned the transitional reliefs will have been obtained. If Fox's judgment is approved there will be no charge to capital transfer tax as the beneficiaries will already have had interests in possession. Difficulties will arise if the trustees wish to appoint the funds upon Accumulation and Maintenance Settlements or upon other trusts. The position is very unsatisfactory.

Income tax

Subject to the decision in *Pearson* v *IRC* (discussed above), where a beneficiary has an interest in possession he will be currently entitled to the income (or would be if there were any income), or to use of the property of the trust. Where income does arise, this will form part of his total income whether he receives it or not. The trustees will not be liable to the additional rate charge (15 per cent) because the beneficiary will be entitled to the income and the trustees have no discretion as to who to pay it to unless they revoke the interest in possession (FA 1973 s16(2)(*a*) and (*b*)).

It should also be noted that, following the case of *Archer-Shee* v *Baker* [1927] AC 844; 11 TC 764 (HL), where securities are held by the trustees for A for life the source of A's income will be the securities themselves; the trust does not form a source of income in itself. This decision is inconsistent with generally accepted trust principles (see *A Periodical Menace to Equitable Principles* LQR 1928 Vol 44, p468 by H G Hanbury; and *The Nature of the Trust Beneficiary's Interest* CBR Vol 45 1967, p219 by D W M Waters).

It was held in the case of *Lord Tollemache* v *IRC* (1926) 11 TC 277 that sums which the beneficiary is entitled to have expended by the trustees for his benefit are taxable upon him. In that case the trust directed the trustees to allow the appellant to occupy and enjoy certain property. It was held that the appellant was assessable to super-tax on the annual value of the property occupied by him, and on the rates, etc paid by the trustees (this was a case under the old Sched A which taxed the annual value of houses; Sched A has now been abolished). The present position is that if there is no actual outlay by the trustees on such matters as rates there is no charge on a beneficiary to income tax on his beneficial enjoyment of the trust property.

Example—T is entitled to live in Greenacres for the rest of his life rent free. He is to be responsible for all outgoings such as rates, electricity, etc. T will not be chargeable to any income tax on his use and enjoyment of Greenacres.

Because the life tenant is taxable on the income of the trust as and when it arises, regardless of whether he actually receives it, there is no scope for accumulating income and capitalizing it, unless the trust falls within the *Pearson* v *IRC* situation (see p51 above). If the entitlement to the income is taken away for any reason this could have serious capital transfer tax consequences as it would result in the termination of an interest in possession.

Capital Transfer Tax

Setting up the Trust

The transfer of funds into the settlement will be a transfer of value by the settlor. However, if the settlor has an interest in possession in the entire fund, or his wife (unless she is not domiciled in the United Kingdom) has such an interest, there will be no charge to capital transfer tax (FA 1975, Sched 5, para 3(1)). If the settlor or his spouse has only an interest in possession in a part and his children, say, have an interest in the rest, there will be a chargeable disposal of that latter part.

The domicile of the settlor is important. If he is domiciled in the United Kingdom then there is a capital transfer tax disposal by him wherever the property is situate. If the settlor is domiciled outside the United Kingdom, only property within the United Kingdom is taxable.

After the Trust is Created: Interests in Possession

The person beneficially entitled to the interest in possession in the settled property is treated for capital transfer tax purposes as if he were beneficially entitled to the property in which the interest subsists (FA 1975, Sched 5, para 3(1)). Thus, the trustees can transfer the share of the trust fund, to which the person with the interest in possession is entitled, to that person, free of capital transfer tax.

If a person is entitled to an interest in possession in half the trust fund or some other proportion, then he will be treated as being the owner of half the trust fund or the appropriate proportion, as the case may be.

Death of person entitled to an interest in possession—Subject to exceptions mentioned later, on the death of such a person he will be treated for capital transfer tax purposes as beneficially entitled to the trust fund supporting his interest in possession. This will be brought into his estate and added to his cumulative total of transfers for the purposes of charge. There is no relief for the fact that the amount of income or benefit he might have derived from his interest in possession might have been very small.

Example—T is a tenant for life of trust fund worth £1 million. He has over the years received the total income derived from the trust fund, amounting to a mere £1,000, the trustees having invested in capital growth assets. On the death of T the £1 million will be brought into his estate for the purposes of capital transfer tax.

Problems sometimes arise when a surviving spouse wants to give her principal residence to her children to get the advantages of the lifetime reduced rates for capital transfer tax and also take all future growth in the value of the property out of her estate. The transfer will usually be free of capital gains tax (FA 1965, s29). The problem is that if she wishes to remain living there she cannot be given the right to live there for life by lease or otherwise as this could create an interest in possession so that there will be a charge on her death. She will not normally want to pay a full rental for the use of the property for life, so taking her out of capital transfer tax under FA 1975, Sched 5, para 1(3), since this would create unearned income in the hands of the children. If she could trust the children the answer would be to give her a revocable licence to live in the house rent free.

Termination or disposition of interest in possession—The person beneficially entitled to an interest in possession can be chargeable to capital transfer tax if he disposes of his interest or the interest itself comes to an end. The rate of tax charged on the disposal or termination of the interest in possession is determined by the beneficiary's cumulative total of transfers at that time.

Example—Mr T, who is entitled to an interest in possession, gives this interest to his son. Mr T will be chargeable to capital transfer tax as if he had made a gift of the part of the capital of the trust fund in which his interest in possession subsisted.

Example—Mrs T is entitled to live in a house left to her by her husband until she remarries or dies, whereafter it will go to her children. On her remarriage her interest in possession will come to an end and there will be a charge to capital transfer tax.

The following are exceptions to the charge on the termination of an interest in possession:

(1) If the person whose interest in the property comes to an end becomes on the same occasion beneficially entitled to the property, or to another interest in possession in the property, tax will not be charged except to the extent that the value of the property to which he becomes entitled is less than the value of the property in which he had an interest in possession (FA 1975, Sched 5, paras 4(3) and 10(*b*).

Example—X is the life tenant of a fund worth £1 million. This is transferred to him by the trustee. There will be no charge to capital transfer tax.

(2) If the interest comes to an end by being disposed of by the person beneficially entitled to it, and the disposal is for a consideration in money or money's worth, tax shall be chargeable as if the value of the property in which the interest subsisted was reduced by the amount of the consideration paid for the interest under the trust; but in determining that amount the value of a reversionary interest in the property or of any interest in other property comprised in the same settlement shall be left out of account (FA 1975, Sched 5, para 4(4)).

Example—Y sells his life interest under a trust for its full actuarial value of £100,000. The trust fund in which his life interest subsists is worth £500,000. Y has made a gift of £400,000 and will be chargeable to capital transfer tax accordingly.

(3) If the interest comes to an end during the settlor's life and on the same occasion the property in which the interest subsisted reverts to the settlor, tax shall not be chargeable unless the settlor or his spouse had acquired the reversionary interest in the property for a consideration in money or money's worth (FA 1975, Sched 5, para 4(5) as amended by FA 1978 s69(1) and see also FA 1975 s22(2) as amended).

Example—A had settled property on B for life with a reversion back to A on B's death. There will be no capital transfer tax payable on B's death if A survives B.

(4) If the interest comes to an end, and on the same occasion the settlor's spouse becomes beneficially entitled to the settled property, then if—

(i) the settlor's spouse is then domiciled in the United Kingdom; and

(ii) neither the settlor nor the settlor's spouse had acquired a reversionary interest in the property for a consideration in money or money's worth, tax will not be chargeable under this paragraph. The references in this paragraph to the settlor's spouse include, in a case where the settlor has died less than two years before the interest comes to an end or the interest comes to an end before 1 April 1977, references to the settlor's widow or widower (FA 1975, Sched 5, para 4(6), and FA 1976, s110(2).

Example—A settles property upon B for life, with power in the trustees to appoint back to A's spouse, or widow, within two years of A's death. If such an appointment is made, so terminating B's interest in possession, there will be no charge to Capital Transfer Tax.

(5) When the person beneficially entitled to the interest is the surviving spouse of the person who died before 13 November 1974, tax is not chargeable if the termination would have been exempted from estate duty under the old surviving spouse exemption (FA 1975, Sched 5, para 4(7)).

These old estate duty surviving spouse trusts now have considerable tax advantages. It means property is left, usually to the children, on the death of the surviving spouse, free of capital transfer tax and capital gains tax. The trustees should try to build up the value of such trust funds as far as possible.

(6) There will be no charge to capital transfer tax if there is a disposal of an interest in possession made by one party to a marriage to the other, or to a child of either party, for the maintenance, education or training of the child for a period ending not later than the year in which he attains the age of eighteen or, after attaining that age, ceases to undergo full-time education or training (FA 1975, s46(5)).

Transactions between trustees and beneficiaries (anti-avoidance)—Paragraph 4(9) of Sched 5 to the FA 1975 states that where a transaction is made between the trustees of the settlement and a person who is, or is connected with—

(1) the person beneficially entitled to an interest in the property; or

(2) a person beneficially entitled to any other interest in that property or to any interest in any other property comprised in the settlement; or

(3) a person for whose benefit any of the settled property may be applied, and, as a result of the transaction, the value of the first-mentioned property is less than it would be but for the transaction, a corresponding part of the interest shall be deemed for the purposes of these provisions to have come to an end, unless the transaction is such that, were the trustees beneficially entitled to the settled property, it would not be a transfer of value.

This anti-avoidance provision could apply where the trustees grant a lease of settled property on favourable terms to a person connected with a beneficiary. The reference in the section to 'transactions' would appear to involve two parties getting together to reduce the value of the fund so that the provision may not apply where the trustees unilaterally reduce the value of the trust fund.

Relief for successive charges on interests in possession—If the same property comprised in a settlement suffers multiple charges to capital transfer tax as a result of quick successive terminations or dispositions of interests in possession there are reliefs available. For instance, if there is a fund for A for life, then B for life, C for life, and D absolutely, there will be charges on each death.

If the period between the termination or disposition is not more than four years, tax shall be charged as if the value of the property were reduced—

(1) by 80 per cent if that period is one year or less;

(2) by 60 per cent if that period is more than one year but not more than two years;

(3) by 40 per cent if that period is more than two years but not more than three years; and

(4) by 20 per cent if that period is more than three years (FA 1975, Sched 5, para 5(1)).

Paragraph 5(2) of Sched 5 of the FA 1975 and the FA 1976, s97(2) adapt these quick succession rules to cover charges under the transitional estate duty rules.

After the Trust is Created: Reversionary Interests (s51(1))

There are, of course, future interests under a settlement. If property is held by A for life and then to B, B has a reversionary interest. If it is held for A for life and then B for life and then C absolutely, both B and C have reversionary interests.

Transfers of a reversionary interest are excluded from the tax except in the following cases:

(1) where it has at any time been acquired (whether by the person entitled to it or by a person previously entitled to it) for a consideration in money or money's worth; or

(2) where it is an interest expectant on the determination of a lease which is treated as a settlement for the purposes of the tax (broadly a lease for the life of a person, unless it was granted for full consideration in money or money's worth); or

(3) where the person who made the settlement, or his spouse, is beneficially entitled to the reversionary interest, except where the reversion arises under a settlement made before 16 April 1976 (FA 1975, s24(3) (as amended)).

Where a person entitled to an interest (whether an interest in possession or not) in any settled property acquires a reversionary interest expectant (whether immediately or not) on the interest, the reversionary interest is not part of his estate for the purposes of capital transfer tax. Thus if he pays anything for that reversionary interest he will be treated as having made a gift.

These interests are dealt with in detail in Chapter 4, p41 et seq.

Capital gains tax

The usual capital gains tax provisions apply to fixed interest trusts as apply to discretionary trusts, ie, there will be disposals when assets are put into the trust, when a beneficiary becomes absolutely entitled as against the trustees, and also when trustees dispose of assets in the normal course of the administration of the trust (see Chapter 2, p28).

Where a person becomes absolutely entitled to trust assets on the death of a life tenant there will be no charge to capital gains tax (although there could be a charge to capital transfer tax), and the new base for capital gains tax will be the value as at the date of death (FA 1965, s25(3), and FA 1971, Sched 12, para 6).

Example—Chargeable assets are held in trust for Mary for life and then for John absolutely. When the assets were put into the trust they were worth £100,000. At Mary's death they were worth £300,000. There will be no capital gains tax payable on Mary's death and John's base value will be £300,000, so that if he subsequently sells them for £350,000 he will pay capital gains tax on only £50,000.

On the termination at any time after 6 April 1965 of a life interest in possession in all or any part of the settled property, the whole or a corresponding part of each of the assets forming part of the settled property and not ceasing at that time to be settled property, shall be deemed for the purposes of capital gains tax to have been disposed of and immediately re-acquired by the trustees for a consideration equal to the whole or a corresponding part of the market value of the assets. However, where the life interest terminates on the death of the life tenant the deemed disposal and re-acquisition will not give rise to a charge to tax (FA 1965, s25(4) as amended by FA 1971, Sched 12, paras 7–9).

Example—Chargeable assets are held in trust for A for life, then for B for life, then for C absolutely. When A dies the base value is uplifted under the FA 1965, s25(4), and the FA 1971, Sched 12, paras 7–9, as above. When B dies, the base is again uplifted, this time under the FA 1965, s25(3) and the FA 1971, Sched 12, para 6.

A life interest in relation to a settlement—

(1) includes a right under the settlement to the income of, or the use or occupation of, settled property for the life of a person other than the person entitled to the right, or for lives;

(2) does not include any right which is contingent on the exercise of the discretion of the trustee or the discretion of some other person; and

(3) does not include an annuity, notwithstanding that the annuity is payable out of or charged on settled property or the income of settled property.

It will thus be seen that for capital gains tax purposes, where there is a life tenant, the gain will be eliminated as at the date of the death of the life tenant, and the person who takes the property will have the new base value. This is highly beneficial. The problem is that in order to get this elimination of inherent capital gains it means that the property must be held by the life tenant for the purposes of capital transfer tax so that there will be a charge to capital transfer tax on that occasion.

The reference to 'a life interest' is not identical to the reference to 'an interest in possession' in the capital transfer tax legislation, so that the separate definitions should be examined. The Revenue however, did state, in connection with their press release of 12 February 1976 (see above, p50) that their view of an interest in possession applied equally to the FA 1965, s25(4), which refers to a life interest in possession.

Revertor to Settlor Situation

If property is settled by S on T for life, with revertor to S, we have already seen that no capital gains tax is payable when the property comes back to S. To prevent S getting an uplift for capital gains tax on the assets he settled, the legislation provides that the base value is in effect rolled over, so that if the assets when settled were worth £10,000, and at the death of T were worth £30,000, S's base value for capital gains tax purposes will be £10,000.

Private Residences

Section 29 of the FA 1965 gives a general exemption from capital gains tax for the disposal by an individual of his principal private dwelling-house. This exemption is extended by s29(9) to cover a gain accruing to a trustee on a disposal of settled property where, during the period of the ownership of the property by the trustee, it had been the only or main residence of a person entitled to occupy it under the terms of the settlement. This exemption clearly covers the case of a life tenant who lives in such a house under the terms of the trust.

A case which has caused some difficulty in this area is *Sansom* v *Peay* [1976], STC 494. In that case the taxpayers were trustees of a discretionary trust which, by its terms, permitted beneficiaries to reside in a dwelling-house as their main residence. They claimed exemption under the FA 1965, s29(9), claiming that they were 'entitled to occupy it under the terms of the settlement'. Brightman J held that they were so entitled. The difficulty with this case lies in its possible capital transfer tax repercussions. The case indicates that the beneficiaries had an interest in possession, so that on the death of the beneficiaries capital transfer tax could be payable (FA 1975, s22), and the grant of such a right by discretionary trustees could create an interest in possession. The Revenue had indicated prior to this decision that such an exercise of power would not create an interest in possession (LSG, 6 August 1975) but this statement may now not be followed.

It is an uncertain area of the law. Trustees should not allow such an interest to arise or should consider charging the beneficiary for the right to live in the property until such time as this area of the law is clarified.

The case also affects the position under the FA 1965, s25, where an 'uplift' on the death of a life tenant is possible for capital gains tax purposes, provided the beneficiary has a right under the settlement to the income of, or the use or occupation of, settled property, for his life. It may be that certain 'discretionary trusts' will now enable an 'uplift' to take place on a death, since the wording of the FA 1965, s25(10)(*a*) and the FA 1965, s29(9) is similar.

Development land tax

The usual development land tax consequences will apply. If the trustees dispose of an interest in land by commencing a project of material development or selling the property, or leasing or otherwise realizing development gain, they could be chargeable to development land tax. They will have the £10,000 annual exemption, and until March 1980 the reduced rate of 66⅔ per cent will apply to the next £150,000 of realized development value. Transfers to a beneficiary of an interest in land will not give rise to a charge to development land tax, although when the beneficiary subsequently disposes of the land he will take the trustees original base cost (see above, p32).

Stamp duty

The usual stamp duty provisions will apply with regard to these types of trusts (see Chapter 2, at p11).

Tax planning

Where there are adult beneficiaries, so that a qualifying accumulation and maintenance settlement cannot be used, these trusts can be useful where it is desired that property should be left in trust for persons; the alternative to a discretionary trust would mean that the disadvantages which those trusts suffer would have to be tolerated.

There are no income tax advantages to be obtained from interest in possession trusts, unless the decision of Fox, J in *Pearson* v *IRC* (see above, p51) is held to be good law on appeal. Because of the capital transfer tax penalty of the life tenant's liability to capital transfer tax on the entire fund, although he only receives the income, it might well be that the use of these trusts is now restricted only to those cases where people genuinely, for non-tax reasons, want to keep property in trust for adults.

The exceptional situations where property is left to a spouse for life and also the revertor to settlor situations can be advantageous.

Other tax points which should be remembered are:

(1) The transfer of interests in possession or reversionary interests (if not in

the hands of a purchaser) will be free of capital gains tax. In this sense a high income taxpayer is able to capitalize future income payments (FA 1965, Sched 7, para 13(1)).

(2) Transfers of trust assets to persons with interests in possession in those assets are free of capital transfer tax.

(3) The gift of a reversionary interest can be free of capital transfer tax and capital gains tax (suffering only ad valorem stamp duty).

(4) The trusts can be quite useful where no income arises, eg, X could settle a house for A for life, with remainder to B. A could enjoy the house as his residence with no adverse income tax consequences and could have it transferred to him free of capital transfer tax and capital gains tax if it is his principal private residence (FA 1965, s29(9)).

(5) By giving an interest in possession to a person on his or her deathbed, one is able to wash the gain for capital gains tax purposes when the donee dies. This could possibly be useful in husband and wife situations. The gain is also washed if property is held by husband and wife as joint tenants. On the death of one of the spouses the other spouse will have his or her capital gains tax base, as to the one half that accrues to him or her, uplifted as at the date of the death of the deceased spouse (FA 1965, s24(1) and (9), Sched 6, para 30, and Sched 7, para 20).

CHAPTER 6

SETTLEMENTS WITHOUT INTERESTS IN POSSESSION (DISCRETIONARY TRUSTS)

It is generally believed that discretionary trusts have been almost 'outlawed' by the introduction of capital transfer tax. This is not entirely the case, but it is correct to say that under the estate duty regime they were given extra favourable treatment. The capital transfer tax rules have merely tried to tax them in a fair manner, especially as between them and fixed trusts. In doing this, however, arbitrary rules have had to be introduced and these can produce injustice.

Discretionary trusts still have the following advantages:

(1) Income can be accumulated, capitalized, and paid out to beneficiaries free of all income tax, provided these powers are given to the trustees.

(2) If a discretionary beneficiary dies no capital transfer tax is payable. Thus, if the proposed beneficiaries are elderly or unwell it might be advantageous to have a discretionary trust rather than any other type of trust.

(3) Small discretionary trusts can be useful vehicles for capitalizing income without suffering from significant capital transfer tax liabilities. For instance, a taxpayer who has made no previous chargeable transfers could exhaust his zero-rate band of £25,000 by creating a discretionary trust of that value. No capital transfer tax will be charged on the creation; a nil rate will apply to distribution payments up to the initial value and thereafter the settlement will have its own cumulative rate (FA 1975, Sched 5, para 7). Alternatively, the taxpayer could use up his £2,000 annual exemption to create a number of small discretionary settlements. If the settlor has made no chargeable transfers the creation of the settlement for £2,000 would be an exempt transfer, and the trust will be able to make a transfer of £25,000 without a charge arising.

(4) The income and capital of the fund can be used by the trustees in a flexible manner so as to produce the most tax advantageous distributions, considering the circumstances of the beneficiaries at any given time.

(5) If a close company has its shares in a discretionary trust it might be difficult for the Revenue to apportion the company's income under the FA 1972, Sched 16 to any particular discretionary beneficiary.

(6) If it is desired to set up a trading trust, a discretionary trust might be the

best vehicle, if the beneficiaries are too old to enable an accumulation and maintenance settlement to be set up.

What is a trust without an interest in possession—A Discretionary Trust?

Such trusts are often referred to as 'discretionary trusts'. They are trusts where there is no interest in possession (see above, p49). The usual case arises where the trustees have power to apply income to beneficiaries in their discretion, with no beneficiary having an immediate entitlement to the trust income.

Example—Property is held on trust to pay the income to X and Y with power to accumulate the income for twenty-one years. This could amount to a trust with an interest in possession if the decision of Fox J in *Pearson* v *IRC* (1978), STC 627, is not overturned on appeal to the higher courts (see p51).

Example—Property is held on trust to pay income to A, B or C as the trustees shall in their discretion decide. Failing the exercise of their discretion the income is to be accumulated. A, B and C do not have interests in possession, as they have no entitlement to any income.

Income tax

Discretionary trusts will usually come within the provisions of the FA 1973, s16, so that the trustees will be liable for tax at the basic rate plus the additional rate of 15 per cent.

Section 16 applies to income arising to trustees in any year of assessment so far as it—

(1) is income which is to be accumulated or which is payable at the discretion of the trustees or any other person (whether or not the trustees have power to accumulate it); and

(2) is neither (before being distributed) the income of any person other than the trustees nor treated for any purposes of the Income Tax Acts as the income of a settlor; and

(3) is not income arising under a trust established for charitable purposes only, or income from investments, deposits or other property held for the purposes of a fund or scheme established for the sole purpose of providing relevant benefits within the meaning of the FA 1970, s26; and

(4) exceeds the income applied in defraying the expenses of the trustees in that year which are properly chargeable to income (or would be so chargeable but for any express provisions of the trust).

Thus, if the trustees of a discretionary trust have the power to accumulate income for the benefit of a beneficiary who only has a contingent right to the income, the income can be accumulated, capitalized and paid out to a beneficiary free of any further income tax (see Chapter 3).

When attempting to benefit from the income tax advantages of being able to accumulate income and capitalize it, one has to take into account the capital transfer tax disadvantages which these trusts suffer.

Capital transfer tax

Discretionary trusts are not favourably treated by the capital transfer tax legislation but there are instances where they can still be of advantage.

The general rule is that there is a charge to capital transfer tax when the trust property ceases to be held upon discretionary trust. This gives rise to an actual or deemed 'capital distribution' (see p66). If on a distribution the beneficiary pays the tax there is no grossing-up (FA 1975, Sched 5, paras 6(4)(*a*) and 6(5) as amended). If the trustees pay the tax there will be grossing-up. If a beneficiary obtains an interest in possession, normally the tax will be payable out of the property so held or by the beneficiary so that there will be no grossing-up. Where the funds are appointed upon accumulation and maintenance settlements, by virtue of Sched 5, para 15(3) there is a notional chargeable transfer by the trustees of a gross sum equal to the value of the property so appointed.

Paragraph 6(3) of Sched 5 of the FA 1975 contains an anti-avoidance provision similar to that applicable to trusts with interests in possession (FA 1975, Sched 5, para 4(9)). The provision causes a charge to arise where transactions are entered into which have the result of reducing the value of the settled property.

There are also specific provisions dealing with additions to settlements by the settlor after 26 March 1974 (Sched 5, para 9), and with capital distributions made after the termination of the interest of the settlor or the settlor's spouse in the settlement (Sched 5, para 10, as amended by FA 1976, Sched 14, para 14). The treatment of these settlements for capital transfer tax purposes differs materially depending on whether the settlements were made after 26 March 1974, or before 27 March 1974.

Pre-27 March 1974 Discretionary Trusts

These trusts are treated as separate persons from the settlor and beneficiaries. The trustees have a separate scale of rates from the settlor or any other individual. It is as if the settlor has created another person with his own set of tax rates (the lifetime scale applies with the first £25,000 taxed at nil per cent), and to this extent these trusts serve a very useful function.

When a Charge Arises

Capital Distributions—There can be a charge to the tax when capital distributions are made to beneficiaries. In this connection, a payment out of capitalized income is a payment out of capital. A capital distribution is defined as a distribution payment out of settled property in which no interest in possession subsists (FA 1975, Sched 5, para 6(1)). A distribution payment is defined as any payment which—

(1) is not income of any person for any of the purposes of income tax, and would not for any of those purposes be income of a person not resident in the United Kingdom if he were so resident; and

(2) is not a payment in respect of costs or expenses (FA 1975, Sched 5, para 11(7)).

The term 'payment' includes the transfer of assets other than money.

Creation of Interest in Possession—Capital transfer tax can be payable where an interest in possession is created in the settled fund. On the creation of such an interest in possession the trustees are deemed to have made a capital distribution (FA 1975, Sched 5, para 6(2)). Also where the whole or any part of the settled property ceases to be so settled, otherwise than by virtue of any payment or transfer of assets made by the trustees, then, if—

(1) paragraph 6(2) does not apply; but

(2) a person at that time becomes entitled to (or immediately thereafter has) an interest in the property which would be an interest in possession if held beneficially by an individual, a capital distribution is deemed to have been made (FA 1978, s70(1)). This is a wide anti-avoidance section aimed at preventing trustees and beneficiaries from avoiding charges to capital transfer tax on the reconstruction or termination of discretionary trusts.

Ten-Year Charge—Every ten years the entire fund of a discretionary trust is treated as notionally distributed (ie, a capital distribution of an amount equal to the value of the fund is treated as having been made), and the charge is at 30 per cent of the rate at which tax would have been chargeable, at lifetime rates, if the whole of the trust property were distributed.

The first ten-year period is to commence on the date of the original settlement, but there are to be no charges before 1 April 1980. Thus, one takes the first ten-year period from the date of the trust and if this falls before 1 April 1980 one takes a further ten-year period. If that falls after 31 March 1980, that will be the first day of the charge. If that second ten-year period falls before 1 April 1980 one must take a further ten-year period and so on, until one has a first periodic charge date after 31 March 1980. So, for example, if a trust was set up on 30 March 1970 the first anniversary will be on 30 March 1980. As this is before 1 April 1980 the first periodic charge for which the trust will be liable will be on 30 March 1990. If a trust was set up on 30 April 1970 the first periodic charge will be on 30 April 1980.

Wherever property becomes liable to tax on a capital distribution made within twenty years of a periodic charge, the trustees will be able to use the amount of the periodic charge as a tax credit (FA 1975, Sched 5, para 13).

Accumulation and Maintenance Settlements—Where there is a discretionary trust and it is converted into an accumulation and maintenance settlement within the FA 1975, Sched 5, para 15 (as amended), a capital distribution is treated as having been made (FA 1975, Sched 5, para 15(3)).

Annual Charge (Non-resident trusts only)—For non-resident trust funds the ten-year 30 per cent charge applies in the normal way. There is, however, in addition, an annual charge of 3 per cent of the full tax at the end of each of the ten years except the last. This charge only applies, like the 30 per cent charge, to discretionary trusts. The 3 per cent tax can also be used as a credit against the 30 per cent tax payable at the end of the ten years. The charge only applies in respect of a year ended after 31 December 1975 (FA 1975, Sched 5, para 12(2)).

Transitional Relief for Settlements Made Before 27 March 1974

In the case of a settlement made before 27 March 1974, capital distributions made or treated as made before 1 April 1980 are charged at a reduced rate. This relief does not apply unless the beneficiary concerned is domiciled in the United Kingdom and had not at or before that time acquired an interest under the settlement for a consideration in money or money's worth directly or indirectly from a person not so domiciled (FA 1975, Sched 5, para 14(5), as amended by FA 1978, s69(3)).

Where the charge arises on the creation of an accumulation and maintenance settlement, the reduction is available only if all of the existing beneficiaries are so domiciled in the United Kingdom. It is vital, therefore, when trying to make use of the capital transfer tax reduced transitional rate relief, that the domiciles of the beneficiaries are checked out.

If capital distributions are made, the charge will be only on the amount of the following fractions of the tax which would otherwise be chargeable on such capital distributions:

Date of distribution	Proportion of the tax normally chargeable that will be payable
Up to 31 March 1976	10%
Up to 31 March 1977	12½%
Up to 31 March 1978	15%
Up to 31 March 1979	17½%
Up to 31 March 1980	20%

Tables relating to distributions up to 31 March 1979 and 31 March 1980 are set out in Appendix I.

How to Deal with Discretionary Trusts Made Before 27 March 1974

United Kingdom discretionary trusts bascially suffer capital transfer tax in two ways:

(1) if the trustees transfer any capital from the trust to a beneficiary, or hold the property upon new trusts, such as an accumulation and maintenance settlement, there will be a charge to capital transfer tax; and

(2) if the trustees decide not to transfer any capital, then every ten years the entire fund of the discretionary trust is notionally treated as having been transferred out and a tax charge equal to 30 per cent of lifetime rates will arise.

These tax penalties can be avoided by either transferring the trust fund absolutely to beneficiaries (and therefore breaking the trust), or by remodelling or reconstructing the trust, usually by deed of appointment, so that the trust remains in being but ceases to be a discretionary trust by virtue of the alteration of the beneficial interest thereunder.

The problem which arises when appointing out the trust fund absolutely to a beneficiary is that the trustees could be liable to capital gains tax on the difference between the market value of chargeable assets when they first went into the trust and the market value of those assets when they are appointed out to a beneficiary.

The alternative to breaking the trust is for the trustees to reconstruct it. The terms of the trust deed must be carefully examined to make sure the trustees have the power to carry out a trust reconstruction. The reconstruction will not cause a liability to capital gains tax to arise, provided the trustees of the reconstructed trust cannot be said to have become absolutely entitled to the trust assets as against the trustees of the old trust under the FA 1965, s25(3).

When carrying out a reconstruction the Chancery Division cases before Brightman J of *Hoare Trustees* v *Gardner* (*Inspector of Taxes*) and *Hart* (*Inspector of Taxes*) v *Brisco and Others* [1978] STC 89) must be borne in mind. In those cases the exercise of powers under the original settlements creating 'sub-settlements' resulted in the trustees of the new settlements becoming absolutely entitled to the settled property as against the trustees of the defunct head settlements (called 'spectral settlements' by Brightman J (at p105)). Brightman J stated at p105:

> In my judgment, the question whether a disposition which exercises a fiduciary power is to be viewed as a separate settlement, or as part of a single fiduciary arrangement headed by the disposition which created the power, must be answered in the context of the circumstances of the particular case. The word 'settlement' is not defined in the Finance Act 1965; the nearest one gets to a definition is to be found in the meaning attributed to 'settled property' in section 45, and that does not carry the matter much further. The fact that, on a strict legal analysis, the limitations created under a special power of appointment are to be written into the instrument which created the power does not in my view, inevitably prevent the appointment

from superseding in toto the settlement which created the power so that thereafter there is one settlement only, namely the appointment. This can, in my opinion, be shown by comparing two extreme examples. If a special power of appointment is exercised in such a manner as to vary the age of vesting or to vary the shares in which contingent beneficiaries are to take, all the other trusts, powers and provisions of the settlement remaining intact, I would think it beyond doubt that one would regard the settlement and the appointment as together constituting a single settlement. If, however, a special power of appointment, drawn in an appropriately wide form, is so exercised that the appointed assets become vested in distinct trustees, and all the trusts, powers and provisions of the original settlement are irrevocably gone, completely new trusts, powers and provisions being created in their place, so that no one will ever again need to refer to the original settlement except to confirm that it has ceased to exist, the trustees of the original settlement being functus officio and having nothing whatever to do, I would find it difficult to believe that the original settlement continues in being.... In what sense, I ask myself, can a settlement be said to exist if all the trusts, powers and provisions of that settlement have been irrevocably brought to an end by the appointment.

To avoid the problem created by these cases, Deeds of Appointment should be drafted carefully to ensure that the sub-settlements are part of the head settlements. It is necessary too that the head settlement stays in existence, ie, there should always be an ultimate resulting trust back to the head settlement, the trustees should be the same, the appointment should be drafted so that it cannot be read on its own, and constant references should be made back to the head settlement.

Owing to the uncertainty created in this area of the law by the above two cases, the Inland Revenue issued a statement on 14 November 1978 entitled *Capital Gains Tax Exercise of a Power of Appointment over Settled Property*. The statement reads as follows:

The Board of Inland Revenue have studied the implications of the judgments in two recent tax cases concerning the treatment of resettled property for CGT purposes (*Hart* v *Briscoe* [1978] 2 WLR 832, and *Hoare Trustees* v *Gardner* [1978] 2 WLR 839; tax case leaflet no 2663), where new trustees become absolutely entitled to the settled property as against the old trustees. It may be of help to practitioners to know how the Revenue propose to approach the questions raised by those decided cases.

The Revenue will continue to take the view that where a power of advancement or a general power of appointment is exercised irrevocably the assets to which it applies will normally pass into a new settlement; a charge on a deemed disposal by the trustees of the original settlement will therefore arise under FA 1965, s25(3).

Brightman J indicated in his judgments that the exercise of a special power of appointment could also, exceptionally, result in the creation of a new settlement. The Revenue do not regard that indication as requiring it to change its practice of accepting that, where a special power of appointment is exercised (ie, a power conferred by the original settlement deed to appoint to or among a named or designated group or class of persons), the assets to which the appointment applies will, in normal cases, remain subject to the original settlement as modified by the appointment so that a deemed disposal for the purposes of FA 1965, s25(3) does not result.

If the appointment could be done before the end of March 1980 the transitional reliefs can be used. The reliefs are on a sliding scale so that the earlier the appointment is made the cheaper it will be.

By reconstructing, trustees will be paying some capital transfer tax now in order to take the trust out of capital transfer tax; in fact, generally, there can only be a charge to capital transfer tax after the reconstruction on the death of a beneficiary who is entitled to the income from the trust for the time being, or if he gives his interest, or part of it, away (FA 1975, Sched 5, para 3(1)).

The reason why the Government has attacked discretionary trusts is that it finds it almost impossible to ascertain on which beneficiary a charge should be imposed. In order to acquire the capital transfer tax reliefs, the legislation makes it necessary for the trustees to decide generally which individuals will benefit immediately or in the future. A trust reconstruction basically designates particular individuals or classes of individuals to have the right to the assets or at least to the income or benefits of the assets.

Normally a reconstruction will be for the benefit of—

(1) the children of the settlor or his grandchildren and other issue; and/or

(2) other relatives or beneficiaries mentioned under the discretionary trust.

If the reconstruction is to be made for the benefit of the children and grandchildren of the settlor it should be in the form of a qualifying accumulation and maintenance settlement so that, broadly, the children will become entitled to all the income which arises from the trust fund when they attain the age of twenty-five years. Before that time the income will be accumulated or paid out to the children at the discretion of the trustees. From that age the income must generally be paid out, but the children will not be entitled as such to the capital. The trustees can have the power to pay capital, ie, the trust assets, to the children in their discretion, but there will be no actual power in the children to call for the trust assets. It is this element in the appointment which enables the capital gains tax liability to be postponed, at the same time obtaining the reliefs from capital transfer tax; ie, the children will become entitled to income at the appropriate time but will not be absolutely entitled as against the trustees to the capital assets. On the death of a child, his children can take his share.

It might well be that in order to have a longer period to accumulate the income, and in order to skip a generation that part of the fund should be put into an accumulation and maintenance settlement for the benefit of the grandchildren of the settlor (see Chapter 7).

If it is desired that persons other than the children or grandchildren of the settlor should be beneficiaries, then, assuming that they are over the age of twenty-five, they will usually be given interests in possession. This will postpone the charge to capital gains tax and enable the trust to make use of the transitional reliefs for capital transfer tax, but there will be no power to accumulate the income, unless *Pearson* v *IRC* is upheld (see p51, above).

Thus, the main advantages of reconstructing these trusts are as follows:

(1) Full use is made of the capital transfer tax reliefs granted by the Government (this will also be the case if the trust is broken)

(2) The capital gains tax liability is postponed.

(3) The trust assets will continue to remain in the names of the trustees.

The main disadvantages of reconstructing are as follows:

(1) Under a discretionary trust, on the death of a beneficiary no capital transfer tax is payable (after a beneficiary becomes entitled to the income under a reconstructed trust there will be a charge to capital transfer tax on that beneficiary's death).

(2) Under the discretionary trust the trustee may be in a position to accumulate the income for twenty-one years and to capitalize it. Under the reconstructed trust, as soon as an interest in possession arises, the power to accumulate income will cease; see, however, *Pearson* v *IRC* (p51, above).

(3) If trustees reconstruct into an accumulation and maintenance trust, the funds are still related property until an interest in possession arises (FA 1975, Sched 10, para 7(2)(*b*)). In this respect little or no purpose, and only expense, is incurred by reconstruction.

(4) It is possible that a change of Government before 1980 might result in these penalties being abolished. The rules might even be changed before 1980 without a change of Government. For instance, from 26 October 1977 trustees were given the new £25,000 threshold plus the 20 per cent or 50 per cent business relief which were not available to trusts reconstructed on or before that date. Thus, trusts worth £25,000 which were constructed before 27 October 1977 will pay capital transfer tax, whereas if the trustees had waited until after 26 October 1977 there would have been no charge.

Some additional reasons for keeping discretionary trusts are—

(1) the trustees cannot afford the capital gains tax on an absolute disposal;

(2) the obvious beneficiary is someone who is already wealthy so that one could move into a tax bracket higher than that of the trustees, especially as individuals are subject to the death scale of capital transfer tax while trustees are not;

(3) the trust contains less than £25,000 of capital, or is so little over this figure that the tax is trivial;

(4) the first periodic charge is a long way off (eg, a 1969 trust is not liable until 1989); and

(5) there will be a distribution within twenty years so that a periodic charge can be credited against the tax thereon.

Appendix II is a report of the type that could be sent to trustees of a discretionary trust setting out the principal points which have a bearing on the decision to reconstruct.

Transfers to Charities and to the Settlor

The exemptions for gifts to charities also apply to distributions from discretionary trusts. These payments are not cumulated with the other distributions from the settlement after 6 April 1976 (FA 1976, s111). Exemption is also given for distributions made to the settlor or the spouse of the settlor. Distributions to the settlor's widow or widower within two years of the settlor's death are similarly exempt. In each case the beneficiary must be domiciled in the United Kingdom. Exemption in this case, however, is not so beneficial as that for charities because the exempt distribution is added to the cumulative total of the settlement, so it will affect the rate of tax on later distributions (see FA 1975, Sched 5, para 6(6), as amended by FA 1976, s110(3) and Sched 15, Pt V). However, the exempt distribution will be treated as having been made after the other tax distributions if the distributions are made on the same day.

Example—Mr X, who is domiciled in the United Kingdom, has a discretionary trust which he set up in 1970. The trustees wish to transfer one-third for the benefit of X's children, one-third to X himself and one-third to charity. Because of the above cumulative provisions the trustees can transfer out property to the charity at any time but the transfer to the children should not take place after the transfer to Mr X. This will prevent the charge to tax on the transfer to the children (which is the only transfer on which tax will actually be paid) being increased by virtue of the amounts transferred to the children being added (to ascertain the appropriate tax rates on the amounts transferred to the children) to the transfer to Mr X himself.

Settlements made after 26 March 1974

A charge to capital transfer tax will arise in the usual way on the creation of the settlement. A charge will generally arise on the distributions from the trust—

(1) when funds are advanced to a beneficiary absolutely—grossing-up in this event will apply if the trustees bear the tax;

(2) when the trust terminates; and

(3) when the trust is reconstructed so as to qualify as an accumulation and maintenance settlement or as a trust with an interest in possession.

As well as the above-mentioned occasions of charge, there will be a periodic charge on the funds remaining in the settlement, at ten-yearly intervals; if the settlement is an overseas settlement an annual charge might also arise (see below, p169).

Distributions from the Trust

The capital transfer tax position of distributions from trusts which are created after 26 March 1974 is based on the position of the settlor when he creates the settlement. The rules are set out in the FA 1975, Sched 5, paras 7, 8 and 11. Very broadly, the rules provide that distributions by the trustees up to the amount put into the settlement (the *Initial Value*) are taxed at a special rate (this is the rate which the settlor would have paid at the time of the settlement on a chargeable transfer equal to the value of the property in the settlement), and thereafter cumulation applies based on the position of the settlor at the time of the settlement.

Although a statement of the principles is simple the implementation of the detailed provisions set out in Sched 5, paras 7, 8 and 11 are complicated. The best way to illustrate the rules is by way of an example.

Example—Mr X on 1 January 1978 has a net cumulative total of gifts, after taking off his annual exemptions, of £90,000 on which he has paid tax of £12,419.

On 1 June 1978 he settles £40,000 upon the trusts of a discretionary settlement.

On 1 January 1979 £10,000 is advanced out of the trust to a beneficiary absolutely.

On 1 June 1979 the balance of the funds now worth £70,000 are appointed out absolutely to the beneficiaries, and the trust is terminated.

(1) The total net transfers by Mr X immediately after he created the settlement amounted to £130,000. The tax on them, borne by Mr X, is £30,217. Mr X will have already paid £12,419 on the first transfer of £90,000 so that the tax attributable to the £40,000 is £17,798 (ie, £30,217–£12,419).

(2) The £40,000 (exclusive of capital transfer tax) is the *Initial Value* of the settlement.

(3) When the transfer of £10,000 is made to a beneficiary on 1 January 1979, the provisions of the FA 1975, Sched 5, para 7 must be examined.

(4) These require the ascertainment of the *Basic rate* of the trust. This is the rate of tax chargeable upon distributions from the trust up to the amount of the *Initial Value*. It is the rate at which tax would have been charged when the settlement was made if the gross amount of the chargeable transfer had been equal to the value of the property originally subject to the settlement. It will thus differ from the rate actually charged on the making of the settlement. In addition, the *basic rate* ignores any personal exemptions available to the settlor.

(5) The formula for ascertaining the basic rate is—

$$\frac{\textit{Notional Tax}}{\textit{Initial Value}} \times \frac{100}{1} = \textit{Basic rate}$$

(6) The *Notional tax* is found by adding the *Initial Value* (£40,000) to the previous grossed-up transfers of the settlor (£90,000 + £12,419), calculating the tax applicable thereto using the gross tables (ie, the tax is £23,972), and deducting therefrom the tax already paid (ie, the tax already paid is £12,419). This gives a *Notional tax* of £11,553.

(7) The amounts for the above formula are thus—

$$\frac{£11{,}553}{40{,}000} \times \frac{100}{1} = 28.88\%$$

(8) The *Basic rate* is therefore 28.88%.

(9) The transfer of £10,000 on 1 January 1979 has to be grossed up as the trustees are bearing the tax. The tax applicable thereto is—

$$£10{,}000 \times \frac{28.88}{71.12} = £4{,}061$$

(10) The value transferred out of the trust on a net gift of £10,000 is therefore £10,000 + £4,061, ie, £14,061.

(11) Thus, out of a total *Initial Value* of £40,000, £25,939 remains after the net transfer of £10,000.

(12) When the trust is terminated on 1 June 1979 it is necessary to find the excess of the trust fund value over what remains of the initial value (ie, £70,000–£25,939). This gives an excess of £44,061. One has to find the tax chargeable on that after adding to it the *Initial Value* (£40,000) and the prior transfers made by the settlor (£90,000 + £12,419). Tax on those sums (£44,061 + £40,000 + £90,000 + £12,419), which total £186,480, amounts to £41,379 using the gross tables.

(13) The next step is to deduct from the £41,379 the *Notional tax* before deducting from it the tax already paid: this is £23,972 (see para (6) above). This gives a tax liability on the excess over the *Initial Value* of £17,407.

(14) The tax payable on the balance of the *Initial value* will be £7,491 (ie, £25,939 × 28.88%). No grossing-up applies, since the trust has come to an end.

(15) Thus, with regard to the £70,000, the trustees will reserve for tax £24,898, leaving a net amount for the beneficiaries of £45,102.

Capital gains tax

The usual capital gains tax provisions will apply to discretionary trusts, ie, there will be a charge to capital gains tax when the trust is set up, when a beneficiary becomes absolutely entitled as against the trustees, and if the trustees make gains in the normal course of their trusteeship. Discretionary beneficiaries do not, as such, have interests under trusts, but if any interests are created then these can be disposed of by the beneficiaries free of capital gains tax (FA 1965, Sched 7, para 13(1)).

The provisions concerning a notional disposal for capital gains tax on the death of a beneficiary will not usually apply as there are no life interests upon which the relief can operate (see above, p31). The rights of the beneficiaries will usually be contingent on the exercise of the discretion of the trustees (see, however, *Sansom* v *Peay* [1976], STC 494, which is discussed at p61, above).

The charge to capital gains tax which arises when an individual becomes absolutely entitled as against the trustee is one of the reasons why, in trying to make use of the transitional reliefs for capital transfer tax (under FA 1975, Sched 5, para 14), one should consider creating interests in possession, or accumulation and maintenance settlements, rather than making absolute appointments.

Development land tax

The usual development land tax consequences will apply. If the trustees disposed of an interest in land by commencing a project of material development, or selling the property, or leasing or otherwise realizing development gain, they could be charged to development land tax (see above, p32).

Stamp duty

The usual stamp duty provisions will apply to discretionary trusts (see above, p11).

Conclusion

The capital transfer tax liabilities imposed upon discretionary trusts now make them rather unattractive vehicles to hold property. There are still the income tax advantages, and trusts which are set up overseas, with overseas settlors, can still be discretionary trusts without any serious tax disadvantages (see p169, below).

The trusts which were set up before 27 March 1974 have served a very useful function for capital transfer tax purposes in creating a 'mirror image' of the settlor, so that two sets of lifetime scales have been created; the old estate duty planning was therefore not done in vain.

There are reliefs from the general penalties suffered by these trusts, such as, the tax-free appointments back to the settlor or his spouse.

It might well be that if income tax saving is dominant, a settlor might wish to set up a discretionary trust to carry out trading activities. This is particularly so if the ages of the beneficiaries are such that one cannot make use of an accumulation and maintenance trust. Wherever it is possible to make use of an accumulation and maintenance trust that should be done. Where it is not possible the general tax position must be examined and it could well be that it still pays to capitalize income at 48 per cent in a discretionary trust and suffer the capital transfer tax disadvantages unless a trust within the decision of *Pearson* v *IRC* (see p51, above) is used.

The mode of valuing shares in a discretionary trust is not based on the loss in value to the trust estate, and so each transfer should be valued separately. Thus, if a pre-27 March 1974 discretionary trust holds 51 per cent of a private trading company, and three life interests are created for individuals in the entire fund, each individual's share is separately valued as a 17 per cent minority holding. It would also appear that, in this case, the full 50 per cent business relief may be available on those minority valuations (FA 1976, Sched 10, para 3(1)(*b*)). Further, if the settlor or his spouse holds shares in the company, their shares will not be related to the trust's shares insofar as the trust makes transfers (FA 1975, Sched 10, para 7(2)(*b*)).

CHAPTER 7

NOMINEESHIP

Nomineeship occurs where property is held in the name of one person for the absolute benefit of another. The nominee must act on the instructions of the beneficiary. He has no active duties to perform, as in the case of trustees of discretionary or fixed interest trusts (see *Christie* v *Ovington* [1875] 1 Ch D 279).

The creation of implied, resulting and constructive trusts will usually result in the trustee being a nominee or bare trustee.

Some uses of nomineeship

The beneficial owner may have the property vested in the name of another for some of the following reasons:

(1) *Secrecy*—The beneficial owner may not want his identity known.

(2) *Convenience*—If there are a large number of trustees of, for instance, a charitable trust, they may want the legal title of the trust property to be in the name of a single, perhaps corporate, trustee for administrative convenience.

(3) *Requirements of law*—Under the Companies Act 1948, s31, if at any time the number of members of a company is reduced, in the case of a private company, to below two, or, in the case of any other company, to below seven, and the company carries on business for more than six months while the number is so reduced, certain penalties can be chargeable. This requirement is, however, satisfied if the legal title alone is in the name of the two persons or seven persons, as the case may be, while the beneficial ownership is with other persons. Appropriate nomineeship documents will have to be executed. There are a number of company law provisions which require the disclosure of beneficial interests in shares: see, for example, the Companies Act 1976, s27, which gives certain companies power to require the disclosure of beneficial interests in their voting shares.

(4) *Persons under disability*—It might be that a transferor wishes to transfer property to infants; in this case the property could be transferred to their parents who could declare that they hold the property for the absolute benefit of the children. The parents would virtually then be nominees, so that if a child were to die the property would form part of his or her estate. This

trust has the added advantage that when the property is ultimately vested in the children no capital gains tax will be payable.

Example—Mr X wishes to transfer property to his minor grandchildren. Half the property is high-income producing and the other half likely to show a high capital appreciation. He transfers the high-income producing half to the parents of the grandchildren upon accumulation and maintenance trusts for the grandchildren, and the balance to the parents to hold as bare trustees for the children. The income in the accumulation and maintenance settlement can be capitalized but any changes of investment will be subject to capital gains tax without the exemption and reliefs for small gains under the FA 1978, s44(1), being available (the less favourable FA 1978, Sched 7, para 6 relief will, however, be available). Disposals of assets under the nominee trust will have the benefit of the capital gains tax exemptions and reliefs applicable to small gains under the FA 1978, s44(1); also, if any income arises from the fund, there will be no aggregation with the parents' income as they (the parents) did not create the trust.

The small gains relief and exemption, it should be noted, is only available to settlements made before 7 June 1978 (FA 1978, Sched 8, para 6(5)).

(5) *Voting control*—A number of beneficial owners may decide that one of their number should have the voting powers of their shares in a company; one person could therefore hold the shares as nominee for the various beneficial owners (see *Booth* v *Ellard* [1978] STC p487).

Tax consequences of nomineeship

The general rule is that 'a bare trusteeship [or nomineeship] is no trusteeship'. The nominee is ignored and the real owner is taxed as if he owned the property. Thus, in *De Pol* v *Cunningham* (1974) 49 TC 445, CA(NI) the taxpayer purchased property with money provided by a third party in circumstances giving rise to a resulting trust for the benefit of the third party. Assessments made on the third party, on the footing that he was the sole beneficial owner, were therefore discharged. For Capital Gains Tax, see the FA 1965, s25(5); for Development Land Tax, see the Development Land Tax Act 1976, s28(1); for Stamp Duty, see the Finance (1909–10) Act 1910, s74(6); for Capital Transfer Tax, see the FA 1975, ss20(2) and 21(3); and for Income Tax, see the words of Sir Wilfred Greene, obiter, in *Corbett* v *IRC* [1938] 1 KB 567, 577, (1937) 4 All ER, 700, 705, 21 TC 449, 460 CA.

CHAPTER 8

THE ACCUMULATION AND MAINTENANCE TRUST: THE SUPERTRUST

These trusts offer considerable capital transfer tax and income tax advantages. The trusts must qualify for capital transfer tax relief under the FA 1975, Sched 5, para 15, as amended by the FA 1976, s106. These trusts are likely to become as popular as discretionary trusts were under Estate Duty.

The capital transfer tax requirements

The capital transfer tax requirements are as follows:

(1) There must be one or more persons who are beneficiaries under the settlement, and those persons must, on or before attaining a specified age not exceeding twenty-five years, become either—

(i) entitled to the settled property or a part of it; or

(ii) obtain an interest in possession (for example, a life interest) in the settled property or a part of it (FA 1975, Sched 5, para 15(1)(*a*)).

(2) Prior to them reaching the age or ages on which they become so entitled, or obtain an interest in possession, there must be no interest in possession in the settled property or a part of the settled property, and the income from the settled property must be accumulated by the trustees so far as not applied for the maintenance, education or benefit of a person who is a beneficiary under the settlement (FA 1975, Sched 5, para 15(1)(*b*)).

(3) In addition to these requirements, one of the following two conditions must also be satisfied—

(i) not more than twenty-five years must have elapsed since the day on which the settlement was made, or if it is later, since the time the conditions in paragraphs (1) and (2) above all became satisfied in respect of the property or part of it (FA 1975, Sched 5, para 15(1)(*c*)(i), added by FA 1976, s106(1); or

(ii) all the persons who are or have been beneficiaries under the settlement are or were either grandchildren of a common grandparent or children, widows or widowers of such grandchildren who were themselves beneficiaries but died before the time when, had they survived, they would have become entitled under the condition in paragraph (1) above (FA 1975, Sched 5, para 15(1)(*c*)(ii), added by FA 1976, s106(1)).

The alternative conditions in paragraph (3) above were added by the FA 1976 to prevent trusts continuing for long periods before the funds vested in the beneficiaries. This was done by the trustees appointing funds away from those members of the class of beneficiaries who were about to become entitled to the trust fund or obtain an interest in possession in the trust fund. The conditions set out in paragraph (3) above have limited the effectiveness of this device.

If the trust is able to satisfy the conditions in paras (1), (2) and (3)(ii), then there is no specific time limit during which the trust will be a qualifying accumulation and maintenance trust; the duration of the qualifying trust will depend upon the ages of the permissible beneficiaries set out in paragraph (3)(ii).

If only the conditions in paragraphs (1), (2) and (3)(i) are satisfied, then the trust has a twenty-five year limitation period. So far as any beneficiary, at the expiry of the twenty-five year period, is not entitled to a part of the fund, or is not entitled to an interest in possession in it, that part will be treated as a trust without an interest in possession which does not qualify as an accumulation and maintenance settlement.

For example, if at the end of the twenty-five year period there is a minor beneficiary who cannot be said to have an interest in possession, his part of the fund will be subject to the discretionary trust penalties, ie, the periodic charge (FA 1975, Sched 5, para 12) and the capital distribution charges (FA 1975, Sched 5, para 6(2)) when the interest in possession ultimately arises. To avoid this problem it will be necessary shortly before the twenty-five years elapse for the trustees to give an interest in possession to that minor beneficiary by giving him an absolute entitlement to the income from his presumptive share, notwithstanding minority. The application of the Trustee Act 1925, s31(2)(ii) would be inconsistent with an interest in possession, and so it must be so excluded.

Child 'Borrowing'

Future born persons can be brought into the class of beneficiaries who benefit under an accumulation and maintenance settlement, but there must be at least one living beneficiary in existence when the trust is set up (FA 1975, Sched 5, para 15(5)).

This could create problems if the settlor wishes to create a trust immediately for the benefit of his future children. He might want to do this in order to create a trust under which the income can be accumulated without suffering the periodic charge (FA 1975, Sched 5, para 12(2)), or a charge when capital is transferred to a beneficiary or when a beneficiary obtains an interest in possession. The problem can possibly be dealt with by using another person's child as the basis for forming a class for one's own children.

Example—David might wish to set up a children's trust but he might have no children in existence. His brother John might have a young child. David could set up a trust and use John's child as the basis of a class. If David had a child before John's child attains an interest in possession, then with an appropriate clause in the deed, the trustees could appropriate the funds to David's child; although the relevant provision is not entirely clear—FA 1975, Sched 5, para 15(1)(*b*)—the Revenue view is that a variation of the shares does not offend the provision. However, if David were to have no children before John's child attains an interest in possession the fund must go to John's child. Thus, David's children born after the interest in possession has vested in John's child cannot benefit under the trust. This is a risk David must take when setting up the trust. There could be a clause inserted in the deed to enable the fund to be appointed away from John's child after he has obtained an interest in possession, but on the exercise of this power a charge to capital transfer tax could arise under the FA 1975, Sched 5, para 4(2).

Definition of Children

For the purposes of these provisions a person's children shall include his illegitimate children, his adopted children and his stepchildren (FA 1975, Sched 5, para 15(6), added by FA 1976, s106(2)).

Tax consequences

The accumulation and maintenance settlement offers considerable capital transfer tax and income tax advantages.

Capital Gains Tax and Stamp Duty

A typical accumulation and maintenance settlement would be one where property is left 'in trust for my children when they shall attain the age of twenty-five' or 'in trust for my grandchildren when they shall attain the age of twenty-five years'.

When the children (or grandchildren, as the case may be) attain the specified age, they can either be given the property absolutely or they can be given an interest in possession. If the beneficiaries are given the property absolutely this could result in a charge to capital gains tax if there are any chargeable assets in the fund (FA 1965, s25(3)). For this reason it would generally be advisable to give an interest in possession to the beneficiaries when they attain the age of twenty-five years, with a power to appoint capital to them. There should be no charge to stamp duty on an absolute appointment of trust funds to a beneficiary apart from a 50*p* deed duty (F (1909–10) A 1910, s74(6) and Stamp Act 1891, Sched 1).

Capital Transfer Tax

If the trust does qualify as an accumulation and maintenance settlement there will be no capital transfer tax payable on the distribution of any capital from the trust to a beneficiary, and there will furthermore be no charge when the interests in possession arise (FA 1975, Sched 5, para 15(2)(*a*)). There will also be no periodic charge (FA 1975, Sched 5, para 15(2)(*b*)). Hence, for capital transfer tax purposes, the creation of the settlement is treated as if it were a direct gift to the beneficiaries who eventually become entitled to the fund or obtain an interest in possession therein.

Income Tax

Until an interest in possession arises with regard to a particular share in the fund, the income of the trust arising from that share can be accumulated for the beneficiary (this can be under the Trustee Act 1925, s31, as amended by the Family Law Reform Act 1969, Sched 3, para 5 (during minority), or, for example, for twenty-one years under the Perpetuities and Accumulations Act 1964, s13). That income will suffer tax at 48 per cent and can then ultimately be paid out to the beneficiary free of all further tax. It is necessary to capitalize the income properly. Also, if the tax rate of the beneficiary, on the income to be paid out to him, would be less than 48 per cent, then the trustees should consider paying the income out to him in the year in which it arises, or, if they have already capitalized it, paying it out regularly so it takes on the nature of income. This should enable the beneficiary to receive the sums as income and make a tax reclaim. This is dealt with in Chapter 3, at p35 (see also *Pearson* v *IRC*, discussed at pp51–53, above).

Death of a Beneficiary

On the death of a beneficiary under an accumulation and maintenance settlement, before he has obtained an interest in possession, there will be no charge to capital transfer tax. After the beneficiary has obtained the interest in possession there will be a charge on his death on the slice of the fund from which his interest in possession derives (FA 1975, Sched 5, para 4(2)). For capital gains tax purposes there will be a notional disposal of the chargeable assets comprised in that slice of the trust fund, but there will be no charge to capital gains tax. The chargeable assets will have as their new base value the market value of those assets as at the date of death. To obtain this uplift it is necessary for the beneficiary to have had a life interest in possession (see Chapter 2, at p31).

Creation

On the creation of an accumulation and maintenance settlement there will be a disposal by the settlor for the purposes of capital transfer tax but he could make use of his annual exemption of £2,000 (FA 1975, Sched 6, para 2(1) as amended by FA 1976, s93(1)), or alternatively he could use up part of the first £25,000 of value which an individual can transfer at a nil rate of capital transfer tax. If the assets settled are chargeable assets then there could be a liability to capital gains tax. There can also be a charge to stamp duty at 2 per cent, depending on the assets settled (F(1909–10) A1910, s74(1)). If the settled assets are cash then there should be no charge to stamp duty apart from the 50*p* deed duty (Stamp Act, Sched 1) or capital gains tax, and, if within the annual exemption of £2,000, there will be no charge to capital transfer tax. If the assets settled are, for example, shares then there could be a charge to capital gains tax, stamp duty and capital transfer tax depending on their value. The capital gains tax charge may be exempt or relieved under the FA 1978, s44 if the amount of the gain is small. It is clear that the types of assets to be settled should be carefully considered.

Development Land Tax

The usual development land tax provisions will apply to these trusts (see above, p32).

Generation skipping

Trusts for the benefit of grandchildren are particularly advantageous because it will usually mean that the trustees can accumulate the income for a longer period than if the trust was set up for the benefit of children, and furthermore it will mean that the assets settled will skip a generation. This is because the assets will not have paid capital transfer tax on the death of the settlor's children.

Relevant trust provisions

Power to Accumulate Income

The trustees will usually be given the power to accumulate the income for twenty-one years from the date of the settlement under the Perpetuities and Accumulations Act 1964, s13. While this power to accumulate is in existence, with regard to the share of a beneficiary, that beneficiary will not obtain an interest in possession (see, however, *Pearson* v *IRC*, at p51, above).

The exact date on which a beneficiary will obtain an interest in possession under an accumulation and maintenance settlement will depend upon a combination of the provisions of the Trustee Act 1925, s31, as amended by the Family Law Reform Act 1969, Sched 3, para 5, the requirements of the FA 1975, Sched 5, para 15 (the beneficiary must obtain an interest in possession on or before the age of twenty-five years to qualify for capital transfer tax relief under the FA 1975, Sched 5, para 15), and the accumulation periods permitted under the LPA 1925 and the Perpetuities and Accumulations Act 1964 (the twenty-one year accumulation period under the Perpetuities and Accumulations Act 1964, s13, is usually incorporated in modern trust deeds).

Under the Trustee Act 1925, s31, as amended by the Family Law Reform Act 1969, Sched 3, para 5, the trustees can accumulate income during the minority (eighteen years) of a beneficiary. If that period expires because a beneficiary attains his majority, the trustees could accumulate for a longer period if the twenty-one year period allowed under the Perpetuities and Accumulations Act is incorporated in the deed.

Example—Matthew sets up a trust for the benefit of his children on attaining the age of twenty-five years, and he incorporates a twenty-one year accumulation period in the deed. If one child is aged two years when the trust is set up, the twenty-one year accumulation period will run out when he is aged twenty-three, so that he will attain his interest in possession at that age even though the trust might refer to the trust fund being held in trust for him when he shall attain the age of twenty-five years. If a child is aged ten when the trust is set up, then it is important that the twenty-one year accumulation period is brought to an end, with regard to the share of that child, fifteen years from the date the trust is set up, so that he attains his interest in possession at the age of twenty-five years. If the accumulation period relating to that share is not brought to an end then he will obtain the interest in possession at the age of thirty-one years and the trust will fail to qualify as an accumulation and maintenance settlement (see, however, *Pearson* v *IRC*, at p51 above). Finally, if a child is aged eleven when the twenty-one year accumulation period runs out then the trustees will nevertheless have the power to accumulate for a further seven years, during that child's minority, under the Trustee Act 1925, s31, as amended by the Family Law Reform Act 1969.

'Specified Age'

There is authority for the statement that where there is an interest contingent on attaining a 'specified age', reference to a 'period' (and not to an age) is not sufficient (*White* v *Whitcher* [1928] 1 KB 453, 13 TC 202). However, the Revenue by concession (IR Press Release, 2 September 1977) have stated that they will regard the requirement of paragraph (1) (at p79, above) as satisfied even if no age is specified, provided that it is clear that a beneficiary will in fact become entitled to the property or an interest in possession by the age of twenty-five years.

Class Closing Provisions

It is important when drafting these settlements to make certain that the class of beneficiaries who can benefit under the trust closes when the first beneficiary attains an interest in possession. If this is not done then the birth of a subsequent child could cause a shifting of part of the interest in possession which vested in the child who first attained the interest in possession, thus causing a possible charge to capital transfer tax (FA 1975, Sched 5, para 4(2)).

A provision could be incorporated in the document, however, to alter the future beneficial entitlement of the beneficiaries who have not attained an interest in possession, but leave unaffected the beneficiary who has attained an interest in possession. For example, there might be three children in existence under a qualifying accumulation and maintenance settlement. Immediately before the first obtains an interest in possession the trustees might decide to apportion one-fifth of the fund to him. If another child is born, the one-fifth share in which the eldest child took an interest in possession will not be affected by the birth, and the trustees can decide how the remaining four-fifths will be divided between the three younger children.

Flexibility

The trustees can be given a discretionary power to select amongst a class of beneficiaries, so long as one or more beneficiaries will on or before attaining twenty-five years become entitled to the property or to an interest in possession in the property (see IR Press Release, 19 January 1976). The trustees can also be given the power to take away an interest in possession after it has vested and appoint it to other beneficiaries (not necessarily the children or grandchildren of the settlor). This power could have adverse capital transfer tax consequences if it is exercised, as it will cause an interest in possession to come to an end. Nevertheless the mere existence of the power would not cause the trust to fail as a qualifying accumulation and maintenance settlement and it could be a useful power to have in the deed. It will be seen that within the limitations set out in the FA 1975, Sched 5, para 15, as amended by the FA 1976, s106, there is great scope for flexibility.

Tax planning

Summary of Tax Advantages

(1) These trusts enable income to be accumulated and capitalized, before an interest in possession arises, and even, perhaps, after, if *Pearson* v *IRC* (see p51 et seq) is correctly decided. The capitalized income can then be paid out to the beneficiaries without further tax.

(2) These trusts have substantial Capital Transfer Tax advantages, in that they do not suffer the penalties which discretionary trusts suffer. On the death of a beneficiary before he obtains an interest in possession, there will be no

charge to Capital Transfer Tax. After he has obtained an interest in possession there could be a charge, but if it is a life interest in possession there will be an uplift in base costs for Capital Gains Tax purposes.

(3) These are ideal trusts to be reconstructed out of pre-27 March 1974 discretionary trusts, to stop the periodic charge from applying and obtain the transitional rates of relief (see p67 et seq).

(4) The trust can be virtually as flexible as a discretionary trust, although some powers may have to be effectively suspended until beneficiaries obtain interests in possession, and others cannot be exercised without adverse tax consequences, eg, the power to take away an interest in possession after it has arisen.

CHAPTER 9

PROTECTIVE TRUSTS

Protective trusts can be very useful as instruments of tax planning. If an interest in possession is to be given to an individual because, for instance, he is over the age of twenty-five, and an accumulation and maintenance settlement would therefore not be applicable, one could give him that interest under a protective trust. It could also be applicable where there was formerly an accumulation and maintenance settlement in existence and an individual has attained the age of twenty-five years; instead of giving the individual an interest in possession, or an absolute interest, an interest under a protective trust could be given to him. The only other alternative would be to give an individual a mere spes as a beneficiary under a discretionary trust but that would suffer the penalties which those trusts suffer.

A protective trust is therefore a compromise between an interest in possession and a discretionary trust. It can give an individual (the principal beneficiary) an interest in possession which can terminate without a charge to tax arising. It can therefore be very useful for spendthrift beneficiaries, or beneficiaries who might become bankrupt.

There is a further advantage in these trusts. On the termination of the interest of the principal beneficiary a discretionary trust will be set up which will be principally for the benefit of the principal beneficiary, his spouse and his issue. The income from the trust can be paid out to these individuals in the absolute discretion of the trustees and is therefore a discretionary trust in the full sense of the word. However, it does not suffer most of the penalties which discretionary trusts normally suffer, eg, the ten year periodic charge is deferred. Thus, settlors who would like to set up discretionary trusts without suffering the penalties imposed on those trusts should consider protective trusts.

What is a protective trust?

These are trusts which have written into them provisions which cause the interests in income of beneficiaries to come to an end should they attempt to alienate those interests or if some outside person, such as a trustee in bankruptcy, should attempt to take the interests.

It was formerly the practice to set out the terms of these protective trusts in great detail in the Trust Deed, but the Trustee Act 1925, s33, now provides that a mere reference to 'protective trusts' will cause the provisions, as set out below, to come into play.

Section 33(1) states that where income, including an annuity or other periodic payment, is directed to be held on protective trusts for the benefit of any person for his life or any less period (such person being described in the section as 'the principal beneficiary'), then, during that period (the 'trust period'), the income is held, without prejudice to any prior interest, on the following trusts:

(i) Upon trust for the principal beneficiary during the trust period or until he does, or attempts to do, any act or thing, or any event happens, other than an advance under any statutory or express power, whereby, if the income were payable during the trust period to the principal beneficiary absolutely during that period, he would be deprived of the right to receive the same or any part thereof;

(ii) If the trust fails or determines during the trust period, then, for the residue of that period, the income is to be held upon trust to be applied as the trustees in their absolute discretion (without being liable to account for the exercise of such discretion) think fit, for the maintenance or support or otherwise for the benefit of all or any of the following persons—

(*a*) the principal beneficiary and his or her wife or husband, if any, and his or her children or more remoter issue, if any; or

(*b*) the principal beneficiary and the persons who would, if he were dead, be entitled to the trust property or the income where there is no wife or husband or issue in existence.

The section is subject to any variations in those basic trusts which may be made in the trust instrument (s33(2)).

It is also provided, in s33(3), that nothing in the section operates to validate any trusts which would, if contained in the instrument creating the trust, be liable to be set aside. Thus, a settlement made by the settlor on himself until bankruptcy, and then on discretionary trusts, may be ineffective (*Re Burroughs-Fowler* [1916] 2 Ch 251).

It will thus be seen that the protective trust consists of the principal beneficiary having an interest in possession which will be brought to an end if he tries to dispose of it or do anything which could deprive himself of it. On that interest being brought to an end a discretionary trust is set up principally to pay the income for the benefit of himself, his spouse, or his issue, and failing them (ie, if there is no spouse or issue) other persons. It will also be noted that the protective trust provisions are only concerned with governing the position with regard to income, ie, it is the income of the fund which is held upon protective trust.

When the trust period, which can be for the life of the principal beneficiary or for a shorter period, comes to an end there will usually then come into existence an interest in possession, so that some beneficiary will be entitled to the income, or there will be an absolute vesting of the income and capital. One might thus have a protective trust for A who is the principal beneficiary, for life, and on his death for his children absolutely when they shall attain the age of eighteen years. In this event A will have a right to the income until his interest shall be alienated, when a discretionary trust under s33 will come into existence. That discretionary trust will cease when A dies and the final trust provisions will come into operation (ie, the property will be held in trust for the children of A until they attain the age of eighteen years).

Capital transfer tax

The governing provisions for capital transfer tax and protective trusts are to be found in the FA 1975, Sched 5, para 18, as amended by FA 1978, s71.

Paragraph 18 applies to settled property held on trusts to the like effect as those specified in the Trustee Act 1925, s33(1). It is felt that it can be assumed that should the trust be the same as those specified the paragraph will also apply. The terms the 'principal beneficiary' and the 'trust period' have the same meaning in the capital transfer tax legislation as they have in the Trustee Act 1925, s33.

When para 18 of the FA 1975, Sched 5, was first enacted, there was much uncertainty as to its exact scope, and an amendment in the Finance Act 1976 did not completely eliminate the problems (Sched 14, para 19). The latest amendments (which appear to have settled the difficulties) have been made by the FA 1978, s71. This section states that the capital transfer tax consequences of a protective trust, or a trust to the like effect, are as follows:

(*a*) there shall be disregarded the failure or determination, before the end of the trust period, of any trusts of the like effect as those in the Trustee Act 1925, s33(1)(i) (ie, the right to income of the principal beneficiary); and

(*b*) the principal beneficiary shall be treated as beneficially entitled to an interest in possession in any property which is for the time being held on trusts to the like effect as those specified in the Trustee Act 1925, s33(1)(ii) (ie, the discretionary trusts which arise if the principal beneficiary's right to income ceases during the trust period).

Section 71 of the FA 1978 shall be deemed to have come into force on 11 April 1978, and applies if the failure or determination of the trusts occurs after that date.

The effect of these provisions is that the forfeiture of the principal beneficiary's right to the income is wholly disregarded for capital transfer tax purposes, so that no cumulation problems should arise. Furthermore, as the principal beneficiary under the subsequent discretionary trust is deemed to have an interest in possession, there can be no periodic charge to capital transfer tax and transfers of funds to that beneficiary will be free of capital transfer tax. It is interesting to note that the principal beneficiary has this deemed interest in possession even though he has no right to the trust income; the trust income may, and in fact is very likely to, be paid to other discretionary beneficiaries under the Trustee Act 1925, s33(1)(ii) trusts.

Example—Mr X puts £100,000 into a protective trust for the life of his son Y, who is married with two children. On the transfer to the settlement there will be a charge to capital transfer tax in the usual way. Five years later Y attempts to alienate his interest under the trust so that his interest terminates. There is no charge to capital transfer tax because of para 18(2)(*a*). The income in the fund is then paid out by the trustees in their absolute discretion to Y and his wife and children for the next twenty years. At the end of the twenty years the trustees decide to transfer the capital of the fund to Y. There will be no charge to capital transfer tax on that distribution payment (para 18(2)(*b*)).

It is sufficient that the protective trust is of the like effect as the one set out in the Trustee Act 1925, s33(1) so that minor variations to the provisions will not prevent the reliefs applying. It will have to be something materially different in the tax consequences of the trust for the Revenue to question the applicability of the reliefs.

The Revenue have indicated in a letter published in the Law Society's Gazette (3 March 1976) that—

(1) the insertion of a power to apply capital for the benefit of the principal beneficiary does not prevent the capital transfer tax reliefs from applying; and

(2) only if there are no beneficiaries, other than the principal beneficiary, alive within the Trustee Act 1925, s33(1)(ii)(*a*) class (spouse and issue) should the beneficiaries in the Trustee Act 1925, s33(1)(ii)(*b*) class (brothers and sisters etc) be in a position to receive income.

An extract from the Revenue letter reads as follows:

> I appreciate so long as the principal beneficiary has no spouse or issue the statutory trusts extend to the next of kin for the time being who might well be brothers and sisters, but this is not the same thing as including them in the primary class of beneficiaries ab initio on the equal footing with the spouse and issue. In that event the brothers and sisters could receive the income of settled property to the entire exclusion of the principal beneficiary his spouse and issue. I confirm that trusts which could produce this result would not be regarded as 'to the like effect' as those specified in Section 33(1) of the Trustee Act 1925.

Finally, under the FA 1975, Sched 6, para 6(3)(*b*)(iv), the marriage settlement exemptions from capital transfer tax can be applicable in certain circumstances where a protective trust is set up broadly for one of the parties to the marriage and the children.

Income tax

There are no income tax savings to be obtained by setting up a protective trust. The interest of the principal beneficiary will require the income arising from it to be paid to the principal beneficiary, and when the discretionary trust subsequently comes into existence it will be subject to the 15 per cent investment income surchage (FA 1973, s16(2)(*a*)). The trustees will not be able to accumulate it because the Trustee Act 1925, s33 requires that the income 'is to be held upon trust to be applied as the trustees in their absolute discretion (without being liable to account for the exercise of their discretion) think fit'.

If the s33 trusts are amended to give the trustees the power to accumulate income in the discretionary trust it is likely that the Revenue will not consider the trust to be of the like effect as a s33 trust and so denying the trust the capital transfer tax reliefs. There is thus no opportunity under these trusts to accumulate income and capitalize it, although while the discretionary trust is in operation the income can be paid to a wide number of children and therefore possibly bring the overall tax charge down. As it will normally be a parent setting up a trust for his own children who are over the age of twenty-five (otherwise an accumulation and maintenance settlement might be more appropriate) the ultimate beneficiaries under the discretionary trust will normally be the grandchildren of the settlor, so that income payments will not be aggregated with the income of the settlor (TA 1970, s437(1)).

Under ss439 and 447 of the TA 1970 it is possible for the settlor to retain a benefit under his settlement if he sets up a trust which is broadly designed to protect the trust property from the creditors of the beneficiaries. Normally the settlor and his spouse must be absolutely excluded from all possible benefits under the trust.

Capital gains tax

When property is put into the settlement a charge to capital gains tax can arise. When a beneficiary becomes absolutely entitled to trust assets as against the trustees, a charge can arise unless the FA 1978, s46 and Sched 8 apply (relief for gifts of business assets) so enabling the gain to be 'rolled over'.

The author is of the view that if the principal beneficiary should die, and the trust period for the purposes of s33 is the period of his life, and the discretionary trusts in s33(1)(ii) have not come into operation, the base value for capital gains tax can be uplifted as at the date of his death under the FA 1965, s25(4) (as amended) or the FA 1971, Sched 12, para 6, as the case may be.

Development land tax

Protective trusts will be liable to this tax in the usual way if the trustees acquire development land and realize development value by a deemed or actual disposal of the land (see Chapter 2, at p32).

Stamp duty

There are no particular exemptions from stamp duty applicable to protective trusts.

On the setting up of the trust the principal charge will be the 2 per cent ad valorem duty payable on the assets transferred, except for cash and other exempt items. On the transfer of assets to beneficiaries there will be no charge to ad valorem duty (see Chapter 2, at p11).

Protective trusts and tax planning

It will clearly be of advantage, where the settlor feels that the interest of a beneficiary is likely to have come to an end, to set up a protective trust. The only alternative would be to set up an accumulation and maintenance settlement, but the problem there is that the beneficiaries might be over the age of twenty-five years. Alternatively, a discretionary trust could be set up and this would suffer the penalties imposed on those trusts such as the periodic charge and the charge to tax on capital distributions.

A significant advantage of these trusts is that on the termination of the interest of the principal beneficiary—and these interests can terminate very easily if the principal beneficiary so chooses—a discretionary trust, as to income, can be set up without any adverse tax consequences, provided the capital of the fund ultimately goes back to the principal beneficiary. Indeed, if the principal beneficiary has no wife and children then one could effectively have a discretionary trust benefiting the persons who are the next of kin of the principal beneficiary for the time being, such as his brothers or sisters.

CHAPTER 10

TRUSTS FOR THE MENTALLY DISABLED

Paragraph 19 of the FA 1975, Sched 5 provides relief from capital transfer tax for discretionary trusts set up only or mainly for the benefit of mentally disabled persons. These provisions were extended by the FA 1977, s51 to cover beneficiaries who are in receipt of an attendance allowance, as defined in the Social Security Act 1975, s35.

None of the other taxes, apart from capital gains tax, provides any particular reliefs or exemptions for such trusts.

What is a trust for the mentally disabled?

The capital transfer tax reliefs to be mentioned apply to settled property held on trusts under which, during the life of a mentally disabled person, no interest in possession in the settled property subsists and which secure that any of the settled property which is applied during the life of the mentally disabled person is applied only or mainly for his benefit (FA 1975, Sched 5, para 19(1)).

A mentally disabled person means a person who by reason of mental disorder, within the meaning of the Mental Health Act 1959, is incapable of administering his property or managing his affairs. In the case of *W* v *L* [1973] 3 All ER 884, the Court of Appeal held that the words relating to mental disorder and mental illness in the Mental Health Act 1959 do not have any particular medical significance but are to be construed in accordance with the ordinary understanding of the words by ordinary people. The Inland Revenue will no doubt require some sort of certificate.

The provision is not clearly drafted. It is not clear whether the requirement that the settled property be applied only or mainly for the benefit of the mentally handicapped person refers only to the capital of the trust, including capitalized income, or just to the income. In the author's view the requirement applies only to the capital of the fund, including capitalized income, but not to uncapitalized income. The reference to 'only or mainly', in the author's view, is a reference to over 50 per cent of the capital of the fund or any capitalized income.

If the reference to over 50 per cent were to be to income this could produce a rather contradictory situation, where in order to set up a mentally handicapped trust no interest in possession must subsist, yet over 50 per cent of the income must be paid to the mentally handicapped person, therefore creating a possible interest in possession. This fortifies the author's view that the reference to the settled property in Sched 5, para 19(1) is a reference only to the capital of the fund and capitalized income.

The trust can be given the power to accumulate income for twenty-one years. Thus, the income as it arises can be paid to persons other than the mentally handicapped person, although, if it is decided to accumulate and capitalize the income, it must be applied only or mainly for the benefit of the mentally disabled person. The mentally disabled person can be of any age when the trust is set up, so that such trusts provide a means of capitalizing income for the benefit of persons over the age of twenty-five years without suffering the penalties which normally apply to trusts where there are no interests in possession.

Capital transfer tax

Where a qualifying mentally disabled trust is set up the following consequences follow:

(1) If the mentally disabled person is the settlor, neither the making of the settlement nor any addition made by him to the settled property shall be a chargeable transfer; the transfer therefore does not enter into the settlor's cumulative total under the FA 1975, s37(1)(*b*).

(2) A distribution payment made to the mentally disabled person shall not be a capital distribution, ie, it is exempt although it still cumulates as a distribution payment.

(3) The periodic charge to capital transfer tax is deferred. This deferment continues until there is a capital distribution (eg, a payment to a beneficiary other than the mentally disabled person), or the property ceases to be held for the benefit of the mentally disabled person.

Income tax

There is an opportunity to capitalize income paying only the basic rate of tax, and the investment income surcharge of 15 per cent, and paying over that income, ultimately, only or mainly for the benefit of the mentally disabled person. Where the income is not accumulated it will be taxable upon the beneficiary who receives it as investment income. The chief advantage of these trusts is that the income can be accumulated and capitalized for an adult person over the age of twenty-five years without suffering the penalties which a trust without interests in possession would usually suffer.

Capital gains tax

When property is put into the trust there will be a charge to capital gains tax and, equally, when a beneficiary becomes absolutely entitled as against the trustees to chargeable assets. It is possible that these gains can be rolled over (that is, the capital gains tax charge postponed) where business assets are transferred (see FA 1978, s46 and Sched 8). These trusts, as well as trusts for persons in receipt of an attendance allowance, enjoy important reliefs and exemptions for small capital gains. Paragraph 5(1) of FA 1978, Sched 7 provides that such trusts, where the settled property and any income arising from the property is applied only or mainly for the benefit of the mentally disabled person or the person in receipt of an attendance allowance, enjoy the same capital gains tax reliefs and exemptions for small gains as individuals. Thus, the first £1,000 of gain per year is exempt, the next £4,000 is taxed at 15 per cent, and where the gain is above £5,000 the tax shall not exceed £600 plus one-half of the excess over £5,000. This effectively provides relief from the full rate of capital gains tax of 30 per cent for gains of less than £9,500 per year (FA 1978, s44(1)–(3)). The exemptions and reliefs available to these trusts are more favourable than those generally available to trusts (FA 1978, Sched 7, para 6).

The reference to 'income arising from the property' in FA 1978, Sched 7, para 5(1) appears to give the mentally disabled person, in an appropriately drawn trust, an uplift for capital gains tax purposes on death (see p31). Such a trust would not qualify for capital transfer tax, as there will be an interest in possession (FA 1975, Sched 5, para 19(1)).

The capital transfer tax and capital gains tax rules do not integrate well and it would appear that a trust cannot qualify fully for both the capital transfer tax and capital gains tax exemptions and reliefs. Presumably this was not intended by Parliament.

Development land tax

These trusts will be liable to this tax in the usual way if the trustees acquire development land and realize any development value (see p32).

Stamp duty

There are no particular exemptions which apply to these trusts with regard to stamp duty. On the setting up of a trust there will be a 2 per cent ad valorem duty payable on the assets transferred unless a certificate for value is appropriate or items exempt from stamp duty are transferred. Transfers of assets to beneficiaries are exempt from ad valorem duty (see p11).

A person in receipt of an attendance allowance

By the FA 1977, s51, the FA 1975, Sched 5, para 19 was extended so that if a person is in receipt of an attendance allowance, trusts of a similar type to those which can be set up for mentally disabled persons, can be set up for such persons and the capital transfer tax reliefs will be available. An attendance allowance means an allowance under the Social Security Act 1975, s35.

Tax planning

The tax advantages obtainable by the setting-up of these trusts can be summarized as follows:

(1) It enables a discretionary trust to be set up without suffering the usual capital transfer tax disadvantages; and

(2) It gives an opportunity to capitalize income only or mainly for the benefit of a mentally disabled person or a person in receipt of an attendance allowance.

(3) If the aim is to obtain the capital gains tax reliefs, a number of such trusts can be set up to obtain multiple reliefs from small gains.

CHAPTER 11

MARRIAGE TRUSTS

There are no special taxation reliefs for marriage settlements although there are Capital Transfer Tax and Stamp Duty exemptions available on the setting-up of such settlements. Individuals who wish to reduce the value of their estates should consider making gifts in consideration of marriage if the opportunity should present itself.

Capital transfer tax

Transfers of value made by gifts in consideration of marriage are exempt from Capital Transfer Tax to the extent that the values transferred by such transfers made by any one transferor in respect of any one marriage (calculated as values on which no tax is payable) do not exceed—

(1) in the case of a gift by a parent of a party to the marriage, £5,000 by way of absolute gift or by way of marriage settlement;

(2) by each remoter ancestor of a party to the marriage, £2,500 by way of absolute gift or by way of marriage settlement;

(3) by each party to the marriage, £2,500 by way of absolute gift or by way of settlement; and

(4) by any other transferor, £1,000, except that in this case it must be by way of outright gift to a party to the marriage.

It is sufficient if the party to the marriage is the illegitimate child or adopted child or step-child of the person making the gift, in ascertaining whether the transferor is the parent or remoter ancestor of the party to the marriage. The gift, whether absolutely or in settlement, must be in consideration of marriage. This has been judicially defined as 'the most valuable consideration imaginable' (*Attorney-General* v *Jacobs-Smith* [1895] 2 QB 341 at p354, per Kay LJ).

The gift in settlement must be made prior to and in contemplation of the marriage and it is essential that the marriage does take place. The settlement could therefore be set up for £1 with the transfer of the trust assets taking place prior to the marriage on condition that it takes place or, alternatively, the assets could be transferred on the wedding day.

In the case of a marriage settlement a disposition shall not be treated as a gift made in consideration of marriage if the persons who are or may become entitled to any benefit under the settlement include any person other than:

(1) the parties to the marriage, issue of the marriage, or a husband or wife of any such issue;

(2) persons becoming entitled on the failure of trusts for any such issue under which trust property would (subject only to any power of appointment to a person falling within para (1) above, or para (3) below), vest indefeasibly on the attainment of a specified age or either on the attainment of such an age or on some earlier event, or persons becoming entitled (subject as aforesaid) on the failure of any limitation in tail;

(3) a subsequent wife or husband of a party to the marriage, or any issue, or the wife or husband of any issue, of a subsequent marriage of either party;

(4) persons becoming entitled under such trusts, subsisting under the Law of England, as are specified in the Trustee Act 1925, s33(1) (protective trusts), the principal beneficiary being a person falling within para (1) above, or para (3) above, or under such trusts, modified by the enlargement, as respects any period during which there is no such issue as aforesaid in existence, of the class of potential beneficiaries specified in s33(1)(ii); or

(5) in respect of a reasonable amount of remuneration, the trustees of the settlement.

References to issue shall apply as if any person legitimated by a marriage, or adopted by the husband and wife jointly, were included among the issue of that marriage (FA 1975, Sched 6, para 6(4)). The £5,000 exemption applies to each parent, so that if all the parents to the parties to the marriage were to make gifts £20,000 can be given and be exempt from capital transfer tax.

Although the above list (1) to (5) sets out the persons who are to be beneficiaries under the marriage settlement, it sets out no further limitations as to the type of trust which need be set up. The trusts can therefore be discretionary trusts or trusts with interests in possession, or trusts incorporating the protective trust provisions. If the trust is a discretionary trust it will suffer the penalties which these trusts suffer, ie, the periodic charge to capital transfer tax and a charge to tax when property is transferred out to beneficiaries. However, because the initial gift into the settlement is exempt (provided the settlor did not exceed the exemption limits of £5,000 and £2,500) the first £25,000 of transfers subsequently made from the settlement will not suffer from the cumulation provision by being cumulated with the settlors' transfers.

If interests in possession are given to the parties to the marriage or other permitted persons within the limitations set out within Sched 6, para 6(3)(*b*), then the usual provisions will apply, ie, on the termination of an interest in possession there will be a transfer of value, and on any transfers of funds absolutely to a person entitled to an interest in possession there will be no charge to capital transfer tax (see above, p54).

The marriage gift exemptions are on top of, and not in place of, any other exemptions available such as the annual £2,000 exemption.

Capital gains tax

There are no particular reliefs from capital gains tax for marriage settlements whether on setting up the settlement or during the administration of the trust or at its termination. Thus, when the trust is set up there could be a charge to capital gains tax and equally when a beneficiary becomes absolutely entitled as against the trustees to chargeable assets (see above, p28).

Stamp duty

A voluntary disposition made in consideration of marriage is not chargeable with ad valorem duty; it will, however, as a Deed, attract the 50*p* fixed duty.

In the author's view if a trust qualifies as a marriage settlement for the purposes of capital transfer tax there will be no ad valorem duty payable on its creation (see FA 1963, s64, F(1909–10) A 1910, s74(5), FA 1975, ss22 and 49(5), and Sched 12, para 1).

Income tax

The usual income tax provisions will apply. If the trust can accumulate income, under the provisions of the FA 1973, ss16 and 17 there will be a charge to 48 per cent tax and the income can be capitalized in the usual way. If there are interests in possession then the trustees will not have power to accumulate the income so that they will then be liable to tax at the basic rate of 33 per cent with the beneficiary either claiming back that tax if his tax rate is low enough or paying the higher rates of tax on the moneys to which he is entitled (see, however, *Pearson* v *IRC* at p51, above).

Under the TA 1970, s447(1), the income of a settlement, in which the settlor or his spouse retains an interest, is treated for all the purposes of the Income Tax Acts as the income of the settlor and not as the income of any other person.

However, the settlor shall not be deemed to have an interest in any income arising under, or property comprised in, a settlement if and so long as that income or property cannot become payable or applicable for his benefit except in four restricted circumstances set out in s447(2). One of these circumstances is in the case of a marriage settlement on the death of both the parties to the marriage and all or any of the children of the marriage. Thus, if the father of one of the parties to the marriage wants to set up a marriage settlement he is able to retain an interest in the settlement to this restricted extent, ie, in the event of such multiple deaths the settled funds can come back to him.

Development land tax

It is not generally envisaged that development land will comprise part of the trust funds of the marriage settlement where the exemption figures are so low, ie, £2,500 and £5,000. Should there be any development land, however, the usual development land tax provisions will apply (see above, p32).

Tax planning

Considering the small amounts which can be given away and be exempt from capital transfer tax it is likely that most transfers in consideration of marriage will be made absolutely and therefore not involving any complicated marriage trusts. Clearly when marriages are to take place and the transferor wishes to reduce the value of his estate, the exemption should be made use of. These gifts are the only real tax advantages of marriage settlements and there are no particular advantages, from the tax point of view, in the settlement itself, unless the settlement is of a small size and does not grow in value to exceed £25,000; even if it does exceed that figure there will be lower tax rates chargeable although the periodic charge will be suffered. Thus, small marriage settlements, where there are no interests in possession, can still be attractive.

CHAPTER 12

TRADING TRUSTS

The trust can be an attractive vehicle for carrying out trading activities. The chief advantage is that, provided the trust has a power to accumulate income, the top rate of tax payable on the profits of the trust will be 48 per cent. This compares with the top rate of tax on companies of 52 per cent, plus the liability of close companies to have their excess of relevant income over distributions apportioned under the provisions of the FA 1972, Sched 16. There are no apportionment provisions in a trust except that at the end of the trust period—usually eighty years—the trust must come to an end, unless it is a charitable trust. The income which arises to the trust can be capitalized, and, depending on the type of trust used to carry out the trade, paid out to the beneficiaries free of further income tax. Also, unlike shares in a company, the interests in a trust can be sold or given away free of capital gains tax. Chargeable capital gains on shares, however, can be eliminated on the death of a shareholder and roll-over may be applicable under the FA 1978, s46 and Sched 8.

The very wide anti-avoidance provisions contained in the TA 1970, s460, do not apply to interests under trusts. Such interests are also much more flexible than shares, and there is no equivalent, in the case of trusts, to the Companies Acts 1948 to 1976, so that this flexibility is not restricted by statute. The trading trust will also have to be compared with the partnership or the sole tradership, where the top rate of tax could be 83 per cent.

It is felt that when any individual is seeking advice on what vehicle he should use to commence trading, as well as the Company and the individual partnership trading concepts, he should consider the trading trust. He could possibly have the three entities trading at the same time, causing profits to accumulate in one or the other depending on which is the most advantageous from the tax point of view.

What is a trading trust?

A trading trust is a trust in which the trustees carry on a trade, profession or vocation for the benefit of the beneficiaries under the trust. They do not merely hold shares or land or other property as investments—they actually trade.

The trust instrument should expressly give the trustees wide powers to trade and must relieve them from liability for any trading losses which may occur.

Income tax

The trustees carrying on a trade will be chargeable to income tax under the TA 1970, Sched D, case 1.

It was held in *Fry* v *Shiel's Trustees* (1914) 6 TC 583 and *M'Dougall* v *Smith* (1918) 7 TC 134 that the income of trustees could not be claimed to be earned income by either the trustees or a beneficiary under the trust where the trustees carry on a trade.

The FA 1971, s32, states that income other than earned income is to be subject to the investment income surcharge, so that as a result of the combination of that provision and the FA 1972, ss16 and 17, accumulated income in a trading trust will be subject to the basic rates of tax, at present 33 per cent, and the investment income surcharge at the full rate of 15 per cent.

It is specifically provided that the provisions which treat a change in the person's carrying on a trade as a discontinuance do not apply when the discontinuance arises through a change of trustees (TA 1970, s154(7)). Similar provisions permitting continuity of relief, where there is a change of trustees, under the stock relief provisions, are contained in FA 1976, Sched 5, para 21(1).

The trustees will be able to deduct the usual trading expenses. However, trustees cannot claim any deduction against income so taxed for expenses incurred by them in relation to the trust (*Aikin* v *MacDonald's Trustees* (1894) 3 TC 306) except in so far as they could have done so if they were beneficially entitled; nor can the trustees claim any personal reliefs in respect of the trust income.

The trustees are able to deduct from their liability to pay the additional 15 per cent payments made in defraying the expenses of the trustees which are properly chargeable to income (FA 1973, s16(2) and see above, p17).

Capital transfer tax

If the trust which is set up is one in which an interest in possession subsists it is felt that there is little to be gained by having a trading trust. This is because the income will not be earned income in the hands of the trustees or the beneficiary, and the income will be added to the beneficiary's income whether he receives it or not (see, however, *Pearson* v *IRC*, at p51 above).

Thus, the type of trust which will need to be set up will have to be one under which the income can be accumulated. The ideal vehicle would be a qualifying accumulation and maintenance settlement under the FA 1975, Sched 5, para 15. The trading income would be taxed at 48 per cent and can ultimately be paid out to the beneficiaries free of further income tax and free of capital transfer tax. If the beneficiaries are over the age of twenty-five the trade could be carried out through a discretionary trust, except that the penalties applicable to those trusts would apply so that one would have to measure the capital transfer tax disadvantages with the income tax advantages.

Another trust which does not suffer the disadvantages of the discretionary trust is a protective trust after the principal beneficiary has attempted to alienate his interest and the discretionary trust comes into operation (see above, p91). The problem is that the power to accumulate would mean altering the Trustee Act 1925, s33 provisions and so the position is not entirely clear. If the accumulations must ultimately be paid out to beneficiaries of the relevant protective trust class these may amount to trusts of a similar nature to those set out in the Trustee Act 1925, s33 and therefore accumulation and capitalization may be possible. However, the position is very unclear and the Revenue are unlikely to allow such a variation of the s33 trusts.

Trusts for mentally incapacitated individuals under the provisions of the FA 1975, Sched 5, para 19, provide scope for the accumulation and capitalization of income (see p94).

The FA 1976, Sched 10, as amended by the FA 1978, s64, provides that where the trustees transfer property (which includes a distribution payment or a deemed capital distribution), consisting of a business or an interest in a business to a beneficiary, the property transferred is treated as reduced for capital transfer tax purposes by 50 per cent. This could be useful if a discretionary trust is used as the trading vehicle.

Capital gains tax

The usual capital gains tax provisions would apply to a trading trust so that if the trustees were to dispose of trust assets they would pay capital gains tax in the usual way. They would be entitled to roll-over relief under FA 1965, s33 (as amended) because they are 'persons' carrying on a trade. There would be a charge to tax when a beneficiary becomes absolutely entitled as against the trustees to chargeable assets (FA 1965, s25(3)) unless the roll-over requirements in the FA 1978, s46 and Sched 8, para 2 are satisfied; in the case of a trading trust they will nearly always be satisfied.

The postponement of payment of tax provisions under FA 1965, Sched 10, para 4, as substituted by FA 1972, s117 and amended by F (No 2) A 1975, s57, which allow capital gains tax on deemed disposals under s25(3) and (4) to be paid by instalments, apply to 'any assets used exclusively for the purposes of a trade, profession or vocation which, immediately before the disposal, was carried on (whether alone or in partnership) by the person by whom the disposal was made or deemed to be made'. Postponement will therefore be available to trustees.

Development land tax

The usual development land tax provisions would apply if the trustees realize material development by way of an actual or deemed disposal of an interest in land (see Chapter 2).

Value added tax

If the trustees carry on a trade and their taxable supplies do not come within the non-registration limits in the FA 1972, Sched 1 (as amended) they will be liable to register for Value Added Tax like any other trader.

Stamp duty

The usual stamp duty provisions will apply (see Chapter 2).

Comparison between a trading trust, a company and a sole tradership (or partnership)

There is set out below a comparison between the three trading entities.

The Trading Trust

(1) The maximum tax rate is 48 per cent. If there is an interest in possession the trustees will be liable only for the basic rate of tax, currently 33 per cent; however, in this case the beneficiaries could be liable for the higher rates of tax and the investment income surcharge (see, however, *Pearson* v *IRC*, discussed at p51 et seq, above).

(2) The trust income is not treated as earned income in the hands of the trustees or beneficiaries although sums paid to employees of, or consultants to, the trust will be earned income in their hands.

(3) The relevant income apportionment provisions (shortfall) do not apply to trading trusts.

(4) Disposals of all types of interests under trusts are generally free of capital gains tax and in addition gifts of reversionary interests are generally excluded from capital transfer tax.

(5) Individual trustees do not have limited liability.

(6) The trading income, in the author's view, should be assessed on a preceding-year basis.

(7) Trusts are chargeable to capital gains tax at 30 per cent with restricted exemptions and reliefs for small gains, except where a trust for the mentally disabled, or for a person receiving an attendance allowance, is set up (FA 1978, s44 and Sched 7).

(8) Section 460 Taxes Act 1970, which is a very wide anti-tax avoidance section involving transactions in securities, has no application to beneficial interests held in trading trusts.

(9) Treasury consent is not required for the transfer of the control and management of a trust from the United Kingdom to overseas.

(10) Retirement relief, for persons aged sixty years or over, under the FA 1965, s34 as amended by the FA 1978, s48 (which can exempt up to £50,000 of capital gains from capital gains tax), in the author's view, has no application to trusts.

(11) A trust must come to an end on or before the expiry of its perpetuity period. The business must then be transferred to the beneficiaries.

Sole Tradership (or Partnership)

(1) The maximum rate of tax payable on the taxable profit of a sole trader or partner is 83 per cent. The basic rate of income tax is 33 per cent. In respect of so much of an individual's total income as does not exceed £750, however, the rate is only 25 per cent. In respect of so much of an individual's total income as exceeds £8,000 the higher rates of tax are payable as set out below:

Part of Excess Over £8,000	*Higher Rate*
The first £1,000	40%
The next £1,000	45%
The next £1,000	50%
The next £1,500	55%
The next £1,500	60%
The next £2,000	65%
The next £2,500	70%
The next £5,500	75%
The remainder	83%

The application of these tables shows that the maximum 83 per cent rate is reached where total income (ie, income after deducting personal allowances and reliefs) exceeds £24,000. Special rules apply to partnerships involving companies (TA 1970, s155).

(2) The income is earned income in the hands of the trader unless he is a sleeping partner who takes no active part in the partnership.

(3) The shortfall provisions are not relevant to partnerships as all partnership profits are taxed upon the partners whether they are retained in the partnership or distributed to the individual partners.

(4) Disposals of shares in partnerships can give rise to charges to capital transfer tax and capital gains tax. Relief for business assets (capital transfer tax) may, however, be available under the FA 1976, Sched 10 (as amended), and capital gains tax 'hold-over' relief may be available under the FA 1978, s46 and Sched 8.

(5) Partners do not have limited liability unless exceptionally a limited liability partnership is set up under the Limited Partnership Act 1907, under which certain partners can have limited liability.

(6) The profits are assessed on a preceding-year basis (TA 1970, s115(1)).

(7) From 1977/78 individuals are exempt from capital gains tax on total net gains arising in the tax year which do not exceed £1,000. Where the net gains are between £1,000 and £5,000, the excess over £1,000 will be charged at 15 per cent. A marginal relief is applicable to gains between £5,000 and £9,500, where liability is based on £600 plus 50 per cent of the excess of the gains over £5,000. If the net gain is in excess of £9,500 the charge will be 30 per cent without any £1,000 exemption.

(8) Section 460 cannot apply to interests held in partnerships or the interests of a sole trader in his business.

(9) Treasury consent is not required for the transfer of the control and management of the business from the United Kingdom to overseas.

(10) Retirement relief under the FA 1965, s34 is available if an individual disposes by way of sale or gift of the whole or part of a business (FA 1965, s34(1)(*a*), as amended by the FA 1978, s48).

(11) A business can keep in existence as long as the sole trader is alive or there are partners for the time being in existence.

Companies

(1) The following are the tax rates applicable to companies. The normal rate of corporation tax for the financial year 1977 (year ended 31 March 1978) is 52 per cent. A reduced rate of 42 per cent applies for the financial year 1977 where the profits of the company do not exceed £50,000 with marginal relief being applicable to profits up to £85,000.

(2) If dividends are paid these will be unearned income, subject to the investment income surcharge in the hands of individuals, as follows:

Taxpayers under 65		*Taxpayers 65 and over*	
Up to £1,700	Nil	Up to £2,500	Nil
£1,701–£2,250	10%	£2,501–£3,000	10%
Over £2,250	15%	Over £3,000	15%

Directors' and employees' salaries will be earned income in their hands. Reasonable salaries can hardly be challenged by the Inland Revenue even if the duties are slight, although the courts expressed doubt as to whether a substantial salary paid to a seventeen year-old schoolgirl director by a family company carrying on the trade of pig dealing was allowable under the TA 1970, s130 (*Copeman* v *Flood (Wm) and Sons Ltd* [1940] KB 24 TC 53).

(3) The company's income can be shortfalled. For close trading companies the exemption limit for apportionment purposes is £25,000 (net of corporation tax) for accounting periods ending after 26 October 1977, with abatement relief up to £75,000 (FA 1978, s35(1) amending the FA 1972, Sched 16, para 9(3)).

(4) Disposals of shares in companies can give rise to a charge to capital transfer tax and capital gains tax. Relief from capital transfer tax may be available, however, under the FA 1976, Sched 10 (as amended) and relief from capital gains tax may be available under the FA 1978, s46 and Sched 8.

(5) A company has limited liability.

(6) Profits are assessed on an actual basis.

(7) Companies are chargeable to corporation tax on their chargeable gains at an effective rate of 30 per cent for the financial year 1977 (TA 1970, s365 and FA 1972, s93 (as amended)) with no reliefs or exemptions for small gains.

(8) Section 460 of the TA 1970 applies to transactions in securities of companies.

(9) Section 482 of the TA 1970 (migration etc of companies) which makes unlawful certain transactions involving the migration etc of companies, without Treasury consent, is restricted to companies and does not apply to trading trusts or sole traders or partnerships.

(10) Retirement relief under the FA 1965, s34(1)(*b*) (as amended by FA 1978, s48) is available to an individual who disposes, by way of sale or gift, of shares or securities in a company.

(11) The life of a company is not limited to any perpetuity period.

Tax planning

It is felt that if a suitable trust is used (basically one which can capitalize income) the concept of a trading trust is very attractive. If the settlor has young children he could set up an accumulation and maintenance settlement which could accumulate the income until they attain the age of twenty-five years. If there are no such persons in existence then a discretionary trust could be used provided the capital transfer tax disadvantages are carefully taken into account. Small discretionary trusts could be quite attractive.

Because the top rate of tax is 48 per cent the concept of the trading trust compares favourable with its nearest competitors—the individual trader and the company. The three entities could be utilized contemporaneously so that between them the most advantageous tax position could be reached.

If it is finally decided in *Pearson* v *IRC* (see p51, above) that an interest in possession trust can subsist even though there is a power to accumulate, such trusts would also be attractive trusts through which to trade.

CHAPTER 13

INSURANCE TRUSTS

This chapter deals with the types of trusts which a person taking out a life assurance policy should consider creating. The types of trusts can be as simple or as complicated as the settlor wishes and in a sense an insurance policy is no different an asset from any other asset which could be settled. It is, however, not an income producing asset and an insurance policy enjoys significant capital gains tax and income tax reliefs and exemptions.

The types of trust are important since the policy trusts can usually be worded to avoid any charge to capital transfer tax when the beneficiary takes the proceeds of the policy. The trusts will normally involve the creation of interests in possession in order to avoid the penalties suffered by discretionary trusts under the Capital Transfer Tax provisions. Alternatively, trusts which qualify as accumulation and maintenance settlements could be used. The trusts can be under the provisions of the Married Women's Property Act 1882, or they can be express trusts.

Insurance policies are a very important tax planning instrument and can be used in a large number of situations. This chapter concentrates on the types of trusts which can be used to mitigate capital transfer tax but certain general aspects of insurance are also discussed.

Income tax

Premium Relief

Since 20 March 1968 the availability of relief for life assurance premiums against the income tax liability of the policy holder has been restricted to premiums paid on 'qualifying policies', which must be taken out on the life of the taxpayer or on the life of his or her spouse.

The qualifying conditions are set out in the TA 1970, Sched 1 and very broadly they require the policy to last for a period of ten years or until earlier death, the premiums generally to be spread evenly over the period, and the capital sum payable on death to be at least 75 per cent of the total premiums. There are exceptions to these rules, for instance a term policy can qualify if it is for less than ten years, provided the surrender value does not exceed the total premiums paid (TA 1970, Sched 1, para 1(4)). Term assurance for less than one year issued after 5 April 1979, however, can never qualify (FA 1976, Sched 4, para 2). If a policy does not qualify there will be no tax relief on the premiums paid.

The premium relief is one-half of the basic rate of income tax, the maximum premium or premiums which qualify for the relief being restricted to one-sixth of the total income of the claimant. For the purposes of calculating the 'income' in establishing the one-sixth limit, charges against income, such as allowable interest, are deductible, but personal reliefs are ignored. If in any year of assessment the total premiums in respect of which relief falls to be granted do not exceed £20, the relief is a deduction equal to the income tax at the basic rate on £10 or on the full amount of the premiums, whichever is the less (TA 1970, s19(1) proviso, as amended).

Schedule 4 of the FA 1976 (as amended by FA 1978, Sched 3) has introduced a new method of granting life assurance relief as from the tax year 1979/80. The new rules provide that the insured will be entitled to deduct from the premiums paid the basic relief which would normally be available (ie, in 1979/80 17½ per cent of the premium). It will be the job of the Life Offices concerned to recover the deductions made by the policy holder from the Revenue. Schedule 2 of FA 1975 and s33 of the FA 1976 also set out new rules for the future certification by the Inland Revenue of life insurance policies. Life assurance relief from 1979/80 will no longer be linked with a percentage of the basic rate of tax as it presently is, so that the basic rate of tax can be varied with the rate of premium relief remaining the same (FA 1976, Sched 4, para 5). The 20 per cent limit mentioned above also ceases to apply.

Under the new rules, from 1979/80 tax relief will be available on premiums of £1,500 or one-sixth of income, whichever is the greater (FA 1976, Sched 4, para 21(2)).

Insurance Policy Gains

When a policy is not a qualifying policy the higher rates can be chargeable when a 'chargeable event', such as a death, a maturity, a surrender or an assignment, occurs (see TA 1970, ss393–402). Even if the policy is a qualifying policy there can be 'chargeable events', but—

(1) in the case of death or maturity, only if the policy is converted into a paid-up policy before the expiry of ten years from the making of the insurance, or, if sooner, of three-quarters of the term for which the policy is to run if not ended by death or disability;

(2) in the case of other chargeable events such as a surrender or assignment, only if it occurs within that time, or the policy has been converted into a paid-up policy within that time.

On the happening of a chargeable event in relation to any policy of life insurance, there shall normally be treated as gains arising in connection with the policy—

(1) if the event is a death, the excess of the surrender value of the policy immediately before the death, plus the amount or value of any relevant capital payments over the total amount previously paid under the policy by way of premiums;

(2) if the event is the maturity of the policy, or the surrender of the policy, the excess of the amount or value of the sum payable or other benefits arising by reason of the event, plus the amount or value of any relevant capital payments, over the total amount previously paid under the policy by way of premiums; and

(3) if the event is an assignment, the excess of the amount or value of the consideration, plus the amount or value of any relevant capital payments or of any previously assigned share in the rights conferred by the policy, over the total amount previously paid under the policy by way of premiums (TA 1970, s395(1)).

'Relevant capital payments' means any benefit of a capital nature paid or conferred under the policy before the happening of the chargeable event, excluding any disability benefit, (TA 1970, s395(4)).

When the taxpayer takes out a policy he should first ascertain whether it is qualifying. If it is, it should give him premium relief. It will also exempt any gain from the higher rates of income tax and the investment income surcharge (no basic rate tax liability arises: TA 1970, s399(1), (4)), unless a chargeable event arises even though it is a qualifying policy. The extent of this charge should then be ascertained taking into account the above rules for ascertaining the amount of the gain and the availability of the rules known as the 'top slicing rules' set out in TA 1970, s400, which can often have the effect of eliminating any tax liability.

Capital gains tax

The capital gains tax position is governed by the FA 1965, s28. It states that no chargeable gain shall accrue on the disposal of, or of an interest in, the rights under any policy of assurance, except where the person making the disposal is not the original beneficial owner and acquired the rights or interest for a consideration in money or money's worth (FA 1965, s28(2)). Thus, in the normal course of things unless a purchaser has intervened there should be no charge to capital gains tax when the policy of assurance falls in.

When the policies are settled, therefore, for the benefit of individuals named under the trusts of the policy, this will not be an acquisition by a purchaser and there will be no charge no capital gains tax on the proceeds on maturity.

Stamp duty

Funding of policies will usually be by way of cash transfers so that no stamp duty will be payable and the same position applies when the policy falls in.

A policy of life insurance bears stamp duty, under the Stamp Act 1891, Sched 1 and the FA 1970, s32 and Sched 7, para 17(1), as follows:

Where the amount insured exceeds £50 but does not exceed £1,000	5*p* for every £100 or part of £100 of the amount insured
Where the amount insured exceeds £1,000	50*p* for every £1,000 or part of £1,000 of the amount insured

(Where the amount insured is £50 or less the duty is nil).

However, under the FA 1966, s47(1) and the FA 1970, Sched 7, para 17(2) the maximum amount chargeable by way of stamp duty on any policy of life insurance made on or after 1 August 1966 for a period not exceeding two years shall be 5*p*. A policy, for the purposes of these provisions, shall be treated as made for a period exceeding two years if it contains any provision whereby it may become available for a period exceeding two years in all. Where a 5*p* policy is subsequently varied there are special provisions to enable the Revenue to obtain the extra duty.

Development land tax

This tax will not usually have any bearing on insurance policy trusts.

Capital transfer tax

Funding the Policy

The funding of the policy will result in chargeable transfers for capital transfer tax unless—

(1) the premiums come within the normal expenditure exemption (FA 1975, Sched 6, para 5);

(2) they fall within the £100 exemption—it is important that such premium be by way of outright gift for the benefit of a specific beneficiary (Sched 6, para 4);

(3) the annual £2,000 exemption is utilized (Sched 6, para 2 (as amended));

(4) the £25,000 nil rate position is used—this is a once and for all lifetime exemption (FA 1975, s37 (as amended));

(5) it is an exempt transfer because it is a transfer to the donor's spouse (Sched 6, para 1); and

(6) it comes within the marriage gift exemptions (Sched 6, para 6) or any of the other exemptions set out in Sched 6 and not specifically mentioned above.

Special Valuation Rules for Capital Transfer Tax and Policies

Special valuation rules apply where an insurance policy is given away. Paragraph 11(1) of the FA 1975, Sched 10, provides that—

(i) in determining, in connection with a transfer of value, the value of a policy of insurance on a person's life, that value shall be taken to be not less than—
(*a*) the total of the premiums or other consideration which, at any time before the transfer of value, has been paid under the policy or any policy for which it was directly or indirectly substituted; less
(*b*) any sum which, at any time before the transfer of value, has been paid under, or in consideration for the surrender of any right conferred by, the policy or a policy for which it was directly or indirectly substituted.

If the surrender value is greater than the above 'premium value' then the surrender value will be the appropriate value for capital transfer tax purposes.

Paragraph 11(1) does not apply in the case of the transfer of value which a person makes on his death, or of any other transfers of value which do not result in the policy ceasing to be part of the transferor's estate (Sched 10, para 11(2) substituted by FA 1978, s72). This provision was passed to stop tax avoidance schemes which involved the effecting, simultaneously, of an endowment policy with a low sum assured but a high premium, and a term policy with a large sum assured and a low premium. The scheme involved a high value being attributed to the endowment policy even though the market value of that policy was small, at least for capital transfer tax purposes. Section 72 of the FA 1978 effectively stops these schemes. Special rules apply to term policies (para 11(3)), policies which have fallen in (para 11(2)) and unit-linked policies (para 11(4)).

Types of Policy

Policies will normally be taken out to raise a particular sum at death, so the aim is for the funds to be simply paid out to beneficiaries when the policies fall in. Complex trusts, therefore, are usually considered to be inappropriate. The most suitable trusts are those involving interests in possession, ie, a right to the income for the time being or an entitlement to such income if there were any such income.

Policies put into a discretionary trust might not suffer the usual discretionary trust penalties while the policy value is low, but should it increase in value or should it in fact fall in, there could be capital transfer tax penalties when there are distributions made out of the discretionary trust. The accumulation and maintenance trusts will also be attractive.

Trusts without an Interest in Possession

A discretionary trust is normally not an appropriate vehicle to hold a trust policy as transfers out to beneficiaries will be chargeable to capital transfer tax and also the trust could suffer the periodic charge to capital transfer tax. If the payments into the trust are exempt, however, for one of the reasons mentioned at p112 above ('Funding the Policy'), then one can possibly be in the position of being able to transfer up to £25,000 out of the trust free of capital transfer tax.

With regard to pre-26 March 1974 policies, these could be reconstructed to create accumulation and maintenance trusts, or interests in possession. This should be done to make use of the transitional reliefs available under the FA 1975, Sched 5, para 14. There will usually be a power of appointment in the trust deed to enable this to be done.

The Board of Inland Revenue has indicated that with respect to discretionary trust policies subsisting on 26 March 1974 the payment of further premiums will not cause the policy to be subject to the treatment contained in the FA 1975, Sched 5, para 7; thus further premiums will not constitute a new discretionary trust.

Accumulation and Maintenance Settlements

If a policy is held for the children of the life assured on attaining the age of twenty-five years absolutely, with power to accumulate the income until the children attain that age, this trust will qualify as an accumulation and maintenance settlement under the FA 1975, Sched 5, para 15, as amended. If a child dies under the age of twenty-five years there will be no charge to capital transfer tax assuming there is an overriding power to accumulate the trust income, if any (but see *Pearson* v *IRC*, discussed at p51, above). If a child dies after the age of twenty-five the policy will be chargeable to capital transfer tax as part of his estate.

It might well be that the power to accumulate under the trust comes to an end before a child attains the age of twenty-five years. For example, if the policy is taken out by the life assured on his life for the benefit of X, Y and Z, aged respectively one, three and ten, with the usual twenty-one year accumulation period, the following consequences could ensue.

X's part of the policy will be chargeable on his death from the age of twenty-two years, as the policy will be vested in him when the twenty-one year accumulation period runs out, and the same applies to Y from the age of twenty-four. In the case of Z the trust will be chargeable on his death from the age of twenty-five years, because in order to qualify as an accumulation and maintenance settlement he must obtain an interest in possession, or the funds must be vested in him, from the age of twenty-five years (see, however, the comments on *Pearson* v *IRC* at p51, above).

A policy may be taken out 'for the benefit of the present and future children of the life assured who shall survive the life assured'. In this event the birth of future children will result in a shift in the value, from the present children to the new children, of part of the policy. If the children are under the age of eighteen years they are unlikely to have interests in possession because of the overriding power of accumulation under the Trustee Act 1925, s31. There will only be a charge on the shifting of the interests if the children are over the age of eighteen because they will then have a vested interest in the policy and this will be taken away from them, in part, and given to the children who are subsequently born.

Fixed Interest Settlements

If a policy is held for X absolutely, X is treated as if he owns the same for capital transfer tax purposes, so that on his death the policy will form part of the estate. On the other hand if the policy is held for X if he shall survive the life assured (Y), and failing this to Z, X will have an interest in possession which is liable to be defeated if X does not survive Y. Thus, on the death of X a charge to capital transfer tax can arise either because he had an interest in possession in the policy or because he survives Y; the policy falls in and the proceeds form part of his estate on his death (assuming he has not spent it before he dies).

It might well be that the settlor wishes to benefit his children but nevertheless retain a power to have the funds appointed back to him during his lifetime or indeed have it appointed back to his spouse. The difficulty is that with this power to appoint back, the trust will not be a qualifying accumulation and maintenance settlement so that the children must, in order to avoid the discretionary trust provisions, have an interest in possession. If the children are under the age of eighteen this will mean that the provisions of the Trustee Act 1925, s31 must be excluded.

If the power to appoint back to the settlor is exercised there will be no charge to capital transfer tax because of the FA 1975, Sched 5, para 4(5), as amended, even though the interests in possession of the children have come to an end. Paragraph 4(6) of Sched 5, as amended, will exempt that part of the fund which comes back to the settlor's spouse, but which derived from the settlor's premiums. The paragraph reads as follows:

> If the interest comes to an end and on the same occasion the settlor's spouse becomes beneficially entitled to the settled property, then if—
> (*a*) the settlor's spouse is then domiciled in the United Kingdom; and
> (*b*) neither the settlor nor the settlor's spouse had acquired a reversionary interest in the property for a consideration in money or money's worth;
> tax shall not be chargeable under this paragraph.

A further provision was added by the FA 1976, s110(2). This states that references to the settlor's spouse include, in a case where the settlor has died less than two years before the interest comes to an end or the interest comes to an end before 1 April 1977, the settlor's widow or widower.

Thus, Mr and Mrs X might have taken out a joint policy on their lives, Mr X paying the premiums until his death. On his death it may be desired to appoint the policy or the surrender moneys to Mrs X absolutely. If this is done no capital transfer tax will be payable because of the FA 1975, Sched 5, para 4(6), as amended by the FA 1976, s110(2). If the appointment were made more than two years after Mr X's death the exemption would not be available on the fraction of the policy derived from Mr X.

Conclusions

Assurance trusts must be seen as part of the overall position of tax reliefs and exemptions available on insurance policies. It must also be appreciated that policies can be held upon other types of trust, such as protective trusts or trusts for the mentally disabled, already mentioned in this book.

CHAPTER 14

EDUCATIONAL TRUSTS

Present position of educational trusts

The taxation position of non-charitable educational trusts has never been clear. It had generally been accepted, however, up to the publication of a Revenue Press Release on 14 June 1978, that they could offer significant tax advantages to directors and higher-paid employees where their company set up the trust for their benefit.

The Revenue has indicated that it intends to stop such tax free perks, so it is now necessary to consider the possibility of setting up charitable trusts for education for the benefit of children in general, with preference perhaps being given to children of employees of particular companies.

The position with regard to educational trusts can now be divided into three parts:

(1) non-charitable educational trusts set up before 14 June 1978 where scholarships thereunder were awarded before that date;

(2) non-charitable educational trusts set up on or after 14 June 1978; and

(3) charitable educational trusts, whenever set up.

Although not dealt with in this chapter, it is also possible for a parent to create a settlement for the education of his child for a period ending not later than the date he attains the age of eighteen years, or, after attaining that age, the date he ceases to undergo full-time education or training. The exemption from capital transfer tax in FA 1975, s46(1) could in this event be utilized, provided the conditions of that section are satisfied.

Non-charitable educational trusts prior to 14 June 1978

Introduction

The tax position of such trusts, which has never been free from doubt, is set out below. The Inland Revenue has stated that where an employer sets up and finances an arrangement under which awards are made to the children of directors or higher-paid employees (a higher-paid employee is one earning at or above the rate of £7,500 a year, including any benefits) it will contend that those awards give rise to benefits assessable on the parents; this practice, however, will apply only to scholarships awarded on or after 14 June 1978 and will not affect the income from existing awards (IR Press Release, 14 June 1978). The Revenue Release has not altered the law, and the analysis of the tax position (at p32 below) still applies to non-charitable educational trusts even though they may have been set up after 13 June 1978.

The tax advantages of such educational trusts can be quite exceptional. If the trust is funded by a company the payments can be deductible for Corporation Tax purposes. Furthermore all payments out of the trust to children or grandchildren of employees shall be tax-free in their hands, as being 'scholarship income', which is specifically exempt from income tax under the TA 1970, s375.

The trust is particularly attractive to higher-paid employees, since they would otherwise have to fund the university education of their children out of net income and they would also only have the minimum grant from the Local Authority.

The company, as well as being able to provide a very useful 'perk' to its employees in a tax-free form, is able to claim Corporation Tax relief on the payments to the educational trust.

What is an Educational Trust (Non-Charitable)?

An educational trust is a trust funded by a company, which can be a close company or a non-close company, which holds the trust funds for the purposes of providing scholarship payments for the education of the children or grandchildren of employees. The trust could be a discretionary trust with an eighty year perpetuity period. It can have power to accumulate income for twenty-one years.

The trust will not be a charitable trust so, for instance, any income which arises from the settled funds will be subject to income tax at the basic rate plus the 15 per cent investment income surcharge. The reason why it would not be a charitable trust is that the element of public benefit will be lacking. This is because the trust will be for the benefit of the children and grandchildren of employees of a particular company or a particular group of companies and this is not a sufficiently wide section of the public for establishing a charity.

Income Tax

Position of Trustees—The trustees will not be subject to income tax on the moneys settled by the company because those moneys will be voluntary payments and will therefore have no 'source', which is essential to create an income tax liability. The trust arrangement envisages regular payments from the company and not just one or two large capital payments.

Any income which arises from the settled funds themselves, eg, bank deposits, will be subject to the basic rate of tax plus the 15 per cent additional rate under the FA 1973, s16, assuming a discretionary trust is set up.

Position of Scholars—Section 375 of the TA 1970 is the key provision providing tax exemption for the payments to the scholars. Subsection (1) states 'Income arising from a scholarship held by a person receiving full-time instruction at a university, college, school or other educational establishment shall be exempt from income tax, and no account shall be taken of any such income in computing the amount of income for income tax purposes'. Subsection (2) states 'In this section "scholarship" includes an exhibition, bursary or any other similar educational endowment'. Subsection (3) states 'If any question arises whether any income is income arising from a scholarship held as aforesaid, the Board may consult the Secretary of State for Education and Science'.

'Scholarship income' is not defined. However, it has been held obiter that the payment does not have to be something that would otherwise have been taxable under one of the schedules, ie, it does not have to be income for tax purposes (see *Mapp* v *Oram* (1969) 45 TC 651, per Lord Hodson, at p677).

On the basis of the above section it can be argued that any payments from the trust are exempt from income tax, being scholarship income. It is also felt that the words 'no account shall be taken of such income in computing the amount of income for income tax purposes' override the general provisions for charging benefits to employees and persons connected with them under Sched E in the FA 1976, s61. The Revenue accept this by concession only for trusts set up before 14 June 1978 where the awards are made prior to that date.

It is also felt that s375 overrides the FA 1973, ss16 and 17, so that should regular payments be made out of capital to a beneficiary, with the result that the payments take on the nature of income, it could be argued that no tax should be deducted from payments to the scholars.

Position of Employees—It can be argued that the payment of the scholarship income to a child of an employee is a benefit in kind to the employee under the general Sched E provisions of the TA 1970, s181, or under s195 of that Act. It is felt, however, that the existence of the trust, and the fact that no child is entitled to any payment except by reference to his academic record and merit, is sufficient to demonstrate that although the child would not have benefited unless the parent was an employee, nevertheless he benefited only because of his academic merit and record (see *Barclays Bank Ltd* v *Naylor* (1960) 39 TC 256, and *Hochstrasser* v *Mayes* (1959) 38 TC 673). The employment, in other words, was the causa sine qua non and not the causa causans.

Section 61 of the FA 1976 taxes a director or higher-paid employee on benefits provided for him or for members of this family or household. The cost of providing the benefits will be chargeable as income under Sched E as emoluments. It might be contended that the scholarship income was a benefit provided to the employee since it discharges his own liability to pay the school or college fees for his children. However, the author is of the view that it could be argued that the payments were not 'by reason of his employment' as the amount of the remuneration the employee receives is the same whether he has children or not. The payments to the child depend on the academic merits and record of the child and do not in any real sense relate to the employment (*Hochstrasser* v *Mayes* (1959) 38 TC 673). It can also be argued that the income is scholarship income under the TA 1970, s375 and that this provision overrides the FA 1976, s61.

Position of Company—In order to establish the payments to the trust as being deductible for Corporation Tax purposes they must have been made wholly and exclusively for the purposes of the trade, and they must be of a revenue nature.

It is felt that it can be fairly easily established that the payments were wholly and exclusively for the purposes of the trade because the company is only setting up the trust to make the employment of the directors and employees more attractive. The requirement as to the payments being of a revenue nature should be satisfied by the company making small regular payments to the trust instead of a few large payments.

Capital Transfer Tax

Capital Transfer Tax and the Trust Itself—If the trust is one which satisfies the conditions set out in para 17(1)–(9) of the FA 1975, Sched 5 as amended, then it will not suffer any of the penalties which normally apply to discretionary trusts (FA 1975, Sched 5, para 17(3), and see also p63, above).

The basic requirement is that the settled property is held on trusts which, either indefinitely or until the end of a period (whether defined by date or in some other way), do not permit any of the settled property to be applied otherwise than for the benefit of—

(1) persons of a class defined by reference to employment in a particular trade, profession or undertaking or employment by, or office with, a body carrying on a trade, profession or undertaking; or

(2) persons of a class defined by reference to marriage or relationship to, or dependence on, persons of a class defined as mentioned in paragraph (1) above; or

(3) charities (Sched 5, para 17(1)).

In the case of the proposed educational trust the beneficiaries will come under paragraph (2) above.

A further requirement set out in para 17(2) is that where the class is defined by reference to employment by, or office with, a particular body, the exemptions and reliefs from capital transfer tax only apply if the class comprises all or most of the persons employed or holding office with that body.

Non-Close Company as Settlor—There can be no charge to capital transfer tax on any transfer to the trust by a non-close company. Thus, where such a company is a settlor there will be no difficulties (FA 1975, s20(5)).

Close Company as Settlor—Section 90 of the FA 1976 sets out the conditions which must be satisfied in order that a close company which makes a transfer of value to the educational trust will be exempt from capital transfer tax. Section 90(1) states that a disposition of property made to trustees by a close company, whereby the property is to be held on trusts of the description specified in the FA 1975, Sched 5, para 17(1), is not a transfer of value if the persons for whose benefit the trusts permit the property to be applied include all or most of either—

(1) the persons employed by or holding office with the company; or

(2) the persons employed by or holding office with the company or any one or more subsidiaries of the company.

There are restrictions on the relief where property can be transferred to participators as defined in the FA 1975, s39, and persons connected with the participators (FA 1976, s90(3)). In determining, however, whether the trust permits property to be applied to any participators, no account shall be taken of any power to make a payment which is the income of any person for any of the purposes of income tax, or would be income for any of those purposes of a person not resident in the United Kingdom if he were so resident (s90(4)). Also, if the company is able to get tax relief on its payments to the trust (which it should do) the FA 1976, s89(1) will exempt those payments from capital transfer tax.

Capital Gains Tax

Creation of the Trust—Under the FA 1976, s56, as amended, where a close company disposes of an asset to the trustees in circumstances such that the disposal is a disposition which by virtue of the FA 1976, s90, as amended, is not a transfer of value for the purposes of capital transfer tax, the capital gains tax liability is treated as if it were a no gain/no loss situation, ie, the gain is in effect 'rolled-over'.

A disposal by a company other than the close company is eligible for capital gains tax relief also if—

(1) the disposal is made to trustees otherwise than under a bargain made at arm's-length; and

(2) the trust is one which would give exemption from capital transfer tax under s90 if the company were a close company.

Transfers by Trustees—If the trustees dispose of assets, which are chargeable assets for capital gains tax purposes, in the normal course of dealing with the trust they will be liable to capital gains tax at 30 per cent on the gain, unless the gains are small and the settlement was made before 7 June 1978 (see FA 1978, Sched 7, para 6, and p32, above). There is no general relief from capital gains tax in this area as there is for capital transfer tax.

Stamp Duty

There are no special exemptions from stamp duty for educational trusts. Normally the company would settle cash so that no ad valorem duty should be payable. 50*p* duty will be payable on the settlement. If shares, or property other than cash, are put into the trust they could be liable to ad valorem duty. Transfers of property out to beneficiaries will in all instances be exempt from duty (F (1909–10) A 1910, s74(6)), but they might attract the miscellaneous conveyance or transfer duty of 50*p*. Normally, however, only cash will be transferred out to beneficiaries, and this will not be under deed, so that stamp duty should not present any problems.

Development Land Tax

Educational trusts will be liable for this tax in the usual way. It will not normally be envisaged, however, that educational trusts will ever acquire any land to fund scholarships let alone any land which has development value.

Conclusion

Educational trusts are an attractive proposition especially for large public companies who have a large number of employees. The scholarship income can pay school fees and supplement university grants.

Post-13 June 1978 non-charitable educational trusts

The tax position of such trusts is identical to that discussed at pp116–122 above, except that the Inland Revenue have issued a Press Release setting out their intended practice with regard to such trusts. Thus, only people who wish to contest the matter with the Inland Revenue should consider setting up non-charitable educational trusts after 13 June 1978 or, if a trust has been set up on or before that date, grant awards after that date.

It is also open to the taxpayer to set up a non-charitable educational trust which complies with the Revenue requirements as set out in their Press Release. The general tax position of such trusts, because of their lack of charitable status, will normally make it inadvisable to set them up. For example, the requirements for corporation tax, capital transfer tax and capital gains tax relief for payments to such trusts will not normally be capable of satisfaction.

The full Inland Revenue Press Release, dated 14 June 1978 and entitled

Benefits in Kind—Scholarships for Employees' Children, reads as follows:

> 1. Hitherto the Inland Revenue have not sought to treat, as a benefit taxable under Section 61 Finance Act 1976 on a director or higher paid employee, the provision by his employer of a scholarship to assist in the cost of the education of a member of his family. They have refrained from doing so on the grounds that Section 375 Income and Corporation Taxes Act 1970, which exempts from tax income from scholarships, precluded such a contention.
> 2. The Revenue are now advised that Section 375, whilst exempting from tax the scholarship income in the scholar's hands, does not prevent the cost of providing the scholarship from being a benefit taxable under Section 61. They therefore propose in future to contend for liability under that section, and in accordance with Section 72(3) Finance Act 1976, where a scholarship is awarded to a member of the family or household of a director or higher-paid employee and the award is made by reason of the latter's employment. Thus, where an employer sets up and finances an arrangement under which awards are made to the children of directors or higher-paid employees, the Revenue will contend that those awards give rise to benefits provided by reason of the employment and are therefore assessable on the parents.
> 3. The Revenue will not, however, contend that there is a benefit giving rise to liability under Section 61 where there is only a fortuitous connection between the identity of the recipient of the scholarship and his parent's employment, for example, where a firm sets up a scheme for awarding scholarships which is open to all, but where one of the successful candidates happens to be the child of a higher-paid employee of that firm.
> 4. The new practice will be applied to income from scholarships awarded on or after today, but not to income from existing awards.
> 5. For the purpose of liability under Section 61, a higher-paid employee is one earning at the rate of £7,500 a year, including any benefits.

The following points should be noted in connection with the Revenue Press Release:

(1) It only seeks to tax directors and higher-paid employees on the awards and not other employees whose children might receive awards.

(2) It does not seek to impose a tax liability where the connection between the employer and the grant of the award to a child of an employee is fortuitous.

A further Press Release, issued by way of clarification of that of 14 June, was issued on 20 June 1978 and reads as follows:

> In response to several enquiries that have been received by the Inland Revenue Press Information and Office concerning their press release of 14th June the following clarifications have been given:
> First, the scholarships referred to are for all types of education, whether for school, university or other.
> Secondly, the phrase in paragraph 3 of our release "... open to all", means just that: it does *not* mean merely open to all employees. "All" means the public at large.

Charitable educational trusts

Educational trusts which are established as being charitable, like all charities, will be largely exempt from United Kingdom income taxation and capital gains tax (TA 1970, s360). Such trusts will also be free from capital transfer tax (FA 1975, Sched 5, para 20). There are certain limited reliefs available to such trusts for stamp duty (FA 1974, s49) and development land tax (DLTA 1976, ss24, 25). Such trusts form 'tax havens' within the United Kingdom.

What is a Charitable Educational Trust?

One of the essential requirements of a charitable trust, apart from one for the relief of poverty, is that the trust should confer a benefit upon the public generally or upon some division of it considered in its public capacity, eg, the inhabitants of a particular locality, a public profession, or a class of the public determined by age or poverty. Jenkins LJ described the breadth of the requirement in the following terms: 'An aggregate of individuals ascertained by reference to some personal tie such as the relations of a particular individual, the members of a particular family, the employees of a particular firm, the members of a particular association, does not amount to the public or a section thereof' (*Re Scarisbrick* [1951] 1 All ER 822, at p837).

In the case of *Oppenheim* v *Tobacco Securities Trust Co* [1951] AC 297 it was held that a gift for the education of the children of employees and ex-employees of a firm and its subsidiaries was not charitable. In *Koettgen's Will Trusts* [1954] 2 WLR 166 a trust was established for the commercial education of British-born persons, with a request that preference should be given to the employees of a particular firm including a proviso that no more than 75 per cent of the available income in any year should be applied for the preferred beneficiaries. It was held that the trust was a valid charitable trust. A similar conclusion was arrived at in *Gaffoor (Trustees of the Abdul Gaffoor Trust)* v *Income Tax Commissioner, Colombo* [1961] AC 584.

In the case of *IRC* v *Educational Grants Association* [1967] CH 993, it was held that where between 75 per cent and 85 per cent of the income of a trust for the advancement of education was spent on children of persons connected with a particular company, the income had not been applied for the public benefit and no exemption from income tax could be granted in respect of those payments.

It is thus feasible for a company to set up and fund an educational trust for the inhabitants of a particular area, requesting the trustees to give a preference to the employees of a particular firm.

It is difficult to extract clear principles from the above cases but clearly a proportion of the income must be applied for the benefit of outsiders and this is a matter for the discretion of the trustees taking into account the fact that as in *IRC* v *Educational Grants Association*, if between 75 per cent and 85 per cent of the income is applied to the children of the employees of a particular company the exemption from income tax will be lost. It is suggested that because of the uncertainty in this area, after the trust has been set up guidance should be obtained from the Charity Commission and the Inland Revenue if the trustees are concerned about the effect on the charitable status of the trust of the exercise of their discretions to grant awards to particular children in any year.

Any company setting up a charitable trust should ensure, as in *Koettgen's Will Trusts* above, that at least 25 per cent of the trust income is applied for the benefit of outsiders; how much more the Inland Revenue will require the trust to pay to outsiders is difficult to ascertain.

Funding the Trust

If the company is a non-close company it should fund the trust by way of a seven year covenant which will enable the charity to claim back the basic rate of tax deducted by the company. The payment will be a charge on income (TA 1970, s248(5), (8) and (9)).

The trust could be an exclusive educational trust or it could be a general charitable trust from which the company carries out its general charitable dealings. Without such a trust the company might be disinclined to enter into covenants with particular charities and would thus tend to give irregular donations for which tax relief would generally not be available. If the company is a close company, however, sums given to charities would tend to indicate that it has surplus income available and therefore the company's shortfall position could be aggravated. If the company makes covenanted donations this will be deductible as a charge on income for Corporation Tax purposes, but will once again open the company to possible shortfall assessments.

Press Release of 14 June 1978

The Revenue have stated in their Press Release of 14 June 1978 that they will not contend that there is a benefit giving rise to a liability under the FA 1976, s61, where there is only a fortuitous connection between the identity of the recipient of the scholarship and his parent's employment. For example, a firm sets up a scholarship scheme which is open to all, but one of the successful candidates happens to be the child of a higher-paid employee of that firm. It would thus appear that if a charitable trust is set up open to all, and an award is made in the due exercise of the discretion of the trustees to the child of an employee of the company which created the trust, that there should be no tax liability upon the parent under the FA 1976, s61 when such an award is made.

It might well be that not all educational charitable trusts will satisfy the

Revenue requirements set out in the Press Release. It is, for instance, charitable if a trust is set up for the education of persons in a particular locality; this might not, however, satisfy the Revenue Press Release requirements that the scholarships be open to the 'public at large'.

Conclusions on Educational Trusts

With regard to trusts where scholarships have been awarded on or before 13 June 1978 the position is clear: the Revenue will not seek to tax the award upon the parent of the recipient of the award.

For awards granted after 13 June 1978 by non-charitable educational trusts which do not satisfy the Revenue Release requirements, it would appear that the Revenue will attempt to tax the parent of the recipient. Unless, therefore, the taxpayer wishes to contest the matter with the Inland Revenue, such awards should not be made and such trusts should generally brought to an end. If the matter is to be fought in the courts it could well be that the Revenue are proved wrong in their interpretation. The making of such awards after 13 June 1978 may be, therefore, one of the final opportunities available to the taxpayer to receive them tax-free before amending legislation is passed It is unlikely that such legislation would be retrospective.

The alternative to arguing the matter with the Inland Revenue is to set up a charitable educational trust. These create difficulties where close companies (but not non-close companies) are providing the trust funds, and they also raise difficulties as to the extent that the trustees in the due and proper exercise of their discretion can make awards to children of employees of particular companies when the potential beneficiaries will of necessity have to include a much wider class of persons. These difficulties are not, however, insurmountable, making such trusts attractive vehicles especially where non-close companies are the settlors and the Revenue Statement requirements are clearly satisfied.

CHAPTER 15

EMPLOYEES' TRUST

These trusts can be of considerable use in mitigating tax especially if a company is the settlor. Payments into the trust can be deductible for Corporation Tax purposes and any income arising from the settled funds and accumulated in the trust will only pay tax, in the trust, at 48 per cent. The trust can also be a means whereby company profits can be settled, so creating a fund which can be used to purchase shares in the company on the death of a shareholder or during a shareholder's lifetime.

If the company is a family company the appointment of appropriate trustees could mean that control of the company is effectively kept within the family, although any dividends arising from the shares held by the employees' trust will ultimately have to be paid for the benefit of employees. Whatever is paid to an employee, whether capital, income, or accumulated income, will be taxable in his hands under Sched E as earned income.

The trust can be a discretionary trust for the benefit of employees without suffering the usual capital transfer tax disadvantages and can last for the eighty years perpetuity period with power to accumulate income for twenty-one years.

As well as capital transfer tax reliefs, capital gains tax reliefs are also available for employees' trusts. The employees' trust can be useful too for a company which has shortfall problems, since payments into an employees' trust, provided that they are not capital payments, will be deductible not only for corporation tax purposes but also for the purposes of reducing relevant income which would otherwise be shortfalled.

Income Tax

Payments to the Trust

The payments made to the employees' trust will be deductible from the company's corporation tax liability, and, if the company is a close company, for the purposes of ascertaining the relevant income of the close company. This is because the payments will be made wholly and exclusively for the purposes of the trade of the company and the payments do not fall within any of the disallowance heads in the TA 1970, s130.

It should be noted that in connection with profit-sharing schemes, which are a type of employees' trust, the Revenue in a Press Release dated 20 April 1978 stated that payments by the company to the trustees of the scheme were deductible from company profits. 'This will follow from the existing law without any express provision in the new legislation' (para 17 of the Release). Such a provision was not included in the Bill although it was finally included in the Act (FA 1978, s60).

There should not be just one payment into the trust. There must be a number of payments over the years, since it was held in *British Insulated and Helsby Cables* v *Atherton* ([1926] AC 205; 10 TC 155) that a lump sum paid to form the nucleus of an unapproved pension fund was not deductible from the company's profits. It was also held, in *Rowntree and Co Ltd* v *Curtis* [1925] 1 KB 328; 8 TC 678), that a sum set aside, in order that the income derived from it might be used for invalid employees, was also not allowable because it was a capital payment although made wholly and exclusively for the purposes of the trade. Thus, a number of payments into the employees' trust is essential. In *Heather* v *PE Consulting Group Limited* (1972) 48 TC 293) it was held that annual payments to a trust fund established by a taxpayer company to purchase shares in the company, for the benefit of, among others, employees, were a succession of revenue payments and therefore deductible from the company profits. The payments to the trust were 10 per cent of the company's annual profits, subject to a minimum of £5,000.

It is important that the company does not make annual payments under a covenant. In *Ball (Inspector of Taxes)* v *National and Grindlays Bank Ltd* ([1971] 3 All ER 485), a UK bank carrying on business overseas covenanted to make monthly payments to named trustees for seven years to provide for the education of the children of its expatriate staff. It was held that the payments were not made under a liability for a valuable and sufficient consideration within the TA 1970, s248(5)(*b*) and therefore not a charge on income. The liability must be incurred in return for a consideration, as that word is used in contract law, ie, something in return for something given. Russell L J at p493 H, stated that these payments, had they been voluntary, would have been deductible.

Example—X Limited puts 10 per cent of its taxable profit into an employees' trust which is invested to produce income. It makes no further payment into the fund. It is felt that the Revenue might effectively claim that this was a payment of capital to form the nucleus of a fund and therefore is not deductible for corporation tax purposes.

Example—Y Limited puts 10 per cent of its profits into an employees' trust and thereafter adds regular amounts each year to the fund. These will be income payments and therefore deductible from the company's profits.

Receipt by Trustees of Settled Funds

The settled funds received from the company by the trustees of the employees' trust will not amount to chargeable income in their hands, even though the payments will be out of the company's income and will be regular payments of an income nature. This is because the payments will not amount to taxable annual receipts because they are entirely voluntary and are not made under any binding obligation. The capital transfer tax position is dealt with below, at p131 but for income tax purposes the receipts will be exempt from tax in the hands of the trustees.

Accumulated Income

If the employees' trust is a discretionary trust, any income which arises from the settled funds (but not the settled funds themselves) will be income in a trust within the FA 1973, s16(2)(*a*), and will thus be chargeable to income tax at the basic rate of 33 per cent, plus the investment income surcharge of 15 per cent giving a total rate of 48 per cent.

Payments to Employees

Any receipts by employees from the trust, whether of capital, income or accumulated income, will be chargeable to tax in their hands under Sched E (see *Brumby (Inspector of Taxes)* v *Milner* [1976] STC 534).

Payments to Employees' Children

If children of employees are beneficiaries it can be argued, following *Barclays Bank* v *Naylor* ((1960) 39 TC 256) that payments to the children will be their income and not part of their parents' income. The law in this area however, is, uncertain; there is now a possible charge under the FA 1976, s61.

Capital Transfer Tax

Considerable reliefs from capital transfer tax are available to employees' trusts. The provisions are contained in the FA 1975, Sched 5, para 17, the FA 1976, ss90 and 107, and the FA 1978, s67 and Sched 11.

Exemptions for the Trust Itself

The provisions apply to trusts where property is held indefinitely (eg, a charitable trust for poor employees), or until the end of a particular period (such as the end of an eighty year perpetuity period) or if the trust were to end on the liquidation of the company. The reliefs only apply provided the following persons alone can benefit under the trust:

(1) persons of a class defined by reference to employment in a particular trade, profession or undertaking or employment by, or office with, a body carrying on a trade, profession or undertaking; or

(2) persons of a class defined by reference to marriage or relationship to, or dependence on, persons of a class defined in para (1) above; or

(3) charities (FA 1975, Sched 5, para 17(1)).

One might therefore have a discretionary trust for the benefit of employees, their spouses and children with a perpetuity period of, say eighty years, by which property can either be paid out to employees, their spouses and children, or paid out for charitable purposes (which could include a trust for poor employees, which would be charitable).

Where the chosen class is made by reference to employment by or office with a particular body, the trust will only qualify if the class comprises all or most of the persons employed by or holding office with that body (FA 1975, Sched 5, para 17(2)).

While an employees' trust so qualifies the following consequences ensue:

(1) the trust property shall be treated as comprised in one settlement, whether or not it would fall to be so treated apart from these provisions; and

(2) an interest in possession in any part of the said property shall be disregarded if that part is less than 5 per cent of the whole; and

(3) subject to the provisions of para 17(4) a payment out of the settled property shall not be a capital distribution and shall not be taken into account as a distribution payment (ie, will be exempt from capital transfer tax); and

(4) the rate of tax on any capital distributions (see below, for what is a capital distribution) ignores aggregation with the settlor; and

(5) the periodic charges to capital transfer tax are deferred and become payable only when a capital distribution is made (eg, if the property is paid to the settlor or certain connected persons).

Paragraph 17(4) of the FA 1975, Sched 5, as amended by FA 1978, Sched 11, para 1, states that a distribution shall be a capital distribution and therefore chargeable to capital transfer tax if it is made for the benefit of—

(*a*) a person who is or is connected with a person who directly or indirectly provided any of the settled property otherwise than by additions not exceeding in value £1,000 in any one year; or

(*b*) in a case where the employment in question is employment by a close company, a person who is a participator in relation to that company and either—

> (i) is beneficially entitled to, or to rights entitling him to acquire, not less than 5 per cent of, or of any class of the shares comprised in, its issued share capital; or
>
> (ii) would, on a winding-up of the company, be entitled to not less than 5 per cent of its assets;

but if the trusts are those of a profit-sharing scheme approved under the FA 1978, para (*b*) above does not preclude the application of (3) immediately above in relation to any appropriation of shares in pursuance of the scheme.

It is clear that participators with the requisite 5 per cent do not have to be excluded from the class of beneficiaries. Should they receive a benefit, however, the adverse capital transfer tax consequences will occur, ie, the trust will be treated as having made a capital distribution. Section 107 of the FA 1976 enables the Sched 5, para 17 relief to be applicable where there is a switch from one employee's trust to another within a one month period and, where the relevant conditions are satisfied by both trusts. This can be particularly important where an employee's trust period is coming to an end and it is necessary to create a further settlement which will also qualify as an employees' trust.

Exemptions for transfers to the trust

Section 90 of the FA 1976 (as amended by the FA 1978, s67 and Sched 11) provides relief from capital transfer tax where property is put into an employees' trust.

Dispositions by a Close Company—A disposition of property made to trustees by a close company, whereby the property is held upon the terms of a trust which is exempt from capital transfer tax under the FA 1975, Sched 5, para 17(1), is not a transfer of value if the persons who benefit under the trust include all or most of the following:

(1) the persons employed by, or holding office with, the company; or

(2) the persons employed by, or holding office with, the company or any one or more of the subsidiaries (as defined in the Companies Act 1948) of the company.

The exemption does not apply if the trusts permit any of the property to be applied at any time for the benefit of:

(1) a person who is a participator in the company making the disposition or, as the case may be, the company whose shares are disposed of; or

(2) any other person who is a participator in any close company that has made a disposition whereby property became comprised in the same settlement, being a disposition which but for this provision would have been a transfer of value; or

(3) any other person who has been a participator in any such company as is mentioned in paragraph (1) or (2) immediately above at any time after, or during the ten years before, the disposition made by that company or, as the case may be, the disposition of its shares; or

(4) any person who is connected with any persons within paragraphs (1), (2) and (3), immediately above.

The participators in a company which are referred to above do not include any participator who—

(1) is not beneficially entitled to, or to rights entitling him to acquire, 5 per

cent or more of, or of any class of the shares comprised in, its issued share capital; and

(2) on a winding-up of the company would not be entitled to 5 per cent or more of its assets.

In determining whether the trusts permit property to be applied to participators, no account shall be taken of any power to make a payment which is the income of any person for any of the purposes of income tax, or would be the income for any of those purposes of a person not resident in the United Kingdom if he were so resident. In addition, no account shall be taken of any power to appropriate shares if the trust qualifies as a profit sharing trust under the FA 1978.

Dispositions by an Individual—There are important, but restricted, reliefs from capital transfer tax for transfers by individuals to employees' trusts. The original legislation was contained in the FA 1976, s90(2) effective from after 6 April 1976; this has been substantially amended by the FA 1978, s67 and Sched 11 effective from 10 April 1978.

A transfer of shares or securities by an individual to a settlement is an exempt transfer if—

(1) the trusts of the settlement are within the FA 1975, Sched 5, para 17(1); and

(2) the persons for whose benefit the trusts permit the settled property to be applied include all or most of the persons employed by or holding office with the company (FA 1978, s67(1)).

It is also necessary for the following conditions to be satisfied:

(1) that, following the transfer or within one year thereafter, the trustees hold more than half the ordinary shares and a majority of the voting rights on all questions affecting the company as a whole; and

(2) there are no provisions whereby the condition in (1) above can cease to be satisfied without the consent of the trustees (FA 1978, s67(2)).

Where the company has shares or securities of any class giving powers of voting limited to either or both of the following:

(1) the question of winding-up;

(2) any question primarily affecting shares or securities of that class.

The reference above to 'all questions affecting the company as a whole' is to all such questions except any in relation to which those powers are capable of being exercised (FA 1978, s67(3)).

The relief does not apply if the trusts permit property to be applied for the benefit of—

(1) a participator in the company; or

(2) a participator in any close company that has made a disposition whereby property became comprised in the same settlement, being a disposition which but for FA 1976, s90 would have been a transfer of value; or

(3) a person who has been a participator in the company mentioned in FA 1978, s67(1) or in any such company as is mentioned in (2) immediately above at any time after, or during the ten years before, the transfer to the trust; or

(4) any person who is connected with any person within (1), (2) or (3), immediately above (FA 1978, s67(4)).

The following are not participators:

(1) a person not beneficially entitled to, or to rights entitling him to acquire, 5 per cent or more of, or of any class of the shares comprised in, the company's issued share capital; and

(2) a person who on a winding-up of the company would not be entitled to 5 per cent or more of its assets.

In determining for the purposes of the FA 1978, s67(4) whether trust property can be applied for the benefit of participators or persons connected with them, no account shall be taken of any power to make a payment which is the income of any person for any of the purposes of income tax, or would be the income for any of those purposes of a person not resident in the United Kingdom if he were so resident.

Definitions

The terms 'close company' and 'participator' have the same meaning as in the FA 1975, s39, ie, broadly their Corporation Tax meaning, but including any company which would be close if it were resident in the United Kingdom. 'Ordinary shares' are shares which carry a right, or are convertible into shares which carry a right, to dividends not restricted to fixed rate dividends (ie, including participating preference shares).

Capital gains tax

Disposals by Close Companies and Individual

Special provisions apply where a company or an individual disposes of an asset to the trustees of an employees' trust.

The new substituted s56 (1) of the FA 1976 (subs(1), having been substituted by the FA 1978, Sched 11, para 2(1)) states that where—

> (*a*) a close company within the meaning of the FA 1976, s90 disposes of an asset to trustees in circumstances such that the disposal is a disposition which by virtue of that section is not a transfer of value . . .; or
>
> (*b*) an individual disposes of an asset to trustees in circumstances such that the disposal is an exempt transfer by virtue of the FA 1978, s69
>
> part III of the FA 1965 shall have effect in relation to the disposal [but subject generally to roll-over relief being applicable].

The disposal is treated for capital gains tax purposes as made for a consideration which produces neither a gain nor a loss (ie, the cost of the asset in a simple case), unless the actual consideration is more than that. Where these no-gain/no-loss provisions apply (ie, generally where no consideration is paid for the assets) the trustees will take over the settlor's base cost for capital gains tax purposes. In the case where the consideration paid by the trustees for the assets exceed their base cost the chargeable gain is to be based on the actual consideration, even if this is not market value. In such a case the trustees do not have the donor's base cost as their base cost. A disposal at an undervalue by a close company will not affect the shareholders' base cost for capital gains tax when the shares are ultimately sold (FA 1976, s56(2) and (3)).

Disposals by Non-close Companies

A disposal made after 6 April 1976 by a company other than a close company is eligible for capital gains tax relief as above if—

(1) the disposal is made to trustees otherwise than under a bargain made at arm's length, and

(2) the trust is one which would give exemption from capital transfer tax under s90 if the company were a close company.

(See FA 1976, s56(4)–(7) and FA 1978, Sched 11, para 2(2).)

Stamp duty

There are no special exemptions from stamp duty for employees' trusts. Normally the company would settle cash so that no ad valorem stamp duty should be payable.

50*p* duty will be payable on the settlement deed. If shares or property are put into the trust ad valorem duty could be chargeable. Transfers of property out to beneficiaries will be exempt from ad valorem duty (F (1909–10) A 1910, s74(6)), but they might attract the miscellaneous conveyance or transfer duty of 50*p* in the unlikely event of a deed being used.

Employees' trust set up to buy private company shares

The employees' trust can be a very useful vehicle to create funds to buy shares in a private company. The private company could in fact be the source of the funds because the company could be the settlor.

Company Law Requirements

The usual obstacle to a company providing funds for the acquisition of its shares is the Companies Act 1948, s54, which makes it unlawful for a company to provide financial assistance for the purchase of or subscription for its own shares or those of its holding company. For the purposes of this provision it is immaterial whether the financial assistance by the company is by means of a loan, a guarantee, the provision of security, or otherwise, and whether it was given directly or indirectly. The section was passed because speculators used to find a company with a cash balance or easily realizable assets, buy up the shares in the company for cash, and so arrange matters that the purchase money which they became bound to provide was advanced to them by the company.

An important exception to these provisions is an employees' trust. It is provided that any provision by a company, in accordance with a scheme, of money for the purchase or subscription by trustees of or for fully-paid shares in the company or its holding company to be held by or for the benefit of employees of the company, including a director holding salaried employment in the company, shall not breach s54. The section only refers to employees, so that if the employees' trust is set up with a view to providing funds to acquire shares from the close company, the spouses or dependants of employees cannot benefit under the trust; furthermore it is not possible to add in charities (unless it is a charity for the benefit of poor employees). Thus, although spouses and children of employees can be beneficiaries without prejudicing certain of the tax reliefs of the trust, nevertheless they cannot be beneficiaries if it is intended that the trust be set up to be funded by the company to buy all or some of its shares.

Applying for tax clearance

As a precaution, when a shareholder does sell to such an employees' trust, he should consider applying for a clearance under the TA 1970, s460. The relevant case is s461 (D), ie, the receipt of profits available for distribution. This clearance should usually be forthcoming, in which case the shareholder will only pay capital gains tax on the shares he sells to the trust.

Example—Messrs A, B, C, and D each own 25 per cent of a close company which has been funding an employees' trust out of its profits for a number of years. A wishes to dispose of his shares to B, C and D. Despite the fact that they could borrow money and get income tax relief on the interest under the provisions of the FA 1974 (Sched 1, para 9), B, C and D cannot raise the money to purchase the shares. A could sell his shares to the employees' trust of which B, C and D are trustees; as a precaution he could go for clearance under the TA 1970, s460.

Conclusion

This chapter only dealt with the taxation aspects of employees' trusts. Commercial, pay-code (see the White Paper, *Winning the Battle against*

Inflation Cmnd 7293, July 1978), and other such factors should also be taken into account when deciding to set up such a trust. The general indications are that all political parties encourage the setting-up of employees' trusts so that their tax and other advantages are likely to continue for some time.

CHAPTER 16

PROFIT SHARING SCHEMES

Profit sharing schemes enable employees to have £500 worth of shares appropriated to each of them per year free of income tax. The shares should be held in the names of trustees for ten years or until death but there are graduated reliefs available where the shares as disposed of after five years, but before the ten years. The schemes involve a mixture of profit sharing and share incentive schemes, and trust and contract law. The schemes must be approved by the Inland Revenue. The relevant provisions are contained in the FA 1978, ss53–61 and Sched 9, and the schemes can only come into operation after 5 April 1979.

As to whether a company creates a scheme will depend on whether it wishes to go through the complications of setting up a scheme which provides only modest tax-free bonuses to employees. If a company is losing employees or wishes to encourage them to work harder the scheme could be attractive. The schemes are part of the concept of greater employee-participation in industry. Commercial, pay-code and company law factors and requirements must also be taken into account when deciding whether or not to go ahead with a scheme and when drafting the trust document; these factors are not dealt with in this book.

References, in this chapter, unless otherwise stated, are to the FA 1978.

The scheme

The scheme will usually involve a company creating and funding a trust, which uses its settled funds to acquire shares, by buying them or subscribing for them, in the company. The trustees will then appropriate the shares to the employees of the company who will have, for income tax purposes, the beneficial interest in the shares, although for capital gains tax purposes they will be the absolute beneficial owners, reducing the trustees to bare nominees. The participants in the scheme will be bound in contract to permit the shares to remain in the hands of the trustees for five years. Thereafter the income tax reliefs will be available on any disposal of the shares with a total exemption from income tax being available if the shares are retained by the trustees for ten years.

In order to obtain the tax reliefs for the scheme it is necessary to obtain Inland Revenue approval. To get their approval, the scheme—

(1) must satisfy the requirements set out in Sched 9 to the Act; and

(2) the participants in the scheme must be bound in contract to comply with the four requirements set out in s54(1) of the Act.

The Requirements of Schedule 9

Part I: Approval of Schemes—If a company (called the 'company concerned') establishes a scheme which complies with all the specific requirements of the Finance Act 1978, the Board of Inland Revenue (called 'the Board' in the legislation) must approve the scheme, 'unless it appears to them that there are features of the scheme which are neither essential nor reasonably incidental to the purpose of providing for employees and directors benefits in the nature of interests in shares' (Sched 9, para 1(1)). This very wide requirement would appear to have been put in because the Revenue must approve a scheme if the conditions are satisfied, and it might well be that the legal mind is capable of creating a scheme which satisfies the conditions without in fact being a scheme to benefit employees in the form of shares.

Where the company concerned controls another company or companies, the scheme may extend to all or any of those companies which it controls. This is referred to in the legislation as a 'group scheme'; a 'participating company' in relation to a group scheme means the company concerned or a company of which for the time being the company concerned has control and to which the scheme extends (para 1(2)). The scheme must provide that the initial value (ie, the market value at the date of the appropriation or at an earlier date if the Revenue and the trustees agree) of the shares appropriated to any one participant in a year of assessment shall not exceed £500 (para 1(4)). An application for approval must be in writing and contain such particulars and be supported by such evidence as the Board may require (para 1(5)).

The Board must be satisfied that at any time every person who—

(1) is then a full-time employee or director of the company concerned or, in the case of a group scheme, a participating company, and

(2) has been such an employee or director at all times during a qualifying period, not exceeding five years, ending at that time, and

(3) is chargeable to tax in respect of his office or employment under Sched E, Case 1, will be eligible, subject to Pt III of the schedule, to participate in the scheme on similar terms (para 2(1)).

The fact that the number of shares appropriated to participants varies by reference to pay, length of service, or similar factors shall not be regarded as meaning that the participants are not eligible to participate in the scheme on similar terms (para 2(2)).

The scheme must provide for the establishment of a body of persons resident in the United Kingdom (called trustees)—

(1) who, out of moneys paid to them by the company concerned or, in the case of a group scheme, a participating company, are required to buy shares which satisfy the conditions in Pt II of the schedule; and

(2) who are required to appropriate shares to individuals who are not ineligible by virtue of Pt III of the schedule; and

(3) whose functions are regulated by a United Kingdom trust which complies with Pt IV of the schedule (para 1(3)).

Special provisions apply if the terms of an approved scheme are contravened (paras 3(1) and (3)) or are altered (para 3(2)). The company concerned can appeal to the Special Commissioners if the Board refuse to approve a scheme or an alteration to a scheme or withdraw an approval (para 4).

Part II: Conditions as to the Shares—The shares in the scheme must form part of the ordinary share capital of—

(1) the company concerned; or

(2) a company which has control (as defined in the Taxes Act 1970, s534) of the company concerned; or

(3) a company which either is or has control of a company which—

(i) is a member of a consortium (as defined in Sched 9, para 17) owning either the company concerned or a company having control of that company; and

(ii) beneficially owns not less than three-twentieths of the ordinary share capital of the company so owned (para 5).

The shares must be either—

(1) shares of a class quoted on a recognized stock exchange; or

(2) shares in a company which is not under the control of another company (para 6).

The shares must be—

(1) fully paid up; and

(2) not redeemable; and

(3) not subject to any restrictions other than restrictions which attach to all shares of the same class (para 7).

Except where the shares are in a company whose ordinary share capital, at the time of the acquisition of the shares by the trustees, consists of shares of one class only, the majority of the issued shares of the same class must be held by persons other than—

(1) persons who acquired their shares in pursuance of a right conferred on them or opportunity afforded to them as a director or employee of the company concerned or any other company and not in pursuance of an offer to the public; and

(2) trustees holding shares on behalf of persons who acquired their

beneficial interests in the shares in pursuance of such a right or opportunity as is mentioned in para (1) above (Sched 9, para 8).

Part III: Individuals Ineligible to Participate—An individual shall not be eligible to have shares appropriated to him under the scheme at any time unless he is at that time or was within the preceding eighteen months a director or employee of the company concerned or, if the scheme is a group scheme, a participating company (para 9).

There are also restrictions on eligibility for participants who have shares appropriated to them under other approved schemes (para 10), and certain participators in close companies (para 11).

Part IV: Provisions as to the Trust Instrument—The trust instrument shall:

(1) provide that as soon as practicable after any shares have been appropriated to a participant, the trustees shall provide him with details, in writing, of the appropriation (para 12);

(2) prohibit a disposal by the trustees of any shares during the period of retention (as defined), except on a reconstruction etc referred to in FA 1978, s54(2)(*a*);

(3) except in two circumstances mentioned in para 13(2), prohibit the trustees from disposing of any shares after the end of the period of retention (as defined);

(4) require the trustees to comply with the various obligations set out in the legislation (see para 14);

(5) oblige the trustees to maintain such records as may be necessary to enable them to carry out their PAYE obligations under the FA 1978, s59 and inform the participant of any relevant facts should he become liable for tax under Sched E, para 15.

The Requirements of Section 54

In order to obtain Revenue approval it is necessary that every participant in the scheme is bound in contract with the company concerned (under the terms of FA 1978, s54(1))—

> (*a*) to permit his shares to remain in the hands of the trustees throughout the period of retention; and
>
> (*b*) not to assign, charge or otherwise dispose of his beneficial interest in his shares during that period; and
>
> (*c*) if he directs the trustees to transfer the ownership of his shares to him at any time before the release date, to pay to the trustees before the transfer takes place a sum equal to income tax at the basic rate on the appropriate percentage of the locked-in value of the shares at the time of the direction; and
>
> (*d*) not to direct the trustees to dispose of his shares at any time before the release date in any other way except by sale for the best consideration in money that can reasonably be obtained at the time of the sale.

The meanings of the various technical terms used above are as follows:

'period of retention'—This is the period which expires on the fifth anniversary of the date when the shares are appropriated or, if it is earlier, the date on which—

(1) the participant ceases to be an employee of the company concerned or the participating companies in a group scheme by reason of injury or disability or on account of his being made redundant within the meaning of the redundancy legislation; or

(2) the participant reaches pensionable age as defined in the Social Security Act 1975, Sched 20; or

(3) the participant dies (s54(4)).

'release date'—This is the tenth anniversary of the date when the shares are appropriated (s54(6)).

'appropriate percentage'—If the sale takes place during the period of retention, this is 100 per cent; if after the period of retention but before the seventh anniversary of the appropriation it is 50 per cent; and if on or after the seventh anniversary but before the tenth anniversary it is 25 per cent (s54(7)).

'the locked-in value'—If the recipient has not received any capital receipts in respect of his shares, this is the market value of the shares at the date of appropriation or such earlier date as the Board and trustees agree in writing (s55(2)). This value will be reduced to the amount of the sale proceeds if this is less. Where there have been a number of allocations of shares, disposals of shares will be deemed to have been made on a first-in first-out basis.

Section 54(2) sets out four instances where the participant can direct or agree with the trustees to enter into transactions concerning the shares without breaching the s54(1) requirements. These relate to reconstruction and amalgamations, compromises and other arrangements, general offers made for the shares, and the sale of the beneficial ownership of the shares by the participant to the trustees after the retention period, for the full value of the shares, as an alternative to directing the trustees to dispose of them to an outsider.

Special provisions apply to company reconstructions and amalgamations which involve scheme shares (see section 57). The intention is to secure that so far as practicable the new shares or securities which replace the original scheme shares receive the same treatment as those original shares.

Income tax

The Participant

When the shares are appropriated under the scheme the beneficial interest passes to the participant but—

(1) the value of the shares at the time of appropriation shall not be treated as income chargeable under Schedule E; and

(2) the participant shall not be chargeable to income tax under Schedule E by virtue of section 79(4) Finance Act 1972 in respect of an increase in the market value of the shares or by virtue of section 67 Finance Act 1976 where shares are appropriated at an undervalue (section 53(3)).

If the trustees dispose of any of a participant's shares before the release date (ie, the tenth anniversary of the appropriation), or, if it is earlier, the date of the participant's death, then, generally, the participant shall be chargeable to income tax under Sched E on the appropriate percentage (100 per cent, 50 per cent or 25 per cent as the case may be) of the locked-in value (usually the market value of the shares when first appropriated) of the shares at the time of the disposal (see s55). If the trustees become entitled before the release date to receive any money or money's worth, such as a payment on the reduction of capital (called a 'capital receipt'), the participant, to whose shares the receipt relates, will be chargeable under Sched E on the appropriate percentage of the amount or value of the receipt (s56(1)). Various receipts are excluded from the definition of a 'capital receipt', the most important being receipts which constitute income in the hands of the recipient for the purposes of income tax, eg, dividends (s56(2) and (3)).

If the capital receipt exceeds the locked-in value, it shall be deemed to be equal to the locked-in value for the purposes of calculating the charge to tax (s56(4)). A receipt shall not be a capital receipt if the entitlement to it arises after the death of the participant to whose shares it is referable (s56(5)).

Special provisions are contained in s58 to charge tax under Sched E, where the value of shares appropriated exceeds the £500 limit and where persons ineligible to participate receive shares. There are also special provisions dealing with rights issues (ss55(4) and (5), and 56(3)).

Dividends on the shares, paid to participants, will be liable to income tax in their hands; it might be that the dividends paid prior to the release date can be treated as earned income but the position is not clear (see *White* v *Franklin* (1965) 42 TC 283, and *Recknell* v *IRC* (1952) 33 TC 201).

The Trustees

When shares have been appropriated the dividends must be paid to the participant in question. Until appropriation, the trust would come within the FA 1973, s16. However, s53(6) exempts the trust from the 15 per cent additional rate of tax on dividends from the scheme shares if the shares are appropriated within eighteen months from their acquisition by the trustees.

In certain cases the trustees can be liable to make deductions under PAYE; details of this are contained in s59.

The Company

Payments to the trust are deductible, as trading expenses or as management expenses, from the profits of the company, provided that one of the following conditions is fulfilled:

(1) that before the expiry of the relevant period the sum is used to acquire shares for appropriation to participants; and

(2) that the sum is necessary to meet the reasonable expenses of the trustees in administering the scheme (s60(1) and (2)).

'The relevant period' means the period of nine months, beginning on the day following the end of the period of account in which the sum in question is charged as an expense of the company incurring the ependiture, or such longer period as the Board may allow, by notice in writing given to that company (s60(3)). The company can be liable to make PAYE deductions on benefits received by participants (see s59).

Capital gains tax

For the purpose of capital gains tax a participant is treated as absolutely entitled to his shares as against the trustees (s53(5)). Thus, the capital gains tax legislation shall apply as if the property were vested in, and the acts of the trustees in relation to the shares were the acts of, the participant; acquisitions from and disposals to the participant by the trustees being disregarded accordingly (FA 1965, s22(5)). The participants should, therefore, benefit from the small gains relief and exemption under the FA 1978, s44.

If any gain accrues to shares between the time of acquisition by the trustees and appropriation, there shall be no charge to capital gains tax, provided the period during which the shares were so appropriated is less than eighteen months (s53(6)(*b*)). If the period is exceeded, the charge would arise under the FA 1965, s25(3).

For the purposes of capital gains tax—

(1) no deduction shall be made from the consideration for the disposal of any shares by reason only that an amount is chargeable to income tax (this is correct since the income tax is actually a deferred charge on the initial market value of the shares which forms the capital gains tax base of the shares);

(2) any charge to income tax under s56 (charge on capital receipts) shall be disregarded in determining whether a distribution is a capital distribution within the FA 1965, Sched 7, para 3; and

(3) nothing in the FA 1978 shall affect the rules applicable to the computation of a gain accruing on a part disposal of a holding of shares or other securities which were acquired at different times (FA 1978, s61(3)).

Roll-over relief should be applicable on transfers of any chargeable assets by the company to the trustees to fund the scheme under the FA 1976, s56, as amended by the FA 1978, Sched 11, para 2 (see above, p133). Normally, one would envisage cash being settled by the company so that the question of capital gains tax would not arise (FA 1965, s22(1)(*b*)).

Capital transfer tax

The profit sharing scheme would qualify as an employees' trust within FA 1975, Sched 5, para 17 (as amended by FA 1978, Sched 11, para 1) (see p129, above). So far as it is necessary, in view of the FA 1976, s89(1) and the FA 1978, s60(1), the trust should satisfy the requirements of the FA 1976, s90 (as amended in particular by the FA 1978, Sched 11, para 3(1) and (2) (see above, p131).

Development Land Tax

Development land tax is not chargeable on the disposal of shares, unlike its predecessor development gains tax (FA 1974, s42). It would thus not appear to be relevant in the context of a profit sharing scheme.

Stamp duty

There are no particular exemptions from stamp duty for profit sharing schemes. The appropriation of the shares and their subsequent transfer into the names of the beneficiaries should be excluded from ad valorem duty under F (1909–10) A 1910, s74(6), as amended. The purchase of scheme shares by the trustees could be liable to ad valorem duty under the first schedule to the Stamp Act 1891. If new shares are issued to the trust, capital duty of 1 per cent will be payable (FA 1973, Sched 19, para 1).

CHAPTER 17

RETIREMENT BENEFIT SCHEMES

Retirement benefit schemes comprise one of the most important and largest groups of trusts in the United Kingdom. It is usual for employers to set up trusts to provide retirement benefits for employees, and if these are Approved Exempt Schemes important tax reliefs will be available. Since the FA 1973 controlling directors are eligible to join such schemes. These schemes have provided directors with a means of mitigating tax as well as providing a tax-free fund available to look after them in their retirement.

Pension law is now very much an area for the specialist and this chapter contains only a brief outline of the subject.

What is a retirement benefit scheme?

A retirement benefit scheme means a deed, agreement, series of agreements, or other arrangements entered into or set up to provide 'relevant benefits' for a single employee or a group of employees (FA 1970, s25). It includes a covenant or agreement to provide 'relevant benefits', even if the employer makes no advance financial provisions by insurance or otherwise.

The term 'relevant benefits' is widely defined in FA 1970, s26(1), and means 'any pension, lump sum, gratuity or other like benefit given or to be given on retirement or on death, or in anticipation of retirement, or, in connection with past services, after retirement or death, or to be given on or in anticipation of or in connection with any change in the nature of the service of the employee in question, except that it does not include any benefit which is to be afforded solely by reason of the disablement by accident of a person occurring during his service or of his death by accident so occurring and for no other reason.'

Revenue approval

Section 19 of the FA 1970 sets out a list of conditions which the retirement benefit scheme must satisfy in order to obtain Revenue Approval. The scheme has to be bona fide established for the sole purpose of providing 'relevant benefits' in respect of services provided by employees, and it must be recognized by the employer and the employees to whom it relates. If the retirement benefit scheme does not satisfy the conditions set out in s19 the

Revenue can still approve the scheme under the discretionary powers which are given to it by s20 of the Act. This is the most common mode of approval and provides scope for obtaining Revenue Approval to attractive pension schemes.

Taxation

If a retirement benefits scheme is approved by the Revenue, the employee is exempt from tax on the moneys provided by the employer pursuant to the scheme (FA 1970, ss23 and 24(1)). To obtain the maximum tax benefit, however, the scheme should be an Exempt Approved Retirement Benefits Scheme (referred to in the legislation as Exempt Approved Schemes (FA 1970, s21(1))).

An Exempt Approved Scheme is—

(1) any approved scheme which is shown to the satisfaction of the Board to be established under irrevocable trusts; or

(2) any other approved scheme as respects which the Board, having regard to any special circumstances, direct that section 21 of the Finance Act 1970 shall apply.

Where there is an Exempt Approved Scheme the following tax consequences will, broadly, follow:

(1) Income derived from the investments of the fund is exempt from tax.

(2) Any sum paid by the employer by way of a contribution under the scheme shall be allowable as a deduction in computing profits. This relief provides one of the most important tax advantages of Exempt Approved Schemes; tax free amounts are paid effectively into a tax free trust.

(3) Employees' contributions shall, in assessing tax under Sched E, be allowable as an expense incurred in the year of assessment in which the contributions are paid. The pensions themselves are treated as earned income.

(4) Capital gains shall not be chargeable to capital gains tax.

There is no exemption from development land tax for pension funds, and they will also be subject to tax on trading profits. They will also normally suffer value added tax on their inputs (ie, outgoings such as actuarial fees). In the *Linotype and Machinery Ltd* case Man/78/4 it was held that professional services provided to a Pension Fund which were paid by the company which set up the fund pursuant to an obligation in the Pension Deed did not enable the company to reclaim the value added tax charged on the professional services. The Court of Appeal case of *Customs and Excise Commissioners* v *British Railways Board* [1976] 1 WLR 1036 was distinguished as turning on its particular facts.

By virtue of the FA 1975, Sched 5, para 16 it can be arranged within the terms of the scheme that the lump sum payment on death will be free of capital transfer tax in the hands of the recipient. This amount could be up to four times the member's salary on his death.

The benefits to members

The types of benefits that can be provided to members of Exempt Approved Schemes are as follows:

(1) a pension up to two-thirds of the individual member's final salary;

(2) the right of a member to commute a portion of his pension for a tax free lump sum up to one and a half times his final salary;

(3) the provision of a pension for a member in the event of his ill-health or early retirement;

(4) a death in service benefit of up to four times his salary at the date of death, together with a widow's pension of up to 4/9ths of his salary at that time; and

(5) a death in retirement pension of up to two-thirds his own pension for the benefit of his widow.

There is also some flexibility in the choice of pension age. This can vary greatly depending upon the type of employment undertaken by the employee concerned. All pensions can be arranged so that they increase in line with the lesser of 8½ per cent per annum and the cost of living. This is understood to be the present position with regard to the Revenue regulations.

Personal pension schemes available to controlling directors are the same as those available to employees, with the exception that where the director, or his immediate family, controls more than 20 per cent of the voting shares, the definition of final pensionable salary must be the average of the last three years' pensionable salary, which may include emoluments which may have fluctuated considerably.

Contributions to the scheme

With regard to contributions to the scheme an individual member may contribute up to 15 per cent of his salary. This is the maximum amount permitted by the Inland Revenue and will be exempt from tax at the member's highest rates. Contributions are not transfers of value for the purposes of capital transfer tax (FA 1976, s89(2)).

Provided maximum benefits for the members are not exceeded, the company is permitted to contribute, as an ordinary annual contribution, an amount needed to secure the benefits the scheme is providing. Special company contributions are permitted although relief against Corporation Tax will probably be spread over a number of years.

Perpetuity period

It is generally considered that a trust establishing a pension scheme, provided that it may be expected to qualify for tax exemption or tax approval, need not contain a rule against perpetuities (Social Security Act 1973, s69). This however is not beyond doubt.

Documentation

The normal method of establishing a pension scheme is by means of an Interim Trust Deed, that is to say, a Deed which declares the intention to establish a scheme but which leaves the full terms of the trust to be defined at a later date by a further deed. This can produce problems, in that care must be taken to ensure that the essential requirements for establishing a valid trust are contained in the deed. Therefore, care should be taken to set out the objects of the trust, albeit in outline, so that the beneficiaries and the nature of their benefits are ascertainable with reasonable certainty, to define the contributions made by the members and to ensure that the payments made by the employer to the trustees by way of contributions are clearly identified as such.

Conclusions

Pension trusts, especially Exempt Approved Schemes, have been encouraged by the Government by the provision of substantial income tax and capital gains tax reliefs. Particularly attractive are the schemes which can be set up for controlling directors and are self-administered; ie, the company can arrange for the trust deed to be drafted and for the appointment of the trustees. Through them, the company can have a say in the investment of the funds which might include, to an extent, an investment in the company's own shares. These schemes can be cheap to administer.

The Inland Revenue have indicated in a four-page Memorandum ('Small Administered Schemes', No 58, February 1979), that they will, broadly, take a more critical approach in looking at schemes which they feel were designed for tax avoidance rather than to provide financial support for members in old age. The Memorandum is necessary reading for all those preparing to set up small self-administered schemes.

CHAPTER 18

CHARITABLE TRUSTS

Charitable trusts are tax havens within the United Kingdom. They are areas of substantial tax exemption not only in the trust itself but also with regard to the setting-up and funding of the trust. There are reliefs, and in some cases total exemption, from capital transfer tax and stamp duty when the trust is set up, and there is total exemption from capital gains tax. The trust is not liable for income tax or capital gains tax once it is set up and there are reliefs for development land tax and rates, although the usual provisions apply for Value Added Tax. Charitable trusts are exempt from capital transfer tax.

In order to obtain the tax reliefs the trust must have exclusively charitable purposes. The settlor, his spouse, and contributors and spouses of contributors, should be effectively excluded from all benefit. The settlor can be the trustee, so effectively keeping control of the settled assets. This can be useful if the shares of a private company are settled. These trusts are normally utilized by persons who have no immediate family to whom they would like the assets to go, or people who do not want the assets to go to any immediate family.

Also, if an open company makes irregular payments of significant sums to charities it would be advisable for it to set up its own charitable trust and to enter into a covenant for seven years to pay sums to the charity. The charitable trust in its discretion can then pay out sums to those charitable objects. Individuals could similarly set up their own charitable trust and covenant to make payments to it. The payments would be deductible for the purposes of basic rate tax only but it would effectively give the covenantor, who could be the trustee of the charity, a discretion as to which charities he wishes to benefit without entering into binding covenants with the separate charities. It is also possible for an individual to lend moneys interest-free to a charity, and thus effectively obtain total tax relief on the interest which would otherwise have arisen on the moneys lent, had he had the moneys on deposit.

What is a charitable trust?

Definition

The term 'charity', because it is not defined in any legislation, can only be examined by reference to the technical meaning given to that expression by English Law.

The basis of the numerous decisions on the meaning of the term 'charity' is to be found in the preamble to the Statute of Elizabeth (43 Eliz 1, c4 1601), commonly known as the Charitable Uses Act 1601. That Statute, except for the preamble, was repealed by the Mortmain and Charitable Uses Act 1888. The 1888 Act was itself repealed by the Charities Act 1960, but the classification to which the preamble gave rise survives in the decided cases. The most quoted classification of charitable purposes is to be found in Lord Macnaghten's speech in the House of Lords, in *IRC* v *Pemsel* [1891] AC 531, at p583; 3 TC 53, at p96. It was stated by Lord Macnaghten that charity should be given its technical meaning under English Law and comprises 'four principal divisions; trusts for the relief of poverty, trusts for the advancement of education, trusts for the advancement of religion and trusts beneficial to the community and not falling under any of the preceding heads. The trusts last referred to are not the less charitable . . . because incidentally they benefit the rich as well as the poor'.

Perpetuity Period

Charitable trusts are not subject to that aspect of the perpetuity rule commonly called the rule against inalienability. The objects of the charity may last forever, but a gift for such purposes will still be valid (*Chamberlayne* v *Brockett* (1872) LR 8 Ch App 206). Thus, one can set up a charitable trust without limiting the trust to the usual eighty year perpetuity period.

Uncertainty of Objects

Another aspect of a charitable trust is that a trust will not fail for uncertainty of objects, provided the settlor clearly intended the funds to go exclusively to charity (see *Moggridge* v *Thackwell* (1803) 7 Ves, 36 (affirmed 1807) 13 Ves 416). If this intention is satisfied, the trust will not fail if the settlor omits to specify the objects with certainty. In such circumstances a cy-pres scheme will be made to render the objects more certain and clearer.

Public Benefit

It is a pre-requisite for a charity, with the exception only of charities for the relief of poverty, that it is set up with a public element of benefit. Thus in *Re Compton* 1945 Ch 123 a trust for the education of the descendants of three named persons was held not to be a charitable trust because the beneficiaries were defined by reference to a personal relationship and therefore it lacked the quality of public benefit. In *Oppenheim* v *Tobacco Securities Trust Co Ltd* ([1951] AC 297) it was held that a trust was not a valid charitable trust if the only nexus between the members of the class of beneficiaries is that they are employees of a particular employer. This is still the case even though the group of persons included in the class might be numerous.

Thus, an aggregate of individuals ascertained by reference to some personal tie, such as the relations of a particular individual or the members of a particular family or company, does not amount to the public or a section thereof for the purposes of the general rule, and accordingly will not be a legal charity (*Re Scarisbrick* [1951] Ch 622, at p649, per Jenkins L J). If the trust is construed so as to grant a mere preference to a limited class, such as employees or relations, the trust will be a valid charity. It succeeded, for example, in *Re Koettgen's Will Trusts* [1954] Ch 252, where a trust was established for the furtherance of the commercial education of British-born persons, with a direction that preference be given to employees of a particular firm. The essential question was whether or not it was a mere expression of preference. If it amounts to an obligation the trust will not be charitable (see above, p124).

As mentioned above, a trust for the relief of poverty does not have to have a public element of benefit. The exception may arise where the personal tie is one of contract or blood. In the case of blood there are the so-called 'poor relations' cases. The case of contract may be exemplified by a trust for the relief of poverty among employees of a particular company. This principle was reaffirmed in *Dingle* v *Turner* [1972] AC 601, where it was held that a trust to apply income in paying pensions to poor employees of the company was a valid charitable trust.

Classification

Trusts for the relief of poverty—In order to qualify it is not necessary that there is an extreme degree of poverty. It is unnecessary to show destitution. Accordingly gifts for such objects as 'ladies of limited means' (*Re Gardom* [1914] 1 Ch 662), or 'decayed actors' (*Spiller* v *Maude* [1881] 32 Ch D 158), and similar purposes can be charitable. All that seems to be required is that the individuals in question be in difficult circumstances or be unable to maintain a reasonable standard of living (*Re Mary Clark Homes* [1904] 2 KB 645).

Trusts for the advancement of education—There must be an intention that learning should be imparted and not simply accumulated. There must be an imparting of the knowledge so that there is a teaching or education of the public [*Re Shaw* [1957] 1 WLR 729]. Recent trends in the cases, however, have tended to widen the field of education; thus, in *Re Dupree's Deed Trusts* [1945] Ch 16, it was held that a trust for chess playing among the boys and youths of Portsmouth was charitable.

Trusts for the establishment or support of Professorships and Lectureships are charitable (*The Abbey Malvern Wells Ltd* v *Ministry of Local Government and Planning* [1951] Ch 728), and so too are stipends for university teachers and fellows of colleges (*Case of Christ's College, Cambridge* (1751) 1 WBl 90). The same principles apply to schools, colleges and universities, and to learned societies and institutions.

Trusts for the advancement of religion—The general rule is that all religions are charitable unless they undermine the morality of the country (*Re Watson* [1973] 1 WLR 1472). However, it was held in *Yeap Cheah Neo* v *Ong Cheng Neo* (1875) LR 6 PC 381 that a trust requiring ancestor worship was not charitable. In *Re Moon's Will Trust* [1948] 1 All ER 300 a bequest for mission work, which the courts construed as meaning Christian mission work, was held to be charitable. Similarly, trusts for the maintenance and repair of a church, stained-glass window, or walls within the church have been held to be charitable, and the same will apply to the churchyard and burial ground even if restricted to a particular religious sect.

Trusts for other purposes beneficial to the community—This is the 'sweeping-up' class in Lord Macnaghten's classification in *Pemsel*'s case.

A trust for the protection of animals generally is a valid charitable trust (*Re Wedgwood* [1915] 1 Ch 113). A trust which promotes the armed forces is also charitable (*Re Stratheden and Campbell* [1894] 3 Ch 265). A gift to a local town or village will generally be charitable as a scheme will be set up which enables the funds to be devoted to exclusively charitable purposes in the locality (see *Re Norton's Will Trusts* [1948] 2 AER 842).

The Recreational Charities Act 1958, which came into force on 3 March 1958, regulates recreational trusts. The Act was passed as a result of the decision in *IRC* v *Baddeley* [1955] AC 572, which cast grave doubt on the charitable status of women's institutes, boys' clubs, welfare trusts and village halls. The Act is intended to give such institutions charitable status. The Act provides that it shall be and shall always be deemed to have been charitable to provide or assist in providing facilities for recreation or other leisure time occupations if the facilities are provided in the interests of social welfare. There is also the overriding proviso that the trust will not be charitable unless it is for the public benefit (s1(1)). Furthermore, the requirement that the facilities must be provided in the interests of social welfare is not satisfied unless—

(1) it is provided with the object of improving the conditions of life for the persons for whom the facilities are primarily intended; and

(2) Either

(i) those persons have need of such facilities by reason of their youth, age, infirmity or disablement, poverty or social and economic circumstances; or

(ii) the facilities are to be available to the members or female members of the public at large.

It is well established in law that a trust designed simply for the promotion of sport is not charitable. Accordingly, in *Re Nottage* [1895] 2 Ch 657 a trust which was established to provide annually a cup for the most successful yacht of the season, the testator stating that his object was to encourage the sport of yacht racing, was held to be not charitable. In the case of *IRC* v *McMullen and Others* [1978] 1 All ER 230 it was held in the High Court that the Football Association Youth Trust was not a charity. The trust deed recited that the Association desired to establish a charitable trust which would have as its main objects the furtherance of education in schools and universities in any part of the United Kingdom, encouraging and facilitating the playing of association football or other games and sports at such schools and universities, and thus assisting to ensure that due attention is given to the physical education and character development of pupils at schools and universities, as well as the development and occupation of their minds. Walton, J did not consider the trust to be charitable because the law did not regard the encouragement of sport as charitable, except where sport was subservient to some wider charitable purpose. He also did not consider that the trust fell within the Recreational Charities Act 1958, since the facilities were not provided with the object of improving the conditions of life for persons for whom the facilities were primarily intended. The decision was affirmed by a majority decision in the Court of Appeal (*The Times*, 19 October 1978, *sub nom IRC* v *Sir Stephen Andrew Stephen and Others*), and leave to appeal to the House of Lords was granted.

It is established that a trust to advance a political purpose will fail as a charity (*Bonar Law Memorial Trust* v *IRC* (1933) 49 TLR 220 and *Re Hopkinson* [1949] 1 AER 346).

The register of charities

Section 4 of the Charities Act 1960 established a register of charities, under the control of the Charity Commissioners, and s5 of the Act provides that:

> An institution shall for all purposes other than rectification of the register be conclusively presumed to be or have been a charity at any time when it is or was on the register of charities.

Most charities with a permanent endowment are required to register and voluntary registration is available in other cases.

The majority of cases concerning charitable status in relation to claims for tax concessions will now probably be resolved by this registration procedure. When setting up new charities the promoters should get the clearance of the Charity Commission and the Inland Revenue at the same time, although it is possible that one body will give approval while the other may refuse. This happened in the case mentioned above of *IRC* v *McMullen* [1978] 1 All ER 230. In that case the Charity Commissioners came to the conclusion that the Football Association Youth Trust was charitable while the Board of Inland Revenue reached an opposite conclusion.

Income tax (investment income)

Reliefs

Charities are exempt from paying income tax on land which they occupy (under Sched B) and on their investment income, whether this is from the rents and profits of land, interest, annuities, dividends, company distributions or other annual payments (TA 1970, s360(1)).

'Charity', for the purposes of these reliefs, means any body of persons or trust established for charitable purposes only (TA 1970, s360(3)).

Under the FA 1973, s16(2)(*c*) income arising under a trust established for charitable purposes is exempt from the additional 15 per cent charge which applies to discretionary and accumulation trusts.

Seven Year Covenant

One of the most important ways of benefiting charities is through a seven year covenant, which enables the charity to claim back the basic rate of tax deducted by the payer. The covenant must be for a fixed period exceeding six years, or for an indefinite period which may exceed six years. The income must be pure income profit in the hands of the charity (*IRC* v *National Book League* [1957] Ch 488).

Interest Free Loans

It is possible to lend money interest-free to a charity and therefore, effectively, get full tax relief on the interest which might otherwise have arisen on the moneys lent. For example, Mr Smith has £10,000 on deposit earning £1,000 interest per annum. If he covenants that sum to charity he can only get relief at the basic rate of tax. If he lends the £10,000 to the charity, repayable at, say, one month's notice, the charity would, in effect, receive the full £1,000 and Mr Smith would pay no tax on it.

Although the position is not entirely clear it is not felt that any problems arise on this arrangement under TA 1970, s451 (sums paid to settlor otherwise than as income), even where the lender was the settlor, because income shall only be deemed not to have been distributed (which can cause a charge to arise under the section) if and only to the extent that it exceeds income arising under the settlement which is exempt from income tax under TA 1970, s360 (see FA 1970, s455(*c*)). The repayment of the loan, therefore (where the lender was the settlor or was a contributor to a charity and could thus be said to be a settlor), should not cause a tax charge to arise under this section. Any such arrangements should also be organized so as not to come within any of the other settlement income tax provisions (see Chapter 2, p11 et seq).

Mixed Loans and Covenants

Donors often wish to pay in advance the future instalments due under a seven year covenant. This can be done by treating the advance payments as loans out of which the annual payment is made when it falls due. If the donor dies during the loan period the balance of the loan must be refunded to the estate of the deceased, unless the moneys are left to the charity in his Will.

Business Donations

In order that a donation to a charity is deductible from a trader's profits it must come within the provisions of the TA 1970, s130. The section provides:

> In computing the amount of profits to be charged under Schedule D Case I no sum shall be deducted in respect of any disbursements or expenses, not being money wholly and exclusively laid out or expended for the purposes of the trade, profession or vocation.

Strictly, a donation to a charity will not be deductible unless the trade derives some benefit, or intended to derive some benefit (although it might not have materialized), from the donation. Thus, donations to a local charity, which is likely to benefit employees, would appear to be allowable.

Significant relief is afforded to traders by extra-statutory concession B7 (1976 list) (Charitable and Benevolent Gifts by Traders). The concession allows tax relief for expenses which would otherwise be prohibited by the TA 1970, s411(8). That section in general disallows tax relief on gifts.

The concession states that expenditure on gifts is not within that provision if—

(1) it is allowable under the TA 1970, s130(a);

(2) the gift is made for the benefit of a body or association of persons established for educational, cultural, religious, recreational or benevolent purposes, and the body or association is—

(i) local in relation to the donor's business activities; and

(ii) not restricted to persons connected with the donor; and

(iii) the expenditure is reasonably small in relation to the scale of the donor's business.

The concession also provides that the payment of an ordinary annual subscription to a local trade association by a non-member is not to be regarded as a gift, provided condition (1) is satisfied.

Payments for technical education related to the trade of the payer may be deductible under the TA 1970, s133.

Section 90 of the Capital Allowances Act 1968 provides that where a person carrying on a trade—

> (*a*) incurs expenditure not of a capital nature on scientific research related to that trade and directly undertaken by him or on his behalf, or

(*b*) pays any sum to any scientific research association for the time being approved for the purposes of section 90 by the Secretary of State or the Minister of Technology, being an association which has as its object the undertaking of scientific research related to the class of trade to which the trade he is carrying on belongs, or

(*c*) pays any sum to be used for such scientific research as is mentioned in (*b*) above to any such university, college, research institute or other similar institution as is for the time being approved for the purposes of section 90 by the Secretary of State or the Minister of Technology,

the expenditure incurred or sum paid, as the case may be, may be deducted as an expense in computing the profits or gains of the trade for the purposes of tax.

If a business makes charitable donations which are not deductible under the above heads, or lends money interest-free to a charity, the shortfall position of the company must be carefully examined. Such payments may help to demonstrate that the company has income available which can be distributed without prejudice to the requirements of the company's business (FA 1972, Sched 16, para 8(1)(*a*)).

Business Covenants

If a company makes a seven-year covenanted donation to a charity, the payments will be allowed as charges on income (TA 1970, s248(5), (8) and (9)), ie, no corporation tax would be payable by the company on that income. The company would make a payment less tax at the basic rate and the charity would then recover the tax from the Inland Revenue. If the company is a close company, however, such covenanted amounts can result in assessments to the higher rates of income tax and the investment income surcharge under the shortfall provisions. These assessments would be by reference to the incomes of the shareholders.

Thus, only non-close companies and close companies where shortfall does not present a problem, eg, where the shares are held by charities, should enter into such covenants.

Income tax (trading income)

Section 360(1)(*e*) of the TA 1970 grants exemption from tax under Sched D in respect of the profits of any trade carried on by a charity, if the profits are applied solely to the purposes of the charity and either—

(1) the trade is exercised in the course of the actual carrying out of a primary purpose of the charity; or

(2) the work in connection with the trade is mainly carried out by beneficiaries of the charity.

This exemption will not extend to fund-raising trades, such as charity shops, carried on by the charity. In such cases it is necessary for the charity to set up a company and for the company to covenant all its net profits to the charity. The charity should own beneficially the company (a holder of less than 5 per cent of the share capital, however, may escape the results of an apportionment of the covenanted amounts under the FA 1972, Sched 16, para 5(4) and 6(2)). If this is done the payments will be charges on income (TA 1970, s248(5)), so that the company can deduct them for tax purposes, and the shareholder being a tax exempt charity, will not have any shortfall problems. This procedure would not operate to exclude from corporation tax chargeable at capital gains tax rates any capital gains made by the company, so that the charity should consider carefully the position before any capital assets are brought into the ownership of the company.

The following extra-statutory concession may be applicable to certain fund-raising activities (Extra Statutory Concession C5 (1976 List) (Trading Activities for Charitable Purposes)):

> Bazaars, jumble sales, gymkhanas, carnivals, fireworks displays, and similar activities arranged by voluntary organizations for the purpose of raising funds for charity may fall within the definition of 'trade' in section 526 of the Income and Corporation Taxes Act 1970, with the result that any profits will be liable to corporation tax. Tax is not, however, charged on such profits provided the following conditions are satisfied:
>
> (i) the organization is not regularly trading;
>
> (ii) the trading is not in competition with other traders;
>
> (iii) the activities are supported substantially because the public are aware that any profits will be devoted to charity;
>
> (iv) the profits are transferred to charities or otherwise applied for charitable purposes.

Capital gains tax

A capital gain is not a chargeable gain if it accrues to a charity and is applicable and applied for charitable purposes (FA 1965, s35(1)). If property held on charitable trust ceases to be so held, then there is a deemed disposal and re-acquisition at market value and any resulting gain will be chargeable to tax (FA 1965, s35(2)).

A disposal to a charity after 21 March 1972 shall be excluded from capital gains tax (FA 1972, s119). This exclusion applies to gifts and to sales at or less than the transferor's base value, computed in accordance with para 4 of the FA 1965, Sched 6 (ie, the acquisition cost and all allowable expenditure). The transaction will be treated as being made for a consideration such that neither a gain nor a loss arises on the disposal. If the charity disposes of the property, its acquisition price will be that of the original donor. However, in most cases the gain will be excluded from capital gains tax since the proceeds are likely to be applicable and applied for charitable purposes, thus coming within the FA 1965, s35(1).

Example—Mr Smith has a picture which he purchased in 1970 for £40,000. It has increased in value ovér the years to £60,000. Mr Smith sells the picture to the charity for £40,000; the charity subsequently sells it for £60,000, applying the net proceeds for charitable purposes. The profit of £20,000 is tax-free in the hands of the charity and Mr Smith pays no tax on the disposal to the charity. Effectively the benefit of the gain, since Mr Smith's acquisition of the picture, is passed on to the charity free of tax.

Capital transfer tax

The Trust

Paragraph 20 of the FA 1975, Sched 5 provides that settled property held for charitable purposes only shall not be subject to any liability on any capital distributions and nor shall such trusts be subject to the periodic charge.

Paragraph 10(2) of the FA 1975, Sched 6, as amended by the FA 1976, s111(1), provides that transfers from discretionary trusts to charities shall not be chargeable as capital distributions and nor shall they be treated as distribution payments (ie, they are totally ignored, not only for the purposes of being chargeable to capital transfer tax, but also for the purposes of ascertaining the cumulative total of transfers).

Position of Donor

Gifts to charities are exempt from capital transfer tax without limit if the donor survives one year or more. If he dies within the year there is exemption for gifts up to a total of £100,000 (FA 1976, Sched 6, para 10). Term insurance should be taken out by the charity to cover this one-year period.

The exemption for transfers to charities will not be available if—

(1) the testamentary or other disposition by which it is given is defeasible; or

(2) the property is an interest in other property and that interest is less than the donor's or the property is given for a limited period; or

(3) the property is an interest in possession in settled property and the settlement does not come to an end in relation to that settled property on the making of the transfer; or

(4) the property is land or building and is given subject to an interest reserved or created by the donor which entitles him, his spouse or a person connected with him, to possession of, or to occupy, the whole or any part of the land or building rent-free or at a rent less than might be expected to be obtained in a transaction at arm's length between persons not connected with each other; or

(5) the property is not land or a building and is given subject to an interest reserved or created by the donor other than—

(i) an interest created by him for full consideration in money or money's worth; or

(ii) an interest which does not substantially affect the enjoyment of the property by the person or body to whom it is given; or

(6) the property or any part of it may become applicable for purposes other than charitable purposes or those of certain exempt bodies.

For the purposes of the conditions above—

(1) any question whether any interest is less than the donor's or whether property is given subject to an interest shall be decided as at a time 12 months after the transfer of value; and

(2) any disposition which has not been defeated at that time and is not defeasible after that time shall be treated as not being defeasible, whether or not it was capable of being defeated before that time.

It is important that the above conditions are strictly complied with. They are set out in the FA 1975, Sched 6, para 15, as amended by the FA 1976, s95.

The related property provisions in the FA 1975, Sched 10, para 7, have been amended by the FA 1976, s103 to cover certain transfers to charities. If an individual or his spouse makes an exempt transfer to a charity after 15 April 1976 the property transferred shall be treated as related property. These provisions will still apply to treat the property as related, even though the charity has disposed of the property within the preceding five years. It seems necessary, if these provisions are to be avoided, for the individual or his spouse to dispose of the property he has retained more than five years after the charity has disposed of the property.

'Charity', for capital transfer tax purposes, has the same meaning as it has in the TA 1970, s360.

Value added tax

There is no general relief for charities as such in the Value Added Tax legislation. A charity which carries on a business is required to be registered for VAT if its taxable turnover is above the exemption limits, in the same way as any other trader is required to register. Certain supplies, however, may be zero-rated under Group 16, FA 1972, Sched 4, which only applies to charities.

Development land tax

The general rule is that charities are liable for development land tax.

There will be no charge, however, on development value accruing to a charity on the disposal of an interest in land which was held by the charity on 12 September 1974, or was held by another charity on that date, and has at no time between that date and the date of the disposal been held otherwise than by a charity (see DLTA 1976, s24). Where the charity acquires an interest in land after 12 September 1974 (otherwise than from another charity where the above provisions apply), and that charity commences development, there will be no deemed disposal provided the property is used for the purposes of the charity. This is merely a deferral of tax, and there will generally be a charge when the property is disposed of to outside parties (DLTA 1976, s25). For the purposes of these provisions property is used for the purposes of a charity if—

(1) it is occupied solely by the charity for its own use, or

(2) it is otherwise used solely for carrying out the charitable purposes of the charity.

Stamp duty

The general doubling of stamp duties in the FA 1974 was expressly made not to apply to gifts to charities. Thus, in the case of a conveyance or transfer to charity the stamp duty is 1 per cent (FA 1974, s49(2)). The relief can only be claimed, however, if the instrument is adjudicated.

If the instrument can be certified under the FA 1963, s55, as amended, the duty can be eliminated or reduced. If the instrument is certified at £15,000 or £20,000, the lower rates will apply. If the instrument is certified at £25,000, the rate of 1 per cent will apply without the need for adjudication.

CHAPTER 19

FOREIGN TRUSTS

Foreign trusts can be useful for mitigating or avoiding capital gains tax, and, if the assets are situated abroad and the settlor is domiciled abroad when the settlement is made, they can be used to avoid charges to capital transfer tax.

Depending on the types of transaction envisaged they can also mitigate stamp duty. They will not normally save any income tax, however, because of the provisions of the TA 1970, s478, and they will also be of little help in reducing any charge to development land tax.

The Double Taxation Treaties with the overseas countries involved, and the relevant Exchange Control legislation and notices, must always be examined where appropriate.

What is an overseas trust?

An overseas trust is basically a trust which is controlled and managed outside the United Kingdom—the United Kingdom for tax purposes does not include the Channel Islands and the Isle of Man.

The various taxes have their own separate rules as to what is an overseas trust, but the general rule is, as mentioned above, that a trust is foreign if it is controlled and managed outside the United Kingdom. The residence or domicile of the settlor or beneficiary can be relevant, as well as the location of the trust assets; the relevance of these factors will depend upon the tax under discussion.

Income tax

If income arises in the United Kingdom from investments, or a trust wholly or partly trades in the United Kingdom or is resident in the United Kingdom, a liability to UK tax could arise (see *Colquhoun* v *Brooks* (1889) 14 App Cas 493, per Lord Herschell, at p504). If there are no such connections with the United Kingdom a liability could still arise under the TA 1970, s478.

Trustees of discretionary trusts are chargeable to the additional 15 per cent pursuant to the FA 1973, s16. The charge theoretically applies to overseas trusts, but problems of collection can arise in practice.

If a UK taxpayer provides overseas companies or trusts with the opportunity to acquire land and make a gain of a capital nature on it, the taxpayer may be assessed to tax under the TA 1970, s488 (see the Chancery decision of *Yuill* v *Wilson* [1977] STC, at p381; the width of the sections has been narrowed by the Court of Appeal, however, [1978] STI, at p581).

Section 478 of the TA 1970 is designed to prevent individuals from transferring assets abroad and enabling the income arising therefrom to accrue to non-residents (for example, non-resident trusts), and therefore to be exempt from UK taxation. The law in this area is now somewhat unclear following the decision in *Vestey* v *IRC* [1977] STC p414, which is being appealed. This case is discussed at p164 below.

The preamble to the TA 1970, s478 states that the section is enacted—

> For the purpose of preventing the avoidance by individuals ordinarily resident in the United Kingdom of liability to income tax by means of transfers of assets by virtue or in consequence whereof, either alone or in conjunction with associated operations, income becomes payable to persons resident or domiciled out of the United Kingdom.

Section 478(1) reads as follows:

> Where by virtue or in consequence of any such transfer, either alone or in conjunction with associated operations, such an individual has, within the meaning of this section, power to enjoy, whether forthwith or in the future, any income of a person resident or domiciled out of the United Kingdom which, if it were income of that individual received by him in the United Kingdom, would be chargeable to income tax by deduction or otherwise, that income shall, whether it would or would not have been chargeable to income tax apart from the provisions of this section, be deemed to be income of that individual for all the purposes of the Income Tax Acts.

The meanings of the important words used in this section will now be examined:

(1) *Where by virtue or in consequence of any such transfer*—The words 'such transfer' refers to the transfer of assets mentioned in the preamble. Section 478(8)(*b*) defines 'assets' to include property or rights of any kind, and 'transfer', in relation to rights, shall include the creation of those rights. Clearly the creation of an overseas settlement will come within the section. The assets being transferred may have been originally situated within or outside the United Kingdom. A transfer from one foreign country to another is sufficient (eg, *Ramsden* v *IRC* (1957) 37 TC 619).

Example—Mr X transfers £100,000 to Jersey trustees. They are to hold the money upon discretionary trust for the benefit of beneficiaries ordinarily resident in the United Kingdom. This transfer of £100,000 will be a transfer within s478.

(2) *either alone or in conjunction with associated operations*—'Associated operations' is defined in s478(4) and means, in relation to any transfer, an operation of any kind effected by any person in relation to any of the assets

transferred or any assets representing, whether directly or indirectly, any of the assets transferred, or to the income arising from any such assets, or to any assets representing, whether directly or indirectly, the accumulations of income arising from any such assets. Death has been held not to be an associated operation (*Bambridge* v *IRC* (1955) 36 TC 313).

In *Fynn* v *IRC* (1958) 37 TC 629, the taxpayer, Mr Fynn, transferred investments to an Eire company in return for shares in the company which he settled on irrevocable trusts for his children. Subsequently, money was lent interest-free by Mr Fynn to the trust. The Revenue contested that this loan, which was repayable on demand, was associated with the transfer of the assets to the company, and was sufficient to give Mr Fynn power to enjoy the income of the company. Upjohn J held on the facts of the case that the transfer of assets and the making of the loan were not associated operations, so that the section was not applicable.

(3) *such an individual*—This means an individual who is ordinarily resident in the United Kingdom, and refers to the individual who has power to enjoy the income and not the individual who set up the trust. The provision cannot render a company liable to an assessment but, in appropriate cases, it can and does render a company's shareholders liable. The individual need not be ordinarily resident in the United Kingdom when the settlement was made but he must be ordinarily resident in the year he is sought to be made liable (*IRC* v *Herdman* (1969) 45 TC 507).

(4) *has, within the meaning of this section, power to enjoy, whether forthwith or in the future, any income*—Section 478(5) states that an individual shall be deemed to have power to enjoy the income if:

> (*a*) the income is in fact so dealt with by any person as to be calculated, at some point of time, and whether in the form of income or not, to enure for the benefit of the individual, or
> (*b*) the receipt or accrual of the income operates to increase the value to the individual of any assets held by him or for his benefit, or
> (*c*) the individual receives or is entitled to receive, at any time, any benefit provided or to be provided out of that income or out of moneys which are or will be available for the purpose by reason of the effect or successive effects of the associated operations on that income and on any assets which directly or indirectly represent that income, or
> (*d*) the individual has power, by means of the exercise of any power of appointment or power of revocation or otherwise, to obtain for himself, whether with or without the consent of any other person, the beneficial enjoyment of the income, or may, in the event of the exercise of any power vested in any other person, become entitled to the beneficial enjoyment of the income, or
> (*e*) the individual is able in any manner whatsoever, and whether directly or indirectly, to control the application of the income.

The words 'power to enjoy' thus have a very wide meaning. It was thought prior to the Chancery Division case of *Vestey* v *IRC* [1977] STC 414, where assets were transferred to a non-resident discretionary trust with a number of beneficiaries ordinarily resident in the United Kingdom, that each and every beneficiary could possibly be taxed upon the income of the trust (see s478(5)(*d*) above, and *Lord Howard de Walden* v *IRC* (1941) 25 TC 121 (CA)).

Vestey v *IRC* [1977] STC 414 and *Vestey* v *IRC* (No 2) [1978] STC 567 concerned an overseas discretionary trust with UK beneficiaries. Capital sums were paid, pursuant to powers of appointment, to the beneficiaries. The Revenue contended that regardless of the amount of the capital appointed, each appointee was liable on the full amount of the trust income, so that the Crown was entitled to as many times the tax on the income as appointees year by year. Walton J allowed the taxpayers' appeal, stating that the section must not be read in such a wide manner. He held that only the capital payments, which were in fact payments out of income, could be taxable and then only in the year of receipt. To enable him to do this the judge had to cut down the language of the section and he quoted the Earl of Loreburn in *Drummond* v *Collins* [1915] AC 1011, at p1017, as authority to enable him to do this (*Vestey and Others* v *IRC* [1977] STC 414, at p429). The case is being appealed by the Revenue direct to the House of Lords under the Administration of Justice Act 1969, s12.

In *Latilla* v *IRC* (1943) 25 TC 107 a share in a mining partnership was transferred to a non-resident company in return for shares and non-interest bearing debentures. It was argued that the income which became payable to the non-resident arose not from the transfer of assets but from the activities of the partners. This contention was rejected by Lord Green, MR, who said that the words of the section were of 'the widest import' (at p116).

(5) *of a person resident or domiciled out of the United Kingdom*—A trust which is controlled and managed outside the United Kingdom will be non-resident for these purposes. Section 478(7) states that for the purposes of this section any body corporate incorporated outside the United Kingdom shall be treated as if it were resident out of the United Kingdom, whether it is so resident or not. It is not necessary that the non-resident person, whose income the person ordinarily resident in the United Kingdom has the power to enjoy, should be resident and domiciled overseas at the time of the transfer; it is sufficient to come within the section, if the person subsequently moves overseas *Congreve* v *IRC* (1946) 30 TC 163.

The increasingly popular non-resident United Kingdom incorporated companies come within the meaning of s478.

(6) *which, if it were income of that individual received by him in the United Kingdom, would be chargeable to income tax by deduction or otherwise*—It is necessary that the amounts which are chargeable to tax are income, so that

if capital gains are made overseas this section will not be applicable.

(7) *that income shall, whether it would or would not have been chargeable to income tax apart from the provisions of this section, be deemed to be income of that individual for all the purposes of the Income Tax Acts*—The individual ordinarily resident in the United Kingdom can be chargeable under the section whether or not he receives the income; this is another one of those notorious deeming provisions to be found in increasing numbers in the United Kingdom tax legislation.

Capital Sums

Section 478(2) states—

> Where, whether before or after any such transfer, such an individual receives or is entitled to receive any capital sum the payment whereof is in any way connected with the transfer or any associated operation, any income which, by virtue or in consequence of the transfer, either alone or in conjunction with associated operations, has become the income of a person resident or domiciled outside the United Kingdom shall, whether it would or would not have been chargeable to income tax apart from the provisions of this section, be deemed to be the income of that individual for all the purposes of the Income Tax Acts.

In this sub-section 'capital sum' means—

(1) any sum paid or payable by way of loan or repayment of loan; and

(2) any other sum paid or payable otherwise than as income, being a sum which is not paid or payable for full consideration in money or money's worth.

This section deals with capital sums. It is aimed to stop schemes which involve the repatriation of the income in a capital form. It was held in *Ramsden* v *IRC* (1957) 37 TC 619 that the word 'loan' does not include a sum left outstanding as unpaid purchase money due from a resident individual to a non-resident company.

Example—Mr X transfers shares to a Jersey discretionary trust for the benefit of Y and Z who are ordinarily resident in the United Kingdom. The dividends are capitalized and paid out in a capital form, by deed of appointment, to Y and Z. Y and Z could be assessed under s478 on the payment, since they will have received a 'capital sum'.

Exclusion for Bona Fide Transactions

Section 478 shall not have effect (subs(3)) if the individual shows in writing, or otherwise, to the satisfaction of the Board either:

> (*a*) that the purpose of avoiding liability to taxation was not the purpose or one of the purposes for which the transfer or associated operations or any of them were effected; or
>
> (*b*) that the transfer and any associated operations were bona fide commercial

transactions and were not designed for the purpose of avoiding liability to taxation.

The jurisdiction of the Special Commissioners on any appeal shall include jurisdiction to review any relevant decisions taken by the Board in exercise of their functions under this sub-section.

Trading Operations

It is clear from the wording of subs(3) above that trading income as well as investment income could come within the section. It should, however, be easier to prove a bona fide commercial transaction set up not to avoid tax in the case of the establishment of an overseas trading operation, than it would be in the case of an investment company.

Thus, a trading trust overseas would have a better chance of coming within the exemption in subs(3) than a trust set up purely for investment.

Conclusions on Section 478

If assets are transferred to non-resident trusts, then, if any individual, ordinarily resident in the United Kingdom, has power to enjoy that income that individual can be taxable upon the income under s478.

It has been suggested that s478 can be avoided by interposing a foreign settlement between the United Kingdom-resident individuals who have power to enjoy the income and an overseas company, allowing the income to accrue in the overseas company. It is felt that the width of the section is sufficient to bring such income into charge to tax upon the beneficiaries of the trust under s478. The decision of *Vestey and Others v IRC* at first instance, however, has made this area of the law uncertain, and the proceedings in the higher courts must be followed.

In the author's view the safest way to avoid s478 is to set up a bona fide overseas trading operation. Alternatively, if it is intended to use overseas operations to avoid tax, then one should not try to avoid income tax but opt instead for capital gains tax or capital transfer tax savings.

Capital gains tax

Gains made by overseas trustees are exempt in the hands of the trustees from United Kingdom capital gains tax because the trustees will not be resident or ordinarily resident in the United Kingdom (FA 1965, s20). However, s42 of the FA 1965 seeks to apportion the gain to beneficiaries under the trust.

Section 42(1) reads as follows:

This section applies as respects chargeable gains accruing to the trustees of a settlement if the trustees are not resident and not ordinarily resident in the United

> Kingdom, and if the settlor, or one of the settlors, is domiciled and either resident or ordinarily resident in the United Kingdom, or was domiciled and either resident or ordinarily resident in the United Kingdom when he made his settlement.

Any beneficiary under the settlement, who is domiciled and either resident or ordinarily resident in the United Kingdom in the year in which the gain is made by the trustees, can have part of that gain apportioned to him in a manner which is just and reasonable. The apportionment will depend on the interest which the beneficiary has under the trust, such as a life interest or an interest in reversion, disregarding, in the case of a defeasible interest, the possibility of defeasance (FA 1965, s42(2)).

There are special rules for discretionary trusts contained in s42(3). It is stated that, for the purposes of the section—

> (*a*) if in any three years ending with that in which the chargeable gain accrues a person has received a payment or payments out of the income of the settled property made in exercise of a discretion he shall be regarded, in relation to that chargeable gain, as having an interest in the settled property of a value equal to that of an annuity of a yearly amount equal to one-third of the total of the payments so received by him in the said three years, and
> (*b*) if a person receives at any time after the chargeable gain accrues a capital payment made out of the settled property in exercise of a discretion, being a payment which represents the chargeable gain in whole or part then, except so far as any part of the gain has been attributed under this section to some other person who is domiciled and resident or ordinarily resident in the United Kingdom, that person shall, if domiciled and resident or ordinarily resident in the United Kingdom, be treated as if the chargeable gain, or as the case may be the part of the chargeable gain represented by the capital payment, accrued to him at the time when he received the capital payment.

Thus, if there is no income in an overseas trust and a chargeable gain is made after a capital payment is made from the trust, subs(3) would appear not to be able to apply.

Section 42(2) is aimed at beneficiaries who have interests in the trust, even though these could be defeated. To come within s42(3), on the other hand, any benefits received by a beneficiary must depend on the trustees being in a position to exercise a discretion (which they must in fact exercise at some time) in favour of a beneficiary.

There is an equivalent provision, in the FA 1965, s41, to charge non-resident companies, but it is noticeable that ss41 and 42 deal with completely separate situations; it might well be that a non-resident trust, which owns a non-resident company that makes a gain, would not cause a charge to arise under these provisions.

Special provisions apply to settlements made before 6 April 1965 (s42(4)).

In this case s42(2) will not apply to a beneficiary whose interest is solely in the income of the settled property (eg, a life tenant) and who cannot, by means of the exercise of any power of appointment or power of revocation or otherwise, obtain for himself, whether with or without the consent of any other person, any part of the capital represented by the settled property; payment of capital gains tax, chargeable on the gain apportioned to a beneficiary in respect of an interest in reversion in any part of the capital represented by the settled property, may be postponed until that person becomes absolutely entitled to that part of the settled property, or disposes of the whole or any part of his interest, unless he can, by means described above, obtain for himself any of it at any earlier time. This section would not appear to have any application to discretionary trusts created before 6 April 1965.

For the purposes of subs(4), property added to a settlement after the settlement is made shall be regarded as property under a separate settlement made at the time when the property is so added. In any case in which the amount of any capital gains tax payable by a beneficiary under a settlement in accordance with the provisions of this section is paid by the trustees of the settlement, such amount shall not for the purposes of taxation be regarded as a payment to such beneficiary (s42(5)). The section does not allow an apportionment of a loss accruing to the trustees (s42(6)).

It can be seen from the above that, provided capital gains are made by an overseas trust and are retained abroad, it is possible to organize matters so that United Kingdom capital gains tax can be postponed almost indefinitely even though all the beneficiaries are resident or ordinarily resident in the United Kingdom. It is even possible to avoid it altogether if one or more of the beneficiaries eventually emigrate or, even without having to take that draconian step, by the United Kingdom beneficiary selling his beneficial interest to a non-resident purchaser.

Exportation of Trusts

The favourable capital gains tax treatment of overseas trusts can often be obtained by the United Kingdom trustees retiring in favour of foreign trustees, so that the trust can become resident outside the United Kingdom. There is nothing in law to prevent this being done, although the law in this area is not entirely settled so that there is a possibility that a beneficiary might apply to the court and have the appointment set aside (Re *Whitehead's Will Trusts* [1971] 2 All ER 1334).

Whether or not capital gains tax is payable when a trust is exported and trust assets disposed of, will depend on how the arrangement is carried out. In *Chinn* v *Collins* and *Chinn* v *Hochstrasser* [1977] STC at p 468, the trustees of an English trust wanted to appoint shares to a beneficiary without paying capital gains tax under the FA 1965, s25(3). The trust was exported to

Guernsey and the shares appointed out contingently to the beneficiary, who assigned his trust interest to a Jersey Company. The beneficiary also contracted to purchase back the shares from the Jersey Company. Templeman J said that on the true facts of the case the assignment and the contract were interdependent and conditional one on the other, so that the beneficiary became absolutely entitled to the shares as against the trustees, causing a charge to capital gains tax to arise under the FA 1965, s42(2). Thus, although the assignment effectively disposed of the beneficiary's interest in the shares, the contract effectively transferred the shares back in equity. The scheme failed also on an alternative ground brought by the Revenue under the FA 1965, s42(7), which extends the meaning of 'settlement' and 'settlor' by incorporating the definition in the TA 1970, s454(3). The Court of Appeal allowed the taxpayer's appeal, holding that the true legal effect was that the beneficiary had not become absolutely entitled to the shares, and the extended meaning of 'settlement' could not be applied to this particular case (STI 1979, p83).

Indemnities will normally have to be given to the retiring trustees. Although exportation may have capital gains tax advantages it will not produce any capital transfer tax advantages, as settlements made by persons domiciled in the United Kingdom remain within the scope of capital transfer tax wherever the settlement is resident.

Capital transfer tax

Since the introduction of capital transfer tax overseas discretionary trusts suffer various penalties. Discretionary trusts in general suffer a charge to capital transfer tax every ten years. When the trustees of a discretionary settlement are not resident in the United Kingdom the settlor, if living, is liable to pay the tax on a transfer every ten years, in the same way as if the trust were resident in the United Kingdom. However, in order to make the charge more effective in every year apart from the last year in the period of ten years ending with the relevant anniversary, the fund is treated as if it were notionally disposed of and will be taxed at a rate of 3 per cent of the rate otherwise chargeable (FA 1975, Sched 5, para 12(3)). The 3 per cent charge will apply on the first anniversary of the trust falling on or after 1 January 1976. Any tax so charged is allowed as a credit against the tax chargeable on the next capital distribution actually made, or treated as made under the ten-year periodic charge, out of the property concerned. To prevent this annual charge arising (or, if it has already arisen, to bring it to an end in the future) the trust could be reconstructed by appointing out interests in possession, by creating accumulation and maintenance trusts, or by appointing property absolutely to the settlor or other beneficiaries under the trust.

The annual charge is inextricably linked with the ten-year charge. If a trust, for example, was set up on 31 July 1962, the first periodic charge will be on 31 July 1982 (there can be no periodic charge before 1 April 1980 (FA 1975, Sched 5, para 12(6)). The first annual charge will be on 31 July 1976. If the trust had been created on 31·July 1968 the first periodic charge will arise on 31 July 1988 and the first annual charge on 31 July 1979. Because of these penalties upon discretionary trusts and because, in the case of a fixed trust, the life tenant would be chargeable to tax as if he owned the trust fund, overseas trusts are not now generally attractive propositions, unless the overseas trust fund can amount to excluded property, and, therefore be totally outside the United Kingdom capital transfer tax regime (it will only be excluded property if the settlor is non-domiciled and the property is situate outside the United Kingdom (FA 1975, Sched 5, para 2(1)(*a*).

A foreign trust, for the purposes of capital transfer tax, is one where the trustees or a majority of them are resident abroad and the general administration of the trust is ordinarily carried on outside the United Kindom (FA 1975, Sched 5, para 12(5)). When the settlement is created the settlor will be liable for capital transfer tax in the usual way. Property comprised in the settlement will be liable to capital transfer tax in the usual way, unless the property is situated outside the United Kingdom and the settlor was not domiciled in the United Kingdom when the trust was set up.

If a chargeable transfer is made by an overseas trust, in theory the trustees of the settlement are liable for the tax (s25(3)(*a*)), although in practical terms it can be obtained from the following persons—

(1) any person entitled (whether beneficially or not) to an interest in possession in the settled property) (FA 1975, s25(3)(*b*));

(2) any person for whose benefit any of the settled property or income from it is applied at or after the time of the transfer (FA 1975, s23(3)(*c*); and

(3) where the chargeable transfer is made during the life of the settlor and the trustees are not for the time being resident in the United Kingdom, the settlor (FA 1975, s25(3)(*d*)).

These rules could operate harshly against a settlor especially if he created the settlement some time ago and the trust has since been exported. The rules were therefore amended in 1976 (FA 1976, Sched 14, para 20), so that no charge on the settlor will arise where:

(1) the settlement was made before 11 December 1974; and

(2) the trustees were resident in the United Kingdom when the settlement was made; and

(3) in the case of a chargeable transfer made after 10 December 1974, the trustees have not been resident in the United Kingdom at any time during the period between that date and the time of the transfer.

Returns by certain persons acting for settlors

Where a person in the course of a trade or profession carried on by him, other than the profession of a barrister, has been concerned with the making, after 26 March 1974, of a settlement, and knows or has reason to believe—

(1) that the settlor was domiciled in the United Kingdom; and

(2) that the trustees of the settlement are not or will not be resident in the United Kingdom;

he shall, within three months of the making of the settlement or, if it was made before the passing of the FA 1975, within three months of the Act, make a return to the Revenue stating the names and addresses of the settlor and the trustees of the settlement (FA 1975, Sched 4, para 4). However, a person shall not be required to inform the Revenue where the settlement was made by will, or another person has informed them.

As previously mentioned para 2 of the FA 1975, Sched 5 states that 'property comprised in a settlement which is situated outside the United Kingdom will be excluded property unless the settlor was domiciled in the United Kingdom at the time the settlement was made'. There is an important exception to this general rule with regard to reversionary interests. If the reversionary interest is situate outside the United Kingdom it is excluded property only if the person beneficially entitled to it is domiciled outside the United Kingdom (FA 1975, s24(2)).

There has been a considerable amount of difficulty in reconciling the FA 1975, s24(2), with the FA 1975, Sched 5, para 2. In the author's view the former section takes precedence over the latter paragraph. This means that a beneficiary domiciled in the United Kingdom who is entitled (without having purchased it) to a reversionary interest in a settlement set up by a United Kingdom settlor will not have that property treated as part of his estate on his death or, if he gives it away, as it is, excluded property (see Chapter 4, at p45).

There are no special rules contained in the Act for determining the location of property so that the position will fall to be determined according to English Law, unless there is a provision in the relevant Double Tax Treaty (see Sched 7, para 7). This is the same rule as formerly applied to estate duty (see *Green's Death Duties*, 7th Edn, p659 et seq, and *Dymond's Death Duties*, 5th Edn, p1256 et seq).

An interesting proposition for a person who is domiciled overseas but intends to become domiciled in the United Kingdom would be for him to set up a trust overseas holding overseas assets. To avoid an ultimate charge upon the United Kingdom beneficiaries they could perhaps become non-domiciled and non-resident when the times comes for the funds to be appointed to them.

Future overseas trusts set up by United Kingdom-domiciled settlors should be avoided if at all possible; overseas relatives or friends should be used to set up such trusts, which own property which is also located overseas, such as shares in an overseas company which might carry out transactions in the United Kingdom. There are considerable problems when there is a United Kingdom settlor.

Development land tax

Section 1(2) of the DLTA 1976 provides that a person (which would include an overseas trust) shall be chargeable to development land tax on the realized development value which accrues to him on the disposal by him of an interest in land in the United Kingdom, and shall be so chargeable whether or not he is resident (for the purposes of income tax or otherwise) in the United Kingdom. Thus, the setting up of an overseas trust will not save development land tax on the disposal of an interest in land in the United Kingdom.

The provisions of the DLTA 1976, s40 could apply if an overseas trust disposes of an interest in land in the United Kingdom, so that a deduction from the sale proceeds might be made by the purchaser. It would have to be shown, before the provision applies, that the usual place of abode of the trustees is outside the United Kingdom.

Stamp duty

As well as applying to United Kingdom instruments, stamp duty applies to foreign property transactions if the instrument is executed in the United Kingdom, and to instruments executed outside the United Kingdom relating to any property situate or matter or thing to be done in the United Kingdom (Stamp Act 1891, s14(1)).

In general, instruments should be stamped within thirty days of execution, except that instruments executed outside the United Kingdom are allowed thirty days from being received in the United Kingdom (Stamp Act 1891, s15(3)(*a*)).

Certain reduced rates of ad valorem stamp duty are applicable to sales of stock or marketable securities to overseas residents under the FA 1974, Sched 11, paras 20–23.

CHAPTER 20

BREAKING AND VARYING TRUSTS

How trusts can be broken or varied

Trusts can be broken or varied in the following ways:

(1) under the terms of the trust instrument, eg, the trustees may be given powers to advance capital to beneficiaries or remodel the trusts of the settlement;

(2) under statutory powers, eg, capital can be advanced to a beneficiary under the Trustee Act 1925, s32;

(3) by the beneficiaries dealing with their interests under the trust; they can, for instance, assign, surrender, disclaim or release their interests, and also (under the rule in *Saunders* v *Vautier* (1841) Cr and Ph 240) if they are all sui juris and agree, the beneficiaries can bring the trust to an end or vary its terms as they please.

(4) By application to the court.

Under the terms of the Trust Instrument

Trustees, particularly of discretionary trusts, are usually given the power to advance capital to beneficiaries in their absolute discretion or remodel the trusts of the settlement. These powers might be exercisable with or without the consent of the settlor or beneficiaries. Where these powers are contained in the Trust Deed then, provided the document has been properly drafted there should be no difficulty should it become necessary for tax planning purposes to alter the trusts of the settlement. This is particularly important with regard to discretionary trusts, and the transitional reliefs from capital transfer tax for such trusts which were set up before 27 March 1974 (FA 1975, Sched 5, para 14).

It is important to keep modern trusts as flexible as possible. This is because of the constantly changing taxation rules which apply to trusts, and also the expense which will be involved if the trustees had to take the matter to court in order to settle the terms of any variation.

Statutory Powers

The most important of these are the power of advancement under the Trustee Act 1925, s32 and the power to pay income under the Trustee Act 1925, s31.

Actions by Beneficiaries

Actions by beneficiaries can involve surrenders of life interests to remaindermen, surrenders of reversionary interests to a life tenant, disclaimers of life interests, releases of annuities, and assignments of life and reversionary interests. If all the beneficiaries under a trust agree, the trust can be brought to an end, regardless of the wishes and intentions of the settlor.

It is important, however, that the beneficiaries are entitled together to all the trust assets. If the trust instrument had provided that the beneficiary, who wishes to bring the trust to an end, did not obtain a vested interest until he survived to a specified date, he would not be able to invoke the rule without the concurrence of the person entitled in default of his attaining that age (*Gosling* v *Gosling* (1859) Johns 265; *Re Lord Nunburnholme* [1912] 1 Ch 489). If the beneficial interest is sold, the purchaser stands in the same position as the vendor, and if the vendor could have brought the trust to an end the purchaser will be able to do so if he is sui juris.

If the beneficial interest is mortgaged, the mortgagee cannot bring the trust to an end as long as the beneficiary who assigned his interest is in a position to redeem the mortgage (*Bell, Re Jeffrey* v *Sayles* [1896] 1 Ch 1). The rule applies whether the beneficiaries hold their interests contemporaneously or are entitled in succession.

The Courts

Inherent Jurisdiction—The Court has an inherent jurisdiction to authorize otherwise unauthorized acts of management or administration (*Chapman* v *Chapman* [1954] AC 429, at pp454 and 455), where an emergency has arisen. This jurisdiction is limited to cases where—

(1) the situation was one which could not have been foreseen or guarded against by the settlor; and

(2) the trustees were embarrassed by the emergency; and

(3) the consent of the beneficiaries could not be obtained.

In the case of *Re New* [1901] 2 Ch 534 trustees were authorized by the court, as a matter of emergency, to concur in a scheme under which the trust shares were exchanged for more realizable shares in a new company. There was no provision in the trust instrument to enable this to be done.

Section 57 of the Trustee Act 1957—The court may empower the trustees in the management and administration of the trust to do any act otherwise unauthorized if in the opinion of the court it is expedient for the trust as a whole that it should be done. The provision is used for a variety of purposes, such as the partitioning of land, the sale of a reversionary interest, or increasing the powers of investment. The section does not apply to trustees of settled land and cannot be used to sanction a variation of beneficial interests.

Section 64 of the Settled Land Act 1925—Under this section the courts are authorized to sanction any transactions affecting or concerning settled land.

Section 24 of the Matrimonial Causes Act 1973—Under the matrimonial legislation the courts can vary certain settlements. The section reads as follows:

> On granting a decree of divorce, a decree of nullity of marriage or a decree of judicial separation or at any time thereafter (whether, in the case of a decree of divorce or of nullity of marriage, before or after the decree is made absolute), the court may make any one or more of the following orders, that is to say—
>
> (*a*) an order that a party to the marriage shall transfer to the other party, to any child of the family or to such person as may be specified in the order for the benefit of such a child such property as may be so specified, being property to which the first-mentioned party is entitled, either in possession or reversion;
>
> (*b*) an order that a settlement of such property as may be so specified, being property to which a party to the marriage is so entitled, be made to the satisfaction of the court for the benefit of the other party to the marriage and of the children of the family or either or any of them;
>
> (*c*) an order varying for the benefit of the parties to the marriage and of the children of the family or either or any of them any ante-nuptial or post-nuptial settlement (including such a settlement made by will or codicil) made on the parties to the marriage;
>
> (*d*) an order extinguishing or reducing the interest of either of the parties to the marriage under any such settlement . . .

Section 103 of the Mental Health Act 1959 (replacing Section 171 of the Law of Property Act 1925)—A Court of Protection may sanction any arrangement of property which the lunatic or defective himself could have done if he had been of sound mind.

Section 53 of the Trustee Act 1925—This provision enables the court to appoint a person to convey property belonging to an infant who is beneficially entitled to the income or capital of trust assets.

Variation of Trusts Act 1958—Prior to 1958 the courts did not have any wide powers to vary the beneficial interests of trusts. The powers mentioned in the preceding paragraphs are of a very limited scope.

After the court's refusal to sanction a variation of the beneficial interests in *Chapman* v *Chapman* [1954] AC 429, which would have been of great benefit to the trust, need was felt for enlargement of the court's powers of varying beneficial interests. For this reason the Variation of Trusts Act 1958 was passed. Under s1 of the Act the court may, if it thinks fit, approve an arrangement varying or revoking all or any of the trusts, or enlarging the powers of the trustees of managing or administering any of the trust property on behalf of four classes of beneficiaries—

(1) infants or other beneficiaries who by reason of some incapacity are incapable of assenting;

(2) persons who may become entitled to an interest in the future, if at the

relevant time they answer a specified description or qualify as members of a specified class;

(3) unborn persons; and

(4) persons who will be interested as discretionary beneficiaries under protective trusts if the interest of the principal beneficiary shall fail or determine.

In the first three cases the court will only approve the arrangement if it is satisfied that it is for the benefit of those beneficiaries on behalf of whom consent is needed. The court can approve an arrangement, even if not for the benefit of persons within the fourth case, although their interests must be considered.

The Act simply empowers the court to give consent on behalf of a person whose consent cannot for some reason be obtained. The court has no power to dispense with the consent of a person able to give such consent and in this case the arrangement cannot go through.

It is clear from the wording of this section that the court can sanction a variation of the beneficial interests of the trust and the fact that the object of the proposal is to minimize taxation is no bar to the court's approval (*Re Robert's Settlement Trust* (1961) TR 401; *Re Clitheroe's Settlement Trusts* [1959] 1 WLR 1159; *Re Lloyd's Settlement* [1967] 2 WLR 1078; and *Re Sainsbury's Settlement*, [1967] 1 WLR 476). There was one notable exception to this, however, in the case of *Re Weston's Settlement* ([1968] 2 WLR 1154; [1968] 1 All ER 720 (Stamp J)), where an application to transfer a trust to Jersey was dismissed. Stamp J in the High Court refused the court's consent, since the scheme was nothing more than a cheap exercise in tax avoidance. Lord Denning in the Court of Appeal felt that the trust should be kept in England: it would be for the beneficiaries' benefit if the trust were 'in this our England which is still the envy of less happier lands' ([1968] 3 All ER (CA) 338 at p342).

In the case of *Re Seale's Marriage Settlement* [1961] Ch 574 and *Re Windeatt's Will Trusts* [1969] 2 AER 324 the courts approved the transfers of the administration of trusts abroad. In the case of *Re Whitehead's Will Trusts, Burke* v *Burke* [1971] 2 All ER 1334, it was held that there was no legal bar to the appointment of foreign trustees provided there was some peculiar circumstance, such as the beneficiaries moving abroad, which made such appointment appropriate.

It should be noted that with regard to capital transfer tax the minimum 10 per cent charge under Sched 5, para 14 was extended for an additional year, ie, up to 31 March 1977, where court proceedings, such as an application under the Variation of Trusts Act, were involved (FA 1975, Sched 5, para 14(3)).

Taxation Consequences

The transactions involved in breaking or varying trusts will usually be capital transactions so that no income tax liability will be involved. There can, however, be liability to income tax; for example, if the assignor of a beneficial interest under the trust is a trader in such interests (he will be liable to income tax under Sched D, case 1) or if a trust is broken and accumulated, but not capitalized, income is paid to the beneficiary.

Trust breaks or variations will also not usually involve development land tax because that tax is not chargeable where consideration does not pass. Thus, if development land is appointed out absolutely to a life tenant and a reversioner, there can be no charge to development land tax.

Reference has already been made to the transitional reliefs available for discretionary trusts set up before 27 March 1974 (FA 1975, Sched 5, para 14, and see above, p67). Where such trusts are varied or terminated before 1 April 1980, the charge to capital transfer tax is reduced by the appropriate fraction. Such transfers can give rise to capital gains tax if property is appointed out absolutely (FA 1965, s25(3)), although there will be no charge to ad valorem duty (F (1909–10) A 1910, s74(6)).

There is set out below the capital transfer tax, capital gains tax and stamp duty consequences of some of the major dealings with fixed interest trusts.

The Property is Divided Between the Beneficiaries

If the fund is divided with the consent of the beneficiaries, for instance, between the life tenant and the reversioner, there will be no charge to capital transfer tax on the life tenant's portion (FA 1975, Sched 5, para 4(3)); however, the property which is taken by the reversioner is treated as if it were a gift by the life tenant. It will therefore be chargeable to capital transfer tax (FA 1975, Sched 5, para 4(4)). This division of the funds will normally be upon actuarial grounds and no ad valorem stamp duty will be payable. If the life tenant survives three years from the break-up of the trust the lifetime rates will apply. This should be compared with the situation if the trust is allowed to continue, whereupon on the death of the life tenant he will be chargeable, without relief, to the death-time rates. By breaking the trust it also enables future growth to be put into the hands of the reversioner rather than waiting until death. One of the difficulties in breaking trusts in this way is that a charge to capital gains tax could arise since the trust will normally be brought to an end. If appropriate, the relief for gifts of business assets contained in the FA 1978, s46 and Sched 8, might enable any gain to be rolled over.

The Life Tenant Assigns his Interest to the Remainderman

This would bring the trust to an end, giving rise to a charge to capital transfer tax (Sched 5, para 4(1) and (2)). There will be ad valorem stamp duty of 2 per cent payable on the assignment of the life interest. If the trust is brought to an end as a result of the assignment there could also be a charge to capital gains tax (FA 1975 (3)). This arrangement enables the trust fund to be put into the hands of the reversioner, who will normally be a younger member of the family, so postponing any charge to capital transfer tax until his death. As there will be a charge on the transfer, it is only future growth which is therefore taken out of charge to tax, plus an opportunity to make use of the lifetime rates. It is possible that the capital gain might be rolled over under the provisions of the FA 1978 (ie, s46 and Sched 8).

Reversioner Assigns his Interest to the Life Tenant

On the assignment of the reversion there will be a charge to ad valorem stamp duty at 2 per cent. There will be no charge to capital transfer tax since the life tenant will be entitled to the entire fund (FA 1975, Sched 5, para 4(3)). On the assignment of the reversion itself there will be no charge to capital gains tax, since that is a disposal of an interest under a trust, but as the disposal will bring the trust to an end there can be a charge at that stage unless it is rolled over under the FA 1978.

If the life tenant buys the interest in remainder the effect is that the life tenant will have made a gift for capital transfer tax purposes of the purchase price (FA 1975, ss20(4) and 23(3)).

Conclusions

The various methods of breaking or varying trusts must be carefully examined from the point of view of their tax and stamp duty consequences.

A problem which often arises is where the life tenants are elderly and they want to pass their assets to their children, who are usually the remaindermen. On the death of the life tenants the entire capital of the fund will be chargeable to capital transfer tax. By dividing the fund up actuarialy during lifetime the future growth will be taken out of the life tenants' estates and the lifetime rates will apply. However, the division could give rise to a charge to capital transfer tax. The power of the remainderman to release his interest to the tenant for life can also be important, since that transaction will not give rise to any charge to capital transfer tax.

It is also important when drafting new trust documents that the maximum flexibility is put into the document, to cater for possible future changes in the tax rules and changes in the position of the settlor. He might first want the trust to be able to protect his assets from the Inland Revenue, then, perhaps from his creditors, and finally from his spouse if there are matrimonial problems.

CHAPTER 21

CONCLUSIONS

With the introduction of capital transfer tax the growth of private family trusts is likely to be restricted. The exception to this is the Accumulation and Maintenance Trust which, because of its capital transfer tax and income tax treatment, is likely to prosper.

Companies are fortunate to be able to set up a wide number of attractive trusts—retirement benefit schemes, charitable trusts, employees' trusts and profit sharing schemes. The profits of a company can be put into these different trusts and could be used to further the well-being of the company, its trading activities, employees and, through a charitable trust, society as a whole. The company might lose the power to benefit directly from the funds which it has settled into these various types of trust, but it will, nevertheless, with appropriately appointed trustees, be in a position to have the economic power and control over the funds which can be used with a view to benefiting the company, albeit indirectly. Thus, moneys put into a self-administered retirement benefit scheme by a company will enable the company to have a degree of control over those funds—for instance, the funds could buy out a competitor—although the company itself cannot actually benefit from the funds. The same applies in the case of a charitable trust where, to an extent, tax-free income can accrue and be used to benefit poor employees and local charities or benefit charities, or charitable purposes in general. Of the four trusts the Employees' Trust is the most flexible, and specific Revenue approval of the trust is not required. It can nevertheless provide the very important function of building up a fund for the benefit of employees for the purpose of buying shares from shareholders who are leaving the company and no longer wish to keep their shares, or from the personal representatives of shareholders who have died. In the author's view companies should consider these four types of trust and, if appropriate, set one or more up.

Another type of trust which is under-used in the United Kingdom is the Trading Trust. This type of trust has been exploited in the United States where it is called the 'Massachusetts Trusts', after the State in which it was used to the fullest extent. The flexibility of the trust enables it to be fully adapted for trading purposes.

When drafting a trust document the equity draftsman must squeeze his trust into the appropriate pigeon hole in order that the correct classification for tax purposes can be made. This might not always be easy and, for instance, difficulty can often be experienced in drafting a qualifying Accumulation and Maintenance Settlement or an Employees' Trust for capital transfer tax purposes. The trust has been described as 'the greatest and most distinctive achievement performed by Englishmen in the field of jurisprudence' (Maitland—*Selected Essay*, 129). It could well be that the elaborate restrictions on trusts required for tax purposes will stunt the growth of this legal institution for many years to come and limit the imagination of lawyers.

APPENDIX I

TRUST TAX AND STAMP DUTY RATES

Income tax

Trustees can be liable to income tax at 33 per cent, or 48 per cent if the trust is an accumulation or discretionary trust (FA 1973, s16 and 17).

Capital gains tax

The rate of capital gains tax applicable to trusts is 30 per cent, with restricted exemptions and reliefs for small gains, except in the case of trusts for the mentally disabled or for persons in receipt of an attendance allowance (FA 1978, Sched 7, paras 5 and 6). Special rules apply, to give reliefs and exemptions, to sales of tangible movable property (FA 1965, s30 and FA 1978, s45).

Capital Transfer Tax

Rates of CTT

Lifetime rates—after 26 October 1977

Cumulative chargeable transfers (gross)	Rate on gross	CTT on band	Cumulative CTT	Cumulative chargeable transfers (net)	Rate on net
£	%	£	£	£	
0— 25,000	0	nil	nil	0— 25,000	nil
25,000— 30,000	5	250	250	25,000— 29,750	1/19
30,000— 35,000	7½	375	625	29,750— 34,375	3/37
35,000— 40,000	10	500	1,125	34,375— 38,875	1/9
40,000— 50,000	12½	1,250	2,375	38,875— 47,625	1/7
50,000— 60,000	15	1,500	3,875	47,625— 56,125	3/17
60,000— 70,000	17½	1,750	5,625	56,125— 64,375	7/33
70,000— 90,000	20	4,000	9,625	64,375— 80,375	1/4
90,000— 110,000	22½	4,500	14,125	80,375— 95,875	9/31
110,000— 130,000	27½	5,500	19,625	95,875—110,375	11/20
130,000— 160,000	35	10,500	30,125	110,375—129,875	7/13
160,000— 210,000	42½	21,250	51,375	129,875—158,625	17/23
210,000— 260,000	50	25,000	76,375	158,625—183,625	1
260,000— 310,000	55	27,500	103,875	183,625—206,125	1 2/9
310,000— 510,000	60	120,000	223,875	206,125—286,125	1½
510,000—1,010,000	65	325,000	548,875	286,125—461,125	1 6/7
1,010,000—2,010,000	70	700,000	1,248,875	461,125—761,125	2⅓
2,010,000+	75			761,125+	3

Death rates—after 26 October 1977

Cumulative chargeable transfers (gross)	Rate on gross	CTT on band	Cumulative CTT	Cumulative chargeable transfers (net)	Rate on net
£	%	£	£	£	
0— 25,000	0	nil	nil	0— 25,000	nil
25,000— 30,000	10	500	500	25,000— 29,500	1/9
30,000— 35,000	15	750	1,250	29,500— 33,750	3/17
35,000— 40,000	26	1,000	2,250	33,750— 37,750	1/4
40,000— 50,000	25	2,500	4,750	37,750— 45,250	1/3
50,000— 60,000	30	3,000	7,750	46,250— 52,250	3/7
60,000— 70,000	35	3,500	11,250	52,250— 58,750	7/13
70,000— 90,000	40	8,000	19,250	58,750— 70,750	2/3
90,000— 110,000	45	9,000	28,250	70,750— 81,750	9/11
110,000— 130,000	50	19,000	38,350	81,750— 91,750	1
130,000— 160,000	55	16,500	54,750	91,750—105,250	1 2/9
160,000— 510,000	60	210,000	264,750	105,250—245,250	1 1/2
510,000—1,010,000	65	325,000	589,750	245,250—420,250	1 6/7
1,010,000—2,010,000	70	700,000	1,289,750	420,250—720,250	2 1/3
2,010,000+	75			720,250+	3

Transitional relief for discretionary settlements

1978–79: 17½% of normal rates

Cumulative chargeable transfers (gross)	CTT Rate on gross	Cumulative chargeable transfers (net)	CTT Rate on net	CTT on band	Cumulative CTT
£000s	%	£ £	fraction	£	£
0—25	nil	0— 25,000.00	nil	nil	nil
25—30	7/8	25,000.00— 29,956.25	7/793	43.75	43.75
30—35	1 5/16	29,956.25— 34,890.63	21/1,579	65.62	109.37
35—40	1 3/9	34,890.63— 39,803.13	7/393	87.50	196.87
40—50	2 3/16	39,803.13— 49,584.38	7/313	218.75	415.62
50—60	2 5/8	49,584.38— 59,321.88	21/779	262.50	678.12
60—70	3 1/16	59,321.88— 69,015.63	49/1,551	306.25	984.37
70—90	3 1/2	69,015.63— 88,315.63	7/193	700.00	1,684.37
90—110	3 15/16	88,315.63— 107,528.13	63/1,537	787.50	2,471.87
110—130	4 13/16	107,528.13— 126,565.63	77/1,523	962.50	3,434.37
130—160	6 1/8	126,565.63— 154,728.13	49/751	1,837.50	5,271.87
160—210	7 7/16	154,728.13— 201,009.38	119/1,481	3,718.75	8,990.62
210—260	8 3/4	201,009.38— 246,634.38	7/73	4,375.00	13,365.62
260—310	9 5/8	246,634.38— 291,821.88	77/723	4,812.50	18,178.12
310—510	10 1/2	291,821.88— 470,821.88	21/179	21,000.00	39,178.12
510—1,010	11 3/8	470,821.88— 913,946.88	91/709	56,875.00	96,053.12
1,010—2,010	12 1/4	913,946.88—1,791,446.88	49/351	122,500.00	218.553.12
2,010+	13 1/8	1,791,446.88+	21/139	—	

1979–80:20% of normal rates

Cumulative chargeable transfers (gross)	CTT Rate on gross	Cumulative chargeable transfers (net)	CTT Rate on net	CTT on band	Cumulative CTT
£000s	%	£ £	fraction	£	£
0—25	nil	0— 25,000	nil	nil	nil
25—30	1	25,000— 29,950	1/99	50	50
30—35	1½	29,950— 34,875	3/197	75	125
35—40	2	34,875— 39,775	1/49	100	225
40—50	2½	39,775— 49,525	1/39	250	475
50—60	3	49,525— 59,225	3/97	300	775
60—70	3½	59,225— 68,875	7/193	350	1,125
70—90	4	68,875— 88,075	1/24	800	1,925
90—110	4½	88,075— 107,175	9/191	900	2,825
110—130	5½	107,175— 126,075	11/189	1,100	3,925
130—160	7	126,075— 153,975	7/93	2,100	6,025
160—210	8½	153,975— 199,725	17/183	4,250	10,275
210—260	10	199,725— 244,725	1/9	5,000	15,275
260—310	11	244,725— 289,225	11/89	5,500	20,775
310—510	12	289,225— 465,225	3/22	24,000	44,775
510—1,010	13	465,225— 900,225	13/87	65,000	109,775
1,010—2,010	14	900,225—1,760,225	7/43	140,000	249,775
2,010+	15	1,760,225+	3/17	—	

Example—The trustees of a 1962 discretionary trust make a net advance of £202,000 to a beneficiary on 1 January 1979. The capital transfer tax is £8,990.62 plus £94.99 (990.62 × 7/73), ie, £9,085.61.

Development land tax

The first £10,000 in any financial year is exempt (DLTA 1976, s12). The next £150,000, up to 31 March 1980, is charged at 66 2/3rds per cent (DLTA 1976, s13, as amended by FA 1978, s76). Thereafter the rate is 80 per cent.

Stamp duty

Subject to any available exemptions (eg, transfer of assets to a beneficiary (F (1909–10) A 1910, s74(6)); or reliefs (eg, if the value of acquired property is £30,000 or less, and is so certified (FA 1963, s55; FA 1974, s49 and Sched 1, para 10(3)) the ad valorem rate on conveyances or transfers on sale or voluntary dispositions is 2 per cent.

There is a sliding scale of duty where the consideration is less than £300 (FA 1974, Sched 11, para 3).

Value added tax

Trusts can be liable to register for VAT where they carry on a business. The standard rate of VAT is 8 per cent and the higher rate, which is applicable to a supply of goods and services of a description specified in F (No 2) A 1975, Sched 7 (as amended), is 12½ per cent.

A particular supply may be zero rated (FA 1972, Sched 4) or exempt (FA 1972, Sched 5), or the supplier may not be liable to register because of the size of his taxable supplies (FA 1972, Sched 1 (as amended)).

Conclusion

It should be noted that certain trusts may be wholly or partly excluded from, or relieved from, one or more of the above six taxes, eg, charitable trusts, exempt approved schemes, unit trusts, profit sharing schemes and employees' trusts.

APPENDIX II

SPECIMEN TRUST RECONSTRUCTION REPORT

This is a report to trustees of a discretionary trust worth £310,000, which was set up in the United Kingdom on 1 June 1972. The beneficiaries include children of varying ages and grandchildren (aged one (born 1 June 1977) and two (born 1 June 1976) of the settlor, and other individuals.

The trustees have power to accumulate income for twenty-one years from the date the settlement was set up (or until a beneficiary attains eighteen years under Trustee Act 1925, s31) and the trust has an eighty year perpetuity period.

It only highlights the principal points to be considered on a reconstruction and does not include all the possibilities which are available.

THE SMITH SETTLEMENT 1972

TAX AND TRUST REPORT

1 January 1979

The Trust

(1) The trust was created on 1 June 1972.

(2) The trust is discretionary which means that the trustees have an absolute discretion as to which of the beneficiaries should receive income or capital. They have the power to accumulate trust income for twenty-one years from the date of the settlement.

(3) The beneficiaries are the settlor's issue and other individuals.

(4) The assets of the trust consist of a portfolio of public company shares. The fund is worth £310,000.

(5) The trust must come to an end at the end of the perpetuity period, ie, 80 years from the date of the settlement.

The Problem

(1) Capital transfer tax, also known as gift tax, was introduced in 1974 and the Government has imposed tax penalties upon discretionary trusts.

(2) The principal penalties are:

(*a*) if the trustees transfer any capital, ie, the shares and the capitalized income, from the trust to beneficiaries they will be chargeable to capital transfer tax; and

(*b*) if the trustees decide not to transfer any capital then every 10 years the entire fund of the discretionary trust is notionally treated as having been transferred out and a tax charge equal to 30 per cent of the rate which would normally be chargeable on such a transfer, becomes chargeable. The first such charge will arise on the trust on 1 June 1982.

Dealing with the Problem

(1) The actions which can be taken to avoid the penalties on the trust are as follows:

(*a*) the shares in the trust can be appointed out absolutely to the beneficiaries thereby breaking the trust; or

(*b*) the trust can undergo a major reconstruction so that the shares remain in the trust but the character of the trust changes so that it ceases to be a discretionary trust.

Breaking the Trust

The problem with appointing out the shares absolutely to a beneficiary is that the trustees will be liable to capital gains tax on the difference between the market value of the shares when they were acquired by the trustees and the market value of the shares when they are appointed out to a beneficiary. That gain will be chargeable on the amounts involved at the full rate of 30 per cent. Furthermore, it will mean that the shares will belong absolutely to the beneficiaries which you might not want.

The alternative to breaking the Trust—Reconstruction

The alternative to breaking the trust is for the trustees to appoint out the shares upon newly constructed sub-trusts. This will not give rise to a liability to capital gains tax and if this appointment could be done before the end of March 1980 the Government has provided substantial reliefs from capital transfer tax. Very broadly these reliefs provide for tax reductions on a reducing scale depending on when the appointment is made. The earlier the appointment is made the cheaper it will be. For instance, if the assets of the trust were valued at £310,000 and the trust is reconstructed before the end of March 1979 the capital transfer tax payable will be £18,178. If we wait until after March 1979 but we transfer before the end of March 1980 the tax payable would be £20,775. After March 1980 the full amount of tax of £103,875 would be payable on the transfer out of the fund.

To put the matter simply, the trustees will be paying a reduced tax now in order to postpone the capital gains tax charge and in order to take the trust out of charge to capital transfer tax. In fact there can only, broadly, be a charge to capital transfer tax after the reconstruction on a death of a beneficiary who is entitled to the income from the trust for the time being.

What will the Reconstruction Involve?

(1) The reason why the Government has attacked discretionary trusts is that they find it almost impossible to tax any particular beneficiary as nobody has any rights under the trust. In order to get the capital transfer tax reliefs it is necessary to decide which individuals are to benefit. The trust reconstruction basically designates, under a Deed of Appointment, particular individuals or classes of individuals to have a right to the dividends arising from the shares in the trust.

(2) The reconstructed trust can, broadly, be for the benefit of:

(*a*) the settlor's children and their issue;

(*b*) the settlor's grandchildren and their issue;

(*c*) other beneficiaries.

The Children's Trust

Under this reconstruction the trustees will hold the assets in trust for the settlor's children and their issue. The settlor's children will be entitled to all the income which arises from the assets, after they attain the age of twenty-five years. The children will not become entitled to the assets themselves. The trustees will have the power to give the assets to the children in their absolute discretion but there will be no actual power in the children to call for the assets. It is this element in the trust which enables the capital gains tax to be postponed, at the same time obtaining the reliefs for capital transfer tax.

On the death of a child his or her share of the trust will pass to his children (ie, the settlor's grandchildren). If he leaves no children it can go to the settlor's surviving children. If there are no children or grandchildren surviving it can go to other persons named in the discretionary trust. Matters are kept very flexible and in fact one would describe the type of trust we are proposing as one which is as near to a discretionary trust as one can get without actually being a discretionary trust. The trustees could, for instance, have power, after a child has attained twenty-five years, to take away the assets which are held for one child and give them to another. That particular power, if ever exercised, could have adverse tax consequences but the existence of the power could prove useful and adds to the flexibility of the arrangement.

Grandchildren's Trust

Under the grandchildren's trust shares would be, broadly, held for the grandchildren with the income (if any) accumulating until they attain the age of eighteen (the twenty-one year accumulation period in the Deed will expire on 1 June 1993 when the grandchildren are aged sixteen and seventeen so that section 31 of the Trustee Act 1925 will be applied). Thereafter, if any income arises, such as dividends, this must be paid to the grandchildren but once again they will never become entitled to the capital unless the trustees exercise their discretion and transfer the capital to them. On the death of a grandchild his children will take his shares in trust. This trust will follow the lineal descendant through until the end of the trust period in 2052 (this is the date the trust must come to an end). This is in effect a 'generation skipping trust'. It enables shares to go to grandchildren without paying tax on the death of their parents. It is a very favourable type of trust as far as tax is concerned.

The trustees will have to decide at some time how they want to treat the grandchildren. Would they like to treat all the grandchildren equally or would they like to treat them according to their separate families? Thus, if one of the children has five children and another child has one, would they like each grandchild to take a sixth or would they like to divide the fund into two so that five of the grandchildren take one-half and the sixth grandchild take the other half.

The Interest In Possession Trust

If you wish persons other than the settlor's children or grandchildren to benefit then these people, if over the age of twenty-five years, can be given a similar interest as you give to the settlor's children when they are over the age of twenty-five years. This would postpone the charge to capital gains tax and at the same time make use of the capital transfer tax reliefs. This is known as an 'interest in possession' trust.

The stamp duty payable by the trustees and beneficiaries on these various transactions will be minimal.

Summary of Main Advantages of Reconstruction

(1) Full use is made of the capital transfer tax reliefs granted by the Government.

(2) The capital gains tax liability is postponed and on the death of a beneficiary who is entitled to the income for the time being the capital gain will be eliminated.

(3) The shares will continue to remain in the names of the trustees.

The Main Disadvantages of Reconstruction

(1)

(*a*) Under the present discretionary trust, if a discretionary beneficiary dies there is no charge to taxation be it capital gains tax, capital transfer tax or income tax.

(*b*) Under the reconstructed trust, after the beneficiaries have become entitled to the income from the trust capital, the capital will be treated as part of their estates and a proportion of the trust fund will be chargeable to capital transfer tax on their deaths.

(2)

(*a*) At present, the income arising in the trust can be accumulated until 1993. This income is taxed at only 48 per cent and once accumulated can then be transferred out to the beneficiary free from further income tax. Alternatively, it does not have to be accumulated: it can be paid out direct to a beneficiary and if that beneficiary has a tax rate of less than 48 per cent he or she can claim back part of the tax suffered by the trust. For example, if we have a beneficiary whose tax rate is 75 per cent we could simply accumulate the income and pay it out to him in the next year and the beneficiary would pay no further tax on it. If another beneficiary has a tax rate of 33 per cent, inclusive of the grossed up payment from the trust, then the trustees would not accumulate the income but would pay it out to him or her as income and he or she could claim back 15 per cent tax from the Revenue, ie, the trust paid 48 per cent tax and the beneficiary's tax rate is 33 per cent, therefore he can claim back 15 per cent. This ability to convert income into capital or leave it as income is one of the chief advantages of the discretionary trust provided of course that income is accruing in the trust.

(*b*) That advantage would be basically lost if we were to carry out the major reconstruction. The reason is that as and when the income arises from the shares this must be paid to the beneficiary who is entitled to the shares because of his interest in possession, regardless of his tax rate, and it will come to the beneficiary as investment income. Thus, beneficiaries with high tax rates would be inclined to leave the income inside the discretionary trust.

(*c*) The problem could be partly cured by leaving in the discretionary trust the shares which are earmarked for a particular beneficiary who has a high rate of income tax and appointing out the balance of the trust fund.

The Trustees' Decision

The trustees must decide on one or other of the following courses or a mixture of them. Either they can—

(1) break the trust; or

(2) reconstruct the trust; or

(3) leave the trust discretionary.

Conclusions

(1) Each year, up until the end of March 1980, it becomes more and more expensive to reconstruct the trust, because no doubt the shares are gradually

going up in value and the Government's reliefs become less and less at the end of March in each year until 1980.

(2) A number of people have opted to apply a wait and see rule especially as the Conservatives have said that they will repeal the legislation on capital transfer tax (this is now unlikely). It is more likely that they would modify some of the provisions. As you know, the FA 1978 reduced the amount of charge to capital transfer tax, and had you reconstructed the trust the day before 29 October 1977 you would not have had those reliefs. There might be further reliefs in the future but it is difficult to predict.

(3) It is clear from this report that the decision to reconstruct or wait depends on the beneficiaries (in particular their ages, their state of health and income tax positions), the value of the trust assets and the long-term aims of the trustees. Unless the beneficiaries in question are not in good health or have income tax problems the arguments in favour of reconstructing the trust are very strong.

(4) To make matters more complicated, there has been a decision in the High Court—*Pearson* v *IRC* (see p51, above)—which appears to enable the trust to be reconstructed so that an interest in possession arises where the trustees still have the power to accumulate and capitalize the trust income. In this event we would be able to reconstruct the trust to avoid the capital transfer tax penalties imposed upon discretionary trusts, yet still be in a position to accumulate and capitalize the trust income for as long as the law allows. In the circumstances, if the capitalization of income is important, it seems wise to wait until we have the decision of the Court of Appeal and House of Lords before we decide what action to take; we hope that these will be available before March 1980.

APPENDIX III

TRUSTS FOR COMPANIES

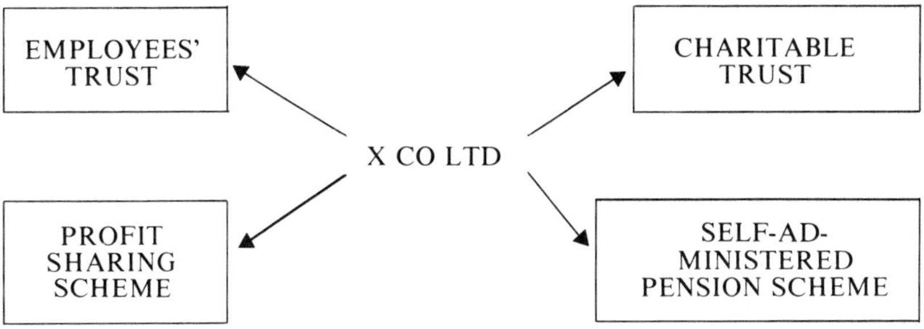

Employees' Trusts

These will be attractive to close and non-close companies. However, close family companies might find them particularly helpful as possible funds to purchase company shares.

Profit Sharing Schemes

These are liable to be attractive mainly to large public companies because of the Revenue requirements.

Charitable Trusts

These are particularly attractive to non-close companies. Part of the funds can be used for the education of company employees' children.

Self-Administered Pension Schemes

These should prove attractive to close and non-close companies.

APPENDIX IV

THE PRINCIPAL TAX AND STAMP DUTY LEGISLATION AFFECTING TRUSTS

INCOME TAX

The principal legislation is to be found in the TA 1970, Pt XVI, and the FA 1973, ss16 and 17.

INCOME AND CORPORATION TAXES ACT 1970

PART XVI

SETTLEMENTS

CHAPTER I

DISPOSITIONS FOR SHORT PERIODS

434. Disposition for period which cannot exceed six years

(1) Any income which, by virtue or in consequence of any disposition made, directly or indirectly, by any person (other than a disposition made for valuable and sufficient consideration), is payable to or applicable for the benefit of any other person for a period which cannot exceed six years shall be deemed for all the purposes of the Income Tax Acts to be the income of the person, if living, by whom the disposition was made, and not to be the income of any other person.

(2) In this Chapter, unless the context otherwise requires, "disposition" includes any trust, covenant, agreement or arrangement.

435. Adjustments between disponor and trustees

(1) Where, by virtue of this Chapter, any income tax becomes chargeable on and is paid by the person by whom a disposition was made, that person shall be entitled—

(*a*) to recover from any trustee or other person to whom the income is payable by virtue or in consequence of the disposition the amount of the tax so paid; and

(*b*) for that purpose to require . . .[1] an inspector to furnish him a certificate specifying the amount of the income in respect of which he has so paid tax and the amount of the tax so paid,

and any certificate so furnished shall be conclusive evidence of the facts appearing thereby.

(2) Where any person obtains in respect of any allowance or relief a repayment of income tax in excess of the amount of the repayment to which he would but for the provisions of this Chapter have been entitled, an amount equal to the excess shall be paid by him to the trustee or other person to whom the income is payable by virtue or in consequence of the disposition, or, where there are two or more such persons, shall be apportioned among those persons as the case may require.

If any question arises as to the amount of any payment or as to any apportionment to be made under this subsection, that question shall be decided by the General Commissioners whose decision thereon shall be final.

(3) Subject to section 529 of this Act, any income which is deemed by virtue of this Chapter to be the income of any person shall be deemed to be the highest part of his income.

[1]Words in subs (1) (*b*) repealed by FA 1971, Sched 6, para 59, and Sched 14, Pt II, with effect from the year 1973–74.

436. Application of Chapter I to dispositions where there is more than one disponor

(1) In the case of any disposition where there is more than one person who made the disposition, this Chapter shall, subject to the provisions of this section, have effect in relation to each person who made the disposition as if he were the only person who had made it.

(2) In the case of any such disposition, references in this Chapter to income payable or applicable by virtue or in consequence of the disposition include, in relation to any person making the disposition, only—

(*a*) income from property which that person has provided directly or indirectly for the purposes of the disposition; and

(*b*) income from property representing that property; and

(*c*) income from so much of any property which represents both property provided as aforesaid and other property as, on a just apportionment, represents the property so provided; and
(*d*) income provided directly or indirectly by that person.

(3) In this section references to property which represents other property include references to property which represents accumulated income from that other property.

CHAPTER II

SETTLEMENTS ON CHILDREN

437. The general rule

(1) Where, by virtue or in consequence of any settlement to which this Chapter applies and during the life of the settlor, any income is paid to or for the benefit of a child of the settlor in any year of assessment, the income shall, if at the time of the payment [the child was unmarried and below the age of eighteen][1] be treated for all the purposes of the Income Tax Acts as the income of the settlor for that year and not as the income of any other person.

(2) This Chapter applies to every settlement, wheresoever it was made or entered into, and whether it was made or entered into before or after the passing of this Act, except a settlement made or entered into before 22nd April 1936 which immediately before that date was irrevocable.

Paragraph 18 of Schedule 14 to this Act shall have effect as respects certain earlier settlements on children.

[(3) Income paid to or for the benefit of a child of a settlor shall not be treated as provided in subsection (1) above for any year of assessment in which the aggregate amount of the income paid to or for the benefit of that child, which, but for this subsection, would be so treated by virtue of this Chapter, does not exceed £5.][2]

(4) . . .[2]

(5) This Chapter shall not apply in relation to any income arising under a settlement in any year of assessment for which the settlor is not chargeable to income tax as a resident in the United Kingdom, and references in this Chapter to income shall be construed accordingly.

---

[1]Substituted by FA 1971, s 16 (2) (*b*).
[2]Substituted for subss (3) and (4) by FA 1971, s16 (2) (*d*).

438. Accumulation settlements

(1) Subject to the provisions of this section, for the purposes of this Chapter—

(*a*) income which, by virtue or in consequence of a settlement to which this Chapter applies, is so dealt with that it, or assets representing it, will or may become payable or applicable to or for the benefit of a child of the settlor in the future (whether on the fulfilment of a condition, or the happening of a contingency, or as the result of the exercise of a power or discretion conferred on any person, or otherwise) shall be deemed to be paid to or for the benefit of that child; and

(*b*) any income dealt with as aforesaid which is not required by the settlement to be allocated, at the time when it is so dealt with, to any particular child or children of the settlor shall be deemed to be paid in equal shares to or for the benefit of each of the children to or for the benefit of whom or any of whom the income or assets representing it will or may become payable or applicable.

(2) Where any income is dealt with as mentioned in subsection (1) of this section by virtue or in consequence of a settlement to which this Chapter applies, being a settlement which, at the time when the income is so dealt with, is an irrevocable settlement—

(*a*) the provisions of subsection (1) of this section shall not apply to that income unless and except to the extent that that income consists of, or represents directly or indirectly, sums paid by the settlor which are allowable as deductions in computing his total income; and

(*b*) any sum whatsoever paid thereafter by virtue or in consequence of the settlement, or any enactment relating thereto, to or for the benefit of a child of the settlor, being a child who at the time of the payment is unmarried and [below the age of eighteen][1], shall be deemed for the purposes of that section to be paid as income, unless and except to the extent that the sum so paid together with any other sums previously so paid (whether to that child or to any other child who, at the relevant time, was unmarried and [below the age of eighteen][1] exceeds the aggregate amount of the income which, by virtue or in consequence of the settlement, has been paid to or for the benefit of a child of the settlor, or dealt with as mentioned in subsection (1) of this section, since the date when the settlement took effect or the date when it became irrevocable, whichever is the later.

(3) In subsection (2) (*b*) above "the relevant time" means—

(*a*) in relation to a payment made after the year 1957–58, except a payment made in the year 1958–59 to or for the benefit of a child born after 6th April 1958, and so made by virtue or in consequence of a settlement made before

9th July 1958, the date when the payment was made.

(*b*) in relation to a payment made in or before the year 1957–58, or a payment made in the year 1958–59 and excepted from paragraph (*a*) above, the commencement of the year of assessment in which the payment was made.

[1]Subs (2) (*b*) substituted by FA 1971, s 16 (2) (*c*).

439. Meaning of "irrevocable"

(1) For the purposes of this Chapter, a settlement shall not be deemed to be irrevocable if the terms thereof provide—

(*a*) for the payment to the settlor or, during the life of the settlor, to the wife or husband of the settlor for his or her benefit, or for the application for the benefit of the settlor or, during the life of the settlor, of the wife or husband of the settlor, of any income or assets in any circumstances whatsoever during the life of any child of the settlor to or for the benefit of whom any income, or assets representing it, is or are or may be payable or applicable by virtue or in consequence of the settlement; or

(*b*) for the determination of the settlement by the act or on the default of any person; or

(*c*) for the payment of any penalty by the settlor in the event of his failing to comply with the provisions of the settlement:

Provided that a settlement shall not be deemed to be revocable by reason only—

(i) that it contains a provision under which any income or assets will or may become payable to or applicable for the benefit of the settlor, or the wife or husband of the settlor, on the bankruptcy of any such child as is mentioned in paragraph (*a*) of this subsection or in the event of an assignment of or charge on that income or those assets being executed by such a child; or

(ii) that it provides for the determination of the settlement as aforesaid in such a manner that the determination will not, during the lifetime of any such child as aforesaid, benefit the settlor or the wife or husband of the settlor; or

(iii) in the case of a settlement to which section 33 of the Trustee Act 1925 applies, that it directs income to be held for the benefit of such a child as aforesaid on protective trusts, unless the trust period is a period less than the life of the child or the settlement specifies some event on the happening of which the child would, if the income were payable during the trust period to him absolutely during that period, be deprived of the right to receive the income or part thereof.

(2) In applying section 438 (2) (*b*) above to a settlement subsisting on 6th April 1958 which would have been revocable if, in paragraph (ii) above, in place of the words

"the settlor or the wife or husband of the settlor"

(which were inserted by section 20 (5) of the Finance Act 1958) there stood

"any person other than such a child, or the wife, husband or issue of such a child" the date when it became irrevocable shall be taken as 6th April 1958.

440. Interest paid by trustees[3]

(1) Where interest is paid by the trustees of a settlement to which this Chapter applies there shall be deemed for the purposes of this Chapter to be paid to or for the benefit of a child of the settlor who at the time of the payment is unmarried and [below the age of eighteen][1] (in addition to any other amount deemed to be so paid) an amount

equal to a fraction $\frac{B}{A}$ of the interest, where—

A is the whole of the income arising under the settlement in the year of assessment, less any expenses of the trustees of the settlement paid in that year which, in the absence of any express provision of the settlement, would be properly chargeable to income, and
B in such part of A as is paid to or for the benefit of any child of the settlor who is unmarried and [below the age of eighteen].[1]

(2) This section shall not apply to interest in respect of which relief from tax—
[2] is allowable under any provision of the Income Tax Acts or to interest payable to the settlor or the wife or husband of the settlor (if living with the settlor).

(3) Nothing in this section shall be construed as affecting the liability of tax of the person receiving or entitled to the interest.

(4) For the purpose of this section—

"income arising under the settlement" has the meaning given by section 454 below, which for that purpose shall be deemed to apply in relation to settlements to which this Chapter applies as it applies in relation to settlements to which Chapter III below applies, and the reference to the trustees' expenses excludes sums mentioned in section 455 (*a*) below (sums distributed to beneficiaries).

[1]Words in subs (1) were substituted by FA 1971, s 16 (2) (*c*).

[2]Words in subs (2) repealed by FA 1971, ss 37 (1), 38 (1) and Sched 6, para 60, with effect from the year 1973–74.

[3]This section was repealed by FA 1972, Sched 28, Pt V, but restored (as amended by FA 1971) by FA 1974, Sched 1, para 27 as regards interest paid after 26 March 1974.

441. Adjustments between disponor and trustees

(1) Where, by virtue of this Chapter, any income tax becomes chargeable on and is paid by the person by whom a settlement was made or entered into, that person shall be entitled—

(*a*) to recover from any trustee or other person to whom the income is payable by virtue or in consequence of the settlement the amount of the tax so paid; and

(*b*) for that purpose to require—[1] an inspector to furnish to him a certificate specifying the amount of income in respect of which he has so paid tax and the amount of the tax so paid,

and any certificate so furnished shall be conclusive evidence of the facts appearing thereby.

(2) Where any person obtains in respect of any allowance or relief a repayment of income tax in excess of the amount of the repayment to which he would but for the provisions of this Chapter have been entitled, an amount equal to the excess shall be paid by him to the trustee or other person to whom the income is payable by virtue or in consequence of the settlement, or, where there are two or more such persons, shall be apportioned among those persons as the case may require.

If any question arises as to the amount of any payment or as to any apportionment to be made under this subsection, that question shall be decided by the General Commissioners whose decision thereon shall be final.

(3) Subject to section 529 of this Act, any income which is deemed by virtue of this Chapter to be the income of any person shall be deemed to be the highest part of his income.

[1]Words in subs (1) (*b*) repealed by FA 1971, Sched 6, para 61 and Sched 14, Pt II, with effect from the year 1973–74.

442. Application of Chapter II to settlements with more than one settlor

(1) In the case of any settlement where there is more than one settlor, this Chapter shall, subject to the provisions of this section, have effect in relation to each settlor as if he were the only settlor.

(2) In the case of any such settlement as aforesaid, only the following can, for the purposes of this Chapter, be taken into account, in relation to any settlor, as income paid by virtue or in consequence of the settlement to or for the benefit of a child of the settlor, that is to say—

(*a*) income originating from the settlor; and
(*b*) in a case in which paragraph (*b*) of subsection (2) of section 438 of this Act applies.

any sums which are under that paragraph to be deemed to be paid as income:

Provided that in applying the said paragraph (*b*) to any settlor—

(i) the references to sums paid by virtue or in consequence of the settlement or any enactment relating thereto include only sums paid out of property originating from that settlor or income originating from that settlor; and
(ii) the reference to income which by virtue or in consequence of the settlement has been paid to or for the benefit of a child of the settlor or dealt with as mentioned in subsection (1) of that section includes only income originating from that settlor.

(3) References in this section to property originating from a settlor are references to—

(*a*) property which that settlor has provided directly or indirectly for the purposes of the settlement; and
(*b*) property representing that property; and
(*c*) so much of any property which represents both property provided as aforesaid and other property as, on a just apportionment, represents the property so provided.

(4) References in this section to income originating from a settlor are references to—

(*a*) income from property originating from that settlor; and
(*b*) income provided directly or indirectly by that settlor.

(5) In subsections (3) and (4) of this section—

(*a*) references to property or income which a settlor has provided directly or indirectly include references to property or income which has been provided directly or indirectly by another person in pursuance of reciprocal arrangements with that settlor but do not include references to property or income which that settlor has provided directly or indirectly in pursuance of reciprocal arrangements with another person; and

(*b*) references to property which represents other property include references to property which represents accumulated income from that other property.

443. Power to obtain information under Chapter II

. . .[1] an inspector may by notice in writing require any party to a settlement to [furnish him within such time as he may direct][2] (not being less than twenty-eight days) with such particulars as [he thinks][2] necessary for the purposes of this Chapter.

[1]Words repealed by FA 1971, Sched 6, para 62 and Sched 14, Pt II, with effect from the year 1973–74.

[2]Words substituted by FA 1971, Sched 6, para 62, with effect from the year 1973–74.

444. Interpretation of Chapter II

(1) In this Chapter "child" includes a stepchild, an adopted child and an illegitimate child . . .[1].

(2) In this Chapter—

"settlement" includes any disposition, trust, covenant, agreement, arrangement or transfer of assets;

"settlor", in relation to a settlement, includes any person by whom the settlement was made or entered into directly or indirectly, and in particular (but without prejudice to the generality of the preceding words of this definition) includes any person who has provided or undertaken to provide funds directly or indirectly for the purpose of the settlement, or has made with any other person a reciprocal arrangement for that other person to make or enter into the settlement;

"income", except in the phrase (occurring in section 437 (1) above) "be treated for all the purposes of the Income Tax Acts as the income of the settlor for that year and not as the income of any other person", includes any income chargeable to income tax by deduction or otherwise and any income which would have been so chargeable if it had been received in the

United Kingdom by a person resident and ordinarily resident in the United Kingdom.

(3), (4)[2].

[1]Words in subs (1) repealed by FA 1971, Sched 14, Pt VII.
[2]Subss (3) and (4) repealed by FA 1971, Sched 14, Pt IV.

CHAPTER III

REVOCABLE SETTLEMENTS, ETC

445. Revocable settlements allowing release of obligation

(1) If and so long as the terms of any settlement (wherever made) are such that—

(*a*) any person has or may have power, whether immediately or in the future, and whether with or without the consent of any other person, to revoke or otherwise determine the settlement or any provision thereof and, in the event of the exercise of the power, the settlor or the wife or husband of the settlor will or may cease to be liable to make any annual payments payable by virtue or in consequence of any provision of the settlement; or
(*b*) the settlor or the wife or husband of the settlor may, whether immediately or in the future, cease, on the payment of a penalty, to be liable to make any annual payments payable by virtue or in consequence of any provision of the settlement,

any sums payable by the settlor or the wife or husband of the settlor by virtue or in consequence of that provision of the settlement in any year of assessment shall be treated for all the purposes of the Income Tax Acts as the income of the settlor for that year and not as the income of any other person:

Provided that, where any such power as is referred to in paragraph (*a*) of this subsection cannot be exercised within the period of six years from the time when the first of the annual payments so referred to becomes payable, and the like annual payments are payable in each year throughout that period, the said paragraph (*a*) shall not apply so long as the said power cannot be exercised.

(2) In subsection (1) above—

(*a*) the references to a power to revoke or otherwise determine a settlement or any provision thereof shall be deemed to include references to any power to diminish the amount of any payments which are or may be payable under the settlement or any provision thereof and to any power to diminish the amount of any annual payments which the settlor or the wife or husband of the settlor is or may be liable to make by virtue or in consequence of any provision of the settlement;

(*b*) the references to the settlor or the wife or husband of the settlor ceasing to be liable to make any annual payments payable by virtue or in consequence of any provision of the settlement shall be deemed to include references to a diminution of the amount of any such annual payments which the settlor or the wife or husband of the settlor is or may be liable to make;

but the sums to be treated under the said subsection (1) as the income of the settlor for any year of assessment and not as the income of any other person shall, where that subsection would not apply but for paragraph (*b*) of this subsection, be such part only of the sums payable as aforesaid by the settlor or the wife or husband of the settlor in that year as corresponds to the diminution mentioned in that paragraph.

(3) Where, in the case of any settlement made before 16th April 1958, any sums payable by the settlor or by the wife or husband of the settlor would, by virtue of subsection (2) above, fall to be treated as the income of the settlor and not as the income of any other person, but would not fall to be so treated apart from that subsection, the sums shall not be so treated if—

(*a*) no power by reason of which they would fall to be so treated has been exercised after 15th April 1958, or is or can become exercisable after 5th April 1959, or such later date as the Board may in any particular case allow, and

(*b*) neither the settlor nor the wife or husband of the settlor has received or is entitled to any consideration or benefit in connection with the fulfilment of the condition set out in paragraph (*a*) of this subsection,

or if the settlement was entered into in connection with any judicial separation or any agreement between spouses to live separate and apart, or with the dissolution or annulment of a marriage.

446. Revocable settlements allowing reversion of property

(1) If and so long as the terms of any settlement (wherever made) are such that—

(*a*) any person has or may have power, whether immediately or in the future, and whether with or without the consent of any other person, to revoke or otherwise determine the settlement or any provision thereof; and

(*b*) in the event of the exercise of the power, the settlor or the wife or husband of the settlor will or may become beneficially entitled to the whole or any part of the property then comprised in the settlement or of the income arising from the whole or any part of the property so comprised,

any income arising under the settlement from the property comprised in the settlement in any year of assessment or from a corresponding part of that property, or a corresponding part of any such income, as the case may be, shall be treated for all the purposes of the Income Tax Acts as the income of the settlor for that year and not as the income of any other person:

Provided that, where any such power as aforesaid cannot be exercised within six years from the time when any particular property first becomes comprised in the settlement, this subsection shall not apply to income arising under the settlement from that property, or from property representing that property, so long as the power cannot be exercised.

(2) In subsection (1) above the references to a power to revoke or otherwise determine a settlement or any provision thereof shall be deemed to include references to—

(*a*) any power to diminish the property comprised in the settlement; and

(*b*) any power to diminish the amount of any payments which are or may be payable under the settlement or any provision thereof to any person other than the settlor and the wife or husband of the settlor.

(3) Where, in the case of any settlement made before 16th April 1958, any income arising under the settlement would, by virtue of subsection (2) above, fall to be treated as the income of the settlor and not as the income of any other person, but would not fall to be so treated apart from that subsection, the income shall not be so treated if—

(*a*) no power by reason of which it would fall to be so treated has been exercised after 15th April 1958 or is or can become exercisable after 5th April 1959, or such later date as the Board may in any particular case allow; and

(*b*) neither the settlor nor the wife or husband of the settlor has received or is entitled to any consideration or benefit in connection with the fulfilment of the condition set out in paragraph (*a*) of this subsection.

447. Settlements where settlor retains an interest

(1) If and so long as the settlor has an interest in any income arising under or property comprised in a settlement (wherever made), any income so arising during the life of the settlor in any year of assessment shall, to the extent to

which it is not distributed, be treated for all the purposes of the Income Tax Acts as the income of the settlor for that year and not as the income of any other person:

Provided that—

(*a*) if and so long as that interest is an interest neither in the whole of the income arising under the settlement nor in the whole of the property comprised in the settlement, the amount of income to be treated as the income of the settlor by virtue of this subsection shall be such part of the income which, but for this proviso, would be so treated as is proportionate to the extent of that interest; and
(*b*) where it is shown that any amount of the income which is not distributed in any year of assessment consists of income which falls to be treated as the income of the settlor for that year by virtue of section 445 or 446 above, that amount shall be deducted from the amount of income which, but for this proviso, would be treated as his for that year by virtue of this subsection.

(2) For the purpose of subsection (1) of this section, the settlor shall be deemed to have an interest in income arising under or property comprised in a settlement if any income or property which may at any time arise under or be comprised in that settlement is, or will or may become, payable to or applicable for the benefit of the settlor or the wife or husband of the settlor in any circumstances whatsoever:

Provided that the settlor shall not be deemed to have an interest in any income arising under or property comprised in a settlement—

(*a*) if and so long as that income or property cannot become payable or applicable as aforesaid except in the event of—

(i) the bankruptcy of some person who is or may become beneficially entitled to that income or property; or
(ii) any assignment of or charge on that income or property being made or given by some such person; or
(iii) in the case of a marriage settlement, the death of both the parties to the marriage and of all or any of the children of the marriage; or
(iv) the death under the age of twenty-five or some lower age of some person who would be beneficially entitled to that income or property on attaining that age; or

(*b*) if and so long as some person is alive and under the age of twenty-five during whose life that income or property cannot become payable or applicable as aforesaid except in the event of that person becoming bankrupt or assigning or charging his interest in that income or property.

448. Settlements: discretionary power for benefit of settlor, etc.

(1) If and so long as the terms of any settlement (wherever made) are such that any person has or may have power, whether immediately or in the future, and whether with or without the consent of any person—

(*a*) to pay or apply to or for the benefit of the settlor or the wife or husband of the settlor the whole or any part of the income or property which may at any time arise under or be comprised in the settlement; or

(*b*) to secure the payment or application to or for the benefit of the settlor or the wife or husband of the settlor of the whole or any part of that income or property,

being a power exercisable at his discretion, any income arising under the settlement in any year of assessment or, as the case may be, any income so arising from the property comprised in the settlement or from a corresponding part of that property, or a corresponding part of any such income, shall (so far is it is not so treated apart from this section) be treated for all the purposes of the Income Tax Acts as the income of the settlor for that year and not as the income of any other person, subject however to the following provisions of this section.

(2) Where the power mentioned in subsection (1) of this section cannot be exercised within six years from the time when any income or class of income first arises under the settlement or from the time when any particular property first becomes comprised in the settlement, then, so long as the power cannot be exercised, that subsection shall not apply to any income arising under the settlement or, as the case may be, any income of that class or income from that property or property representing that property.

(3) Where, under the proviso to section 447 (2) above, the settlor is not deemed to have an interest in any income arising under or property comprised in the settlement, subsection (1) of this section shall not apply to that income or, as the case may be, to income arising from that property.

(4) Where, in the case of any settlement made before 9th July 1958, any income arising under the settlement would, by virtue of the preceding provisions of this section, fall to be treated as the income of the settlor and not as the income of any other person, but would not fall to be so treated apart from those provisions, it shall not be so treated if—

(*a*) no power by reason of which it would fall to be so treated has been exercised after 8th July 1958, or is or can become exercisable after 5th April 1959, or such later date as the Board may in any particular case allow; and

(*b*) neither the settlor nor the wife or husband of the settlor has received or is entitled to any consideration or benefit in connection with the fulfilment of the condition set out in paragraph (*a*) of this subsection.

449. Provisions supplemental to preceding provisions of Chapter III

(1) Tax chargeable . . .[1] by virtue of the preceding provisions of this Chapter shall be charged under Case VI of Schedule D.

(2) In computing the liability to income tax of a settlor chargeable by virtue of any of the said preceding provisions, the same deductions and reliefs shall be allowed as would have been allowed if the income treated as his by virtue of that provision had been received by him.

(3) Where, by virtue of any of the said preceding provisions, any income tax becomes chargeable on and is paid by a settlor, he shall be entitled—

(*a*) to recover from any trustee, or other person to whom income arises under the settlement, the amount of the tax so paid; and

(*b*) for that purpose to require—[1] an inspector to furnish to him a certificate specifying the amount of income in respect of which he has so paid tax and the amount of tax so paid.

Any certificate so furnished shall be conclusive evidence of the facts stated therein.

(4) Where any person obtains, in respect of any allowance or relief, a repayment of income tax in excess of the amount of the repayment to which he would, but for any of the said preceding provisions, have been entitled, an amount equal to the excess shall be paid by him to the trustee or other person to whom income arises under the settlement, or, where there are two or more such persons, shall be apportioned among those persons as the case may require.

If any question arises as to the amount of any payment or as to any apportionment to be made under this subsection, that question shall be decided by the General Commissioners whose decision thereon shall be final.

(5) Subject to section 529 of this Act, any income which is treated by virtue of any of the said preceding provisions as income of a settlor shall be deemed for the purpose of this section to be the highest part of his income.

[1]Words repealed by FA 1971, Sched 6, para 63, and Sched 14, Pt II, with effect from the year 1973–74.

450. Disallowance of deduction from total income of certain sums paid by settlor

(1) Where, by virtue or in consequence of any settlement to which this section applies, the settlor pays directly or indirectly in any year of assessment to the trustees of the settlement any sums which would, but for this subsection, be allowable as deductions in computing his total income for that year—[2] those

sums shall not be so allowable to the extent to which the aggregate amount thereof falls within the amount of income arising under the settlement in that year which has not been distributed, less—

(*a*) so much of any income arising under the settlement in that year which has not been distributed as is shown to consist of income which has been treated as the income of the settlor by virtue of section 445, 446 or 448 above, and

(*b*) the amount of income so arising in that year which is treated as the income of the settlor by virtue of section 447 above.

(2) For the purposes of subsection (1) of this section, any sum paid in any year of assessment by the settlor to any body corporate connected with the settlement in that year shall be treated as if it had been paid to the trustees of the settlement in that year by virtue or in consequence of the settlement.

(3) No relief shall be given under any of the provisions of the Income Tax Acts on account of tax paid in respect of so much of any income arising under a settlement in any year of assessment as is equal to the aggregate amount of any sums paid by the settlor in that year which are not allowable as deductions by virtue of this section.

(4) This section shall apply to any settlement (wherever made) made after 26th April 1938, and where income arising under any settlement (wherever made) made on or before that date is treated as the income of the settlor by virtue of section 445 or 446 above but ceases to be so treated by reason of any variation of the terms of the settlement made after that date, or would have been so treated but for such a variation, this section shall apply to that settlement as from the date when the variation takes effect.

(5) In this section, references to sums paid by a settlor include references to sums paid by the wife or husband of the settlor.

---

[1]Words repealed by FA 1971, Sched 14, Pt II, with effect from the year 1973–74.

---

451. Sums paid to settlor otherwise than as income

(1) Any capital sum paid directly or indirectly in any relevant year of assessment by the trustees of a settlement to which this section applies to the settlor shall—

(*a*) to the extent to which the amount of that sum falls within the amount of income available up to the end of that year, be treated for all the purposes of the Income Tax Acts as the income of the settlor for that year;

(*b*) to the extent to which the amount of that sum exceeds the amount of income available up to the end of that year but falls within the amount of the income available up to the end of the next following year, be treated for the purposes aforesaid as the income of the settlor for the next following year,

and so on.

(2) For the purposes of subsection (1) of this section, the amount of income available up to the end of any year shall, in relation to any capital sum paid as aforesaid, be taken to be the aggregate amount of income arising under the settlement in that year and any previous relevant year which has not been distributed, less—

(*a*) the amount of any other capital sums paid to the settlor in any relevant year before that sum was paid, and
(*b*) so much of any income arising under the settlement in that year and any previous relevant year which has not been distributed as is shown to consist of income which has been treated as income of the settlor by virtue of section 445, 446 or 448 above, and
(*c*) any income arising under the settlement in that year and any previous relevant year which has been treated as the income of the settlor by virtue of section 447 above, and
(*d*) any sums paid by virtue or in consequence of the settlement, to the extent that they are not allowable, by virtue of section 450 above, as deductions in computing the settlor's income for that year or any previous relevant year, and
(*e*) an amount equal to [the sum of tax at the basic rate and tax at the additional rate][2] on—

(i) the aggregate amount of income arising under the settlement in that year and any previous relevant year which has not been distributed, less
(ii) the aggregate amount of the income and sums referred to in paragraphs (*b*), (*c*) and (*d*) of this subsection.

(3) Where any amount is included in a person's income by virtue of section 287 of this Act (assessment in respect of loan from close company) in respect of any loan or advance, there shall be corresponding reduction in the amount (if any) afterwards falling to be so included in respect of it by virtue of this section.

(4) For the purpose of this section, any capital sum paid to the settlor in any year of assessment by any body corporate connected with the settlement in that year shall be treated as having been paid by the trustees of the settlement in that year.

(5) Where the whole or any part of any sum is treated by virtue of this section as income of the settlor for any year, it shall be treated as income of such an amount as, after deduction [of both tax at the basic rate and tax at the

additional rate for that year,][2] would be equal to that sum or that part thereof.

(6) Tax chargeable[1] by virtue of this section shall be charged under Case VI of Schedule D.

(7) In computing the liability to income tax of a settlor chargeable by virtue of this section, the same deductions and reliefs shall be allowed as would have been allowed if the amount treated as his income by virtue of this section had been received by him as income.

(8) This section applies to any settlement wherever made, and whether made before or after the passing of this Act, and in this section—

"capital sum" means—

(i) any sum paid by way of loan or repayment of a loan; and

(ii) any other sum paid otherwise than as income, being a sum which is not paid for full consideration in money or money's worth,

but does not include any sum which could not have become payable to the settlor except in one of the events specified in the proviso to section 447 (2) above, and

"relevant year" means any year of assessment after the year 1937–38, and

references to sums paid to the settlor include references to sums paid to the wife or husband of the settlor.

---

[1]Words repealed by FA 1971, Sched 6, para 64 and Sched 14, Pt II, with effect from the year 1973–74.

[2]Words in subss (2) (*e*) and (5) substituted by FA 1973, s 16 (7).

---

452. Application of Chapter III to settlements where there is more than one settlor

(1) In the case of any settlement where there is more than one settlor, this Chapter shall, subject to the provisions of this section, have effect in relation to each settlor as if he were the only settlor.

(2) References in this Chapter to the property comprised in a settlement include, in relation to any settlor, only property originating from that settlor and references in this Chapter to income arising under the settlement include, in relation to any settlor, only income originating from that settlor.

(3) In considering for the purposes of this Chapter, in relation to any settlor, whether any, and if so, how much, of the income arising under the settlement has been distributed, any sums paid partly out of income originating from that settlor and partly out of other income must (so far as not apportioned by the terms of the settlement) be apportioned evenly over all that income.

(4) References in sections 445 (1) and 450 above to sums payable by virtue or in consequence of any provision of the settlement or sums paid by virtue or in consequence of the settlement include, in relation to any settlor, only sums payable or paid by that settlor.

(5) References in this section to property originating from a settlor are references to—

(*a*) property which that settlor has provided directly or indirectly for the purposes of the settlement; and
(*b*) property representing that property; and
(*c*) so much of any property which represents both property provided as aforesaid and other property as, on a just apportionment, represents the property so provided.

(6) References in this section to income originating from a settlor are references to—

(*a*) income from property originating from that settlor; and
(*b*) so much of any such income of a body corporate as is mentioned in section 454 (1) (*b*) below as corresponds to property originating from the settlor which is comprised in the settlement; and
(*c*) income provided directly or indirectly by that settlor.

(7) In subsections (5) and (6) of this section—

(*a*) references to property or income which a settlor has provided directly or indirectly include references to property or income which has been provided directly or indirectly by another person in pursuance of reciprocal arrangements with that settlor, but do not include references to property or income which that settlor has provided directly or indirectly in pursuance of reciprocal arrangements with another person; and
(*b*) references to property which represents other property include references to property which represents accumulated income from that other property.

453. Power to obtain information for purposes of Chapter III

—[1] an inspector may by notice in writing require any person, being a party to a settlement, to [furnish him within such time as he may direct][2] (not being less than twenty-eight days) with such particulars as [he thinks][2] necessary for the purposes of any of the provisions of this Chapter.

[1]Words repealed by FA 1971, Sched 6, para 65 and Sched 14, Pt II, with effect from the year 1973–74.
[2]Words substituted by FA 1971, Sched 6, para 65, with effect from the year 1973–74.

454. Interpretation of Chapter III

(1) In this Chapter, "income arising under a settlement" includes—

(*a*) any income chargeable to income tax by deduction or otherwise, and any income which would have been so chargeable if it had been received in the United Kingdom; and by a person domiciled, resident and ordinarily resident in the United Kingdom; and

(*b*) where the amount of the income of any body corporate has been apportioned [under Schedule 16 to the Finance Act 1972 or (as respects income of accounting periods ending before 6th April 1973)][2] under section 296 of this Act (close companies), or (as respects income arising before the year 1966–67) under Chapter III of Part IX of the Income Tax Act 1952, for any year or period, or could have been so apportioned if the body corporate were incorporated in any part of the United Kingdom, so much of the income of the body corporate for that year or period as is equal to the amount which has been or could have been so apportioned to the trustees of or a beneficiary under the settlement.

But, where the settlor is not domiciled, or not resident, or not ordinarily resident, in the United Kingdom in any year of assessment, does not include income arising under the settlement in that year in respect of which the settlor, if he were actually entitled thereto, would not be chargeable to income tax by deduction or otherwise by reason of his not being so domiciled, resident or ordinarily resident.

[Where the income of a body corporate has been, or could have been, apportioned under Schedule 16 to the Finance Act 1972 any amount of that income which by virtue of paragraph (*b*) above is to be included in the income arising under a settlement shall be increased by such proportion thereof as corresponds to the rate of advance corporation tax applicable to a distribution made at the end of the accounting period to which the apportionment relates.][2]

(2)[1].

(3) In this Chapter, "settlement" includes any disposition, trust, covenant, agreement or arrangement, and "settlor", in relation to a settlement, means any person by whom the settlement was made; and a person shall be deemed for the purposes of this Chapter to have made a settlement if he has made or entered into the settlement directly or indirectly, and in particular (but without prejudice to the generality of the preceding words) if he has provided or undertaken to provide funds directly or indirectly for the purpose of the settlement, or has made with any other person a reciprocal arrangement for that other person to make or enter into the settlement.

(4) For the purposes of this Chapter, a body corporate shall be deemed to be connected with a settlement in any year of assessment if it is at any time in the year a close company (or only not a close company because it is not resident in the United Kingdom) and the participators then include the trustees of or a beneficiary under the settlement.

(5) In relation to income arising before the year 1966–67 subsection (4) above shall not apply and, for the purposes of this Chapter, a body corporate shall be deemed to have been connected with a settlement in any year of assessment if any of the income thereof for any year or period ending in that year of assessment—

(*a*) has been apportioned to the trustees of or a beneficiary under the settlement under Chapter III of Part IX of the Income Tax 1952, or could have been so apportioned if the body corporate had been incorporated in the United Kingdom, or
(*b*) could have been so apportioned if the income of the body corporate for that year or period had not been distributed to the members thereof and, in the case of a body corporate incorporated outside the United Kingdom, if the body corporate had been incorporated in the United Kingdom.

(6) The provisions of this Chapter shall be in addition to and not in derogation of any other provisions of this Act.

---

[1]Repealed by FA 1971, Sched 14, Pt IV.
[2]Words in subs (1) (*b*) and paragraph at the end of the subsection inserted by FA 1972, s 111 (3) and Sched 24, para 26, with effect from 6 April 1973.

---

455. Ascertainment of undistributed income

For the purposes of this Chapter, income arising under a settlement in any year of assessment shall be deemed not to have been distributed if and to the extent that it exceeds the aggregate amount of—

(*a*)[1] the sums, excluding all payments of interest, paid in that year by the trustees of the settlement to any persons (not being a body corporate connected with the settlement and not being the trustees of another settlement made by the settlor or the trustees of the settlement) in such manner that they fall to be treated in that year, otherwise than by virtue of section 451 above, as the income of those persons for the purposes of income tax, or would fall to be so treated if those persons were domiciled, resident and ordinarily resident in the United Kingdom and the sums had been paid to them therein, and (*b*)[1] subject to section 456 below, any expenses of the trustees of the settlement paid in that year which, in the absence of any express provision of the settlement, would be properly chargeable to income, in so far as such expenses are not included in the sums mentioned in paragraph (*a*) of this section, and

(*c*) in a case where the trustees of the settlement are trustees for charitable purposes, the amount by which any income arising under the settlement in that year in respect of which exemption from tax may be granted under section 360 of this Act exceeds the aggregate amount of any such sums or expenses as aforesaid paid in that year which are properly chargeable to that income.

[1]Words in paras (*a*) and (*b*) were repealed by FA 1972, Sched 28, Pt V and restored by FA 1974, Sched 1, para 27 as regards interest paid after 26 March 1974.

456. Ascertainment of undistributed income: interest paid by trustees[2]

(1) Paragraph (*b*) of section 455 above shall apply to any interest paid by the trustees of the settlement subject to the provisions of this section.

(2) If no sums within paragraph (*a*) of that section were paid to any person other than the settlor, or the wife or husband of the settlor, the whole of the interest shall be excluded from the said paragraph (*b*).

(3) If any sum was so paid, there shall be excluded from the said paragraph (*b*) a fraction $\frac{A-B}{A}$ of the interest where—

A is the whole of the income arising under the settlement in the year of assessment, less the sums referred to in the said paragraph (*b*) apart from this section, and B is so much of the sums within the said paragraph (*a*) as is paid to persons other than the settlor, or the wife or husband of the settlor.

(4) This section shall not apply to interest in respect of which relief from tax[1] is allowable under any provision of the Income Tax Acts or to interest payable to the settlor or the wife or husband of the settlor (if living with the settlor).

(5) Nothing in this section shall be construed as affecting the liability to tax of the person receiving or entitled to the interest.

[1]Words in subs (4) repealed by FA 1971, ss 37 (1), 38 (1) and Sched 6, para 66, with effect from the year 1973–74.

[2]This section was repealed by FA 1972, Sched 28, Pt V, but restored (as amended by FA 1971) by FA 1974, Sched 1, para 27. It only applies to interest paid after 26 March 1974.

CHAPTER IV

"SURTAX" LIABILITY OF SETTLORS IN CERTAIN CASES

457. Settlements made on or after 7th April 1965

(1) Where, during the life of the settlor, income arising under a settlement made on or after 7th April 1965 is, under the settlement and in the events that occur, payable to or applicable for the benefit of any person other than the settlor, then, unless, under the settlement and in the said events, the income either—

(*a*) consists of annual payments made under a partnership agreement to or for the benefit of a former member, or the widow or dependants of a deceased former member, of the partnership, being payments made under a liability incurred for full consideration, or
(*b*) is excluded by subsection (2) below, or
(*c*) is income arising under a settlement made by one party to a marriage by way of provision for the other after the dissolution or annulment of the marriage, or while they are separated under an order of a court or under a separation agreement or in such circumstances that the separation is likely to be permanent, being income payable to or applicable for the benefit of that other party, or
(*d*) is income from property of which the settlor has divested himself absolutely by the settlement, or
(*e*) is income which, by virtue of some provision of the Income Tax Acts not contained in this Chapter, is to be treated for the purposes of those Acts as income of the settlor,

[the income shall, for the purposes of excess liability, be treated as the income of the settlor and not as the income of any other person.

In this subsection "excess liability" means the excess of liability to income tax over what it would be if all income tax were charged at the basic rate to the exclusion of any other rate.][1]

(2) Subsection (1) above shall not apply to income consisting of annual payments made by an individual, in connection with the acquisition by him of the whole or part of a business—

(*a*) to or for the benefit of the individual from whom it is acquired or, if he is dead, to or for the benefit of his widow or dependants, or
(*b*) if the acquisition was from a partnership, to or for the benefit of a former member, or the widow or dependants of a deceased former member, of that or any preceding partnership, or to or for the benefit of an individual

from whom the business or part was acquired by that or any preceding partnership or, if he is dead, to or for the benefit of the widow or dependants of such an individual,

being payments made under a liability incurred for full consideration.

(3) Payments made in respect of any individual under a liability incurred in connection with an acquisition from a partnership shall only be excluded from the operation of subsection (1) above by virtue of subsection (2) (*b*) above if, and to the extent that, they are made in substitution for, or matched by reductions in, other payments which would themselves be excluded from its operation.

(4) Where the right of a former member of a partnership to payments falling due not more than ten years after he ceased to be a member of that partnership has devolved on his death, subsections (1) (*a*) and (2) above shall apply to the payments as they would apply if he had not died.

(5) For the purposes of this section—

(*a*) "former member", in relation to a partnership, means an individual who has ceased to be a member of that partnership on retirement or death,
(*b*) a partnership becomes a "preceding partnership" of another if it transfers its business or part of its business to another and one or more individuals are members of both, and any preceding partnership of the transferor by reference to any part of the business transferred shall also become a preceding partnership of the transferee.

(6) The settlor shall not be deemed for the purposes of this section to have divested himself absolutely of any property if that property or any income therefrom or any property directly or indirectly representing proceeds of, or of income from, that property or any income therefrom is, or will or may become, payable to or applicable for the benefit of the settlor or the wife or husband of the settlor in any circumstances whatsoever:

Provided that a settlor shall not be deemed not to have divested himself absolutely of any property by reason only that the property or income therefrom or any such other property or income as aforesaid may become payable or applicable as aforesaid in the event of—

(*a*) the bankruptcy of some person who is or may become beneficially entitled to any such property or income; or
(*b*) an assignment of or charge on any such property or income being made or given by some such person; or
(*c*) in the case of a marriage settlement, the death of both parties to the marriage and of all or any of the children of the marriage; or

(*d*) the death under the age of twenty-five or some lower age of some person who would be beneficially entitled to that property or income on attaining that age.

[1]Words at the end of subs (1) substituted by FA 1971, Sched 6, para 67, with effect from the year 1973–74.

458. Settlements made before 7th April 1965, but on or after 10th April 1946

(1) Where, during the life of the settlor, income arising under a settlement made before 7th April 1965, but on or after 10th April 1946, is, under the settlement and in the events that occur, payable to or applicable for the benefit of any person other than the settlor, then, unless under the settlement and in the said events, the income either—

(*a*) is payable to an individual for his own use, or
(*b*) is applicable for the benefit of an individual named in that behalf in the settlement or of two or more individuals named in that behalf therein, or
(*c*) is applicable for the benefit of a child or children of an individual named in that behalf in the settlement, or
(*d*) is income from property of which the settlor has divested himself absolutely by the settlement, or
(*e*) is income which, by virtue of some provision of the Income Tax Acts not contained in this Chapter, is to be treated for the purposes of those Acts as income of the settlor,

[the income shall, for the purposes of excess liability, be treated as the income of the settlor and not as the income of any other person.

In this subsection "excess liability" means the excess of liability to income tax over what it would be if all income tax were charged at the basic rate to the exclusion of any other rate][1]:

Provided that the exceptions provided for by paragraphs (*a*), (*b*) and (*c*) of this subsection shall not apply where the named individual or individuals or, in the case of the said paragraph (*c*), either the named individual or the child or any of the children in question, is in the service of the settlor or accustomed to act as the solicitor or agent of the settlor.

(2) The settlor shall not be deemed for the purposes of this section to have divested himself absolutely of any property if that property or any income therefrom or any property directly or indirectly representing proceeds of, or of income from, that property or any income therefrom is, or will or may

become, payable to him or applicable for his benefit in any circumstances whatsoever:

Provided that a settlor shall not be deemed not to have divested himself absolutely of any property by reason only that that property or income therefrom or any such other property or income as aforesaid may become payable to him or applicable for his benefit in the event of—

(*a*) the bankruptcy of some person who is or may become beneficially entitled to any such property or income, or
(*b*) an assignment of or charge on any such property or income being made or given by some such person, or
(*c*) in the case of a marriage settlement, the death of both parties to the marriage and of all or any of the children of the marriage, or
(*d*) the death under the age of twenty-five or some lower age of some person who would be beneficially entitled to that property or income on attaining that age.

[1]Words in subs (1) substituted by FA 1971, Sched 6, para 68, with effect from the year 1973–74.

459. Supplemental provisions for Chapter IV

(1) In this Chapter "income arising under a settlement", "settlement" and "settlor" have the meanings assigned to them for the purposes of Chapter III above by section 454 above.

(2) Section 452 above shall have effect in relation to this Chapter as it has effect in relation to Chapter III above.

FINANCE ACT 1973

PART III

16. Charge to additional rate of certain income of discretionary trusts

(1) So far as income arising to trustees is income to which this section applies it shall, in addition to being chargeable to income tax at the basic rate, be chargeable at the additional rate.

(2) This section applies to income arising to trustees in any year of assessment so far as it—

(*a*) is income which is to be accumulated or which is payable at the discretion of the trustees or any other person (whether or not the trustees have power to accumulate it); and

(*b*) is neither (before being distributed) the income of any person other than the trustees nor treated for any of the purposes of the Income Tax Acts as the income of a settlor; and

(*c*) is not income arising under a trust established for charitable purposes only or income from investments, deposits or other property held for the purposes of a fund or scheme established for the sole purpose of providing relevant benefits within the meaning of section 26 of the Finance Act 1970; and

(*d*) exceeds the income applied in defraying the expenses of the trustees in that year which are properly chargeable to income (or would be so chargeable but for any express provisions of the trust).

(3) This section also applies to sums apportioned to the trustees under paragraph 1 of Schedule 16 to the Finance Act 1972 and treated, under paragraph 5 (2) of that Schedule as applied by subsection (4) below, as income received by the trustees.

(4) Sub-paragraphs (2) and (4) to (8) of paragraph 5 of Schedule 16 to the Finance Act 1972 shall, with the omission in sub-paragraph (2) (*a*) of the words following "the apportionment relates", the substitution of "income" for "total income" and all other necessary modifications, apply to a sum apportioned to trustees as they apply to sums apportioned to an individual; and paragraph 6 of that Schedule shall apply accordingly.

(5) For the purposes of this section amounts paid or credited to trustees in any year of assessment in respect of dividends or interest payable in respect of shares in or deposits with or loans to a building society with which arrangements under section 343 of the Taxes Act are in force for that year shall be treated as income for that year received by the trustees after deduction of income tax from a corresponding gross amount.

In this subsection expressions used in section 343 of the Taxes Act have the same meanings as in that section.

(6) In this section "trustees" does not include personal representatives; but where personal representatives, on or before the completion of the administration of the estate, pay to trustees any sum representing income which, if personal representatives were trustees within the meaning of this section, would be income to which this section applies, that sum shall be deemed to be paid to the trustees as income and to have borne income tax (at the basic rate).

This subsection shall be construed as if it were contained in Part XV of the Taxes Act.

(7)[1].

(8) A notice to trustees under section 8 of the Taxes Management Act 1970 may require a return of the income arising to them to include particulars of the manner in which the income has been applied, including particulars as to the exercise of any discretion and of the persons in whose favour it has been exercised.

17. Payments under discretionary trusts

(1) Where, in any year of assessment, trustees make a payment to any person in the exercise of a discretion exercisable by them or any person other than the trustees, then, if the sum paid is for all the purposes of the Income Tax Acts income of the person to whom it is paid (but would not be his income apart from the payment), the following provisions of this section shall apply with respect to the payment in lieu of section 52 or 53 of the Taxes Act.

(2) The payment shall be treated as a net amount corresponding to a gross amount from which tax has been deducted at a rate equal to the sum of the basic rate and the additional rate in force for the year in which the payment is made; and the sum treated as so deducted shall be treated—

(*a*) as income tax paid by the person to whom the payment is made; and
(*b*) so far as not set off under the following provisions of this section, as income tax assessable on the trustees.

(3) The following amounts, so far as not previously allowed, shall be set against the amount assessable (apart from this subsection) on the trustees in pursuance of subsection (2) (*b*) above:

(*a*) the amount of any tax on income arising to the trustees and charged at the additional as well as at the basic rate in pursuance of section 16 of this Act; and
(*b*) the amount of tax at the additional rate on any sum treated, under paragraph 5 (2) of Schedule 16 to the Finance Act 1972 as applied by section 16 (4) above [or under section 34 (6) of the Finance (No. 2) Act 1975][2], as income of the trustees; and
(*c*) the amount of tax at the basic rate on any amount taken for the purposes of paragraph 5 of Schedule 16 to the Finance Act 1972 as applied by section 16(4) above, to be the amount to be excluded from the income of the trustees in accordance with sub-paragraph (6) of that paragraph; and
(*d*) an amount of tax in respect of income found on a claim made by the trustees to have been available to them for distribution at the end of the year

1972–73, which shall be taken to be two-thirds of the net amount of that income; [and

(*e*) the amount of any tax on income arising to the trustees by virtue of section 38 (2) of the Finance Act 1974 (development gains) and charged at a rate equal to the sum of the basic rate and the additional rate in pursuance of section 43 (1) of that Act;][1]

but tax on any income represented by amounts paid or credited as mentioned in section 16 (5) of this Act after the end of the year 1973–74 shall be taken into account under paragraph (*a*) above only on production of a certificate from the building society concerned specifying those amounts and stating that an amount representing income tax on that income calculated at the basic rate has been or will be accounted for.

(4).

(5) In this section "trustees" does not include personal representatives within the meaning of section 432 (4) of the Taxes Act.

Subs (4) amends TA 1970, s 55.

[1]Para (*e*) of subs (3) inserted by FA 1974, Sched 7, para 8, with effect from 18 December 1973; see FA 1974, s 44 (5).

[2]Words in subs (3) (*b*) inserted by F (No 2) A 1975, s 34 (6).

---

18. Discretionary trusts—relief for overseas tax

(1) Subsection (2) of this section shall apply if a payment made by trustees falls to be treated as a net amount in accordance with section 17 (2) of this Act and the income arising under the trust includes income in respect of which the trustees are entitled to credit for overseas tax under Part XVIII of the Taxes Act (in that subsection referred to as "taxed overseas income").

(2) If the trustees certify—

(*a*) that the income out of which the payment was made was or included taxed overseas income of an amount and from a source stated in the certificate; and

(*b*) that that amount arose to them not earlier than in the year 1973–74 and not earlier than six years before the end of the year of assessment in which the payment was made;

the person to whom the payment was made may claim that the payment, up to the amount so certified, shall be treated for the purposes of the said Part XVIII as income received by him from that source and so received in the year in which the payment was made.

CAPITAL TRANSFER TAX

The principal provisions are contained in the FA 1975, Sched 5. That schedule has been substantially amended by the FA 1976, 1977 and 1978.

FINANCE ACT 1975

SCHEDULE 5

Section 21

SETTLED PROPERTY

Definition of "settlement" and related expressions

1.—(1) The following provisions of this paragraph apply for determining what is to be taken for the purposes of capital transfer tax to be a settlement, and what property is, accordingly, referred to as property comprised in a settlement or as settled property; and who is the settlor and a trustee in relation to a settlement.

(2) "Settlement" means any disposition or dispositions of property, whether effected by instrument, by parole or by operation of law, or partly in one way and partly in another, whereby the property is for the time being—

(*a*) held in trust for persons in succession or for any person subject to a contingency; or

(*b*) held by trustees on trust to accumulate the whole or part of any income of the property or with power to make payments out of that income at the discretion of the trustees or some other person, with or without power to accumulate surplus income; or

(*c*) charged or burdened (otherwise than for full consideration in money or money's worth paid for his own use or benefit to the person making the disposition), with the payment of any annuity or other periodical payment payable for a life or any other limited or terminable period;

or would be so held or charged or burdened if the disposition or dispositions were regulated by the law of any part of the United Kingdom; or whereby, under the law of any other country, the administration of the property is for the time being governed by provisions equivalent in effect to those which would apply if the property were so held, charged or burdened.

(3) A lease of property which is for life or lives, or for a period ascertainable

only by reference to a death, or which is terminable on, or at a date ascertainable only by reference to, a death, shall be treated as a settlement and the property as settled property, unless the lease was granted for full consideration in money or money's worth, and where a lease not granted as a lease at a rack rent is at any time to become a lease at an increased rent it shall be treated as terminable at that time.

(4) In relation to Scotland "settlement" also includes—

(*a*) an entail;

(*b*) any deed by virtue of which an annuity is charged on, or on the rents of, any property (the property being treated as the property comprised in the settlement).

(5) In sub-paragraph (4) above, "deed" includes any disposition, arrangement, contract, resolution, instrument or wiriting.

(6) "Settlor", in relation to a settlement, includes any person by whom the settlement was made directly or indirectly, and in particular (but without prejudice to the generality of the preceding words) includes any person who has provided funds directly or indirectly for the purpose of or in connection with the settlement or has made with any other person a reciprocal arrangement for that other person to make the settlement.

(7) "Trustee", in relation to a settlement in relation to which there would be no trustees apart from this sub-paragraph, means any person in whom the settled property or its management is for the time being vested.

(8) Where more than one person is a settlor in relation to a settlement and the circumstances so require, this Schedule and section 25 (3) (*d*) of this Act shall apply in relation to it as if the settled property were comprised in separate settlements.

(9) In the application of this [Part of this Act][1] to Scotland, any reference to an interest in possession in settled property is a reference to an interest of any kind under a settlement [by virtue of which the person in right of that interest is entitled to the enjoyment of the property or would be so entitled if the property were capable of enjoyment][1] and the person in right of such an interest at any time shall be deemed to be entitled to a corresponding interest in the whole or any part of the property comprised in the settlement.

(10) In the application of this Part of this Act to Northern Ireland this paragraph shall have effect as if references to property held in trust for persons included references to property standing limited to persons and as if the lease referred to in sub-paragraph (3) did not include a lease in perpetuity within the meaning of section 1 of the Renewable Leasehold Conversion Act 1849 or a

lease to which section 37 of that Act applies.

[1]Substituted by FA 1976, Sched 14, para 10.

Excluded property

2.—(1) Where property comprised in a settlement is situated outside the United Kingdom—

(*a*) the property (but not a reversionary interest in the property) is excluded property unless the settlor was domiciled in the United Kingdom at the time the settlement was made; and

(*b*) section 24 (2) of this Act applies to a reversionary interest in the property but does not otherwise apply in relation to the property.

(2) In determining whether property comprised in a settlement which became so comprised before 10th December 1974 is excluded property section 45 of this Act shall be disregarded.

Interests in possession

3.—(1) A person beneficially entitled to an interest in possession in settled property shall be treated as beneficially entitled to the property in which the interest subsists.

(2) Where the person entitled to the interest is entitled to part only of the income (if any) of the property, the interest shall be taken to subsist in such part only of the property as bears to the whole thereof the same proportion as the part of the income to which he is entitled bears to the whole of the income.

(3) Where the part of the income of any property to which a person is entitled is a specified amount (or the whole less a specified amount) in any period, his interest in the property shall be taken, subject to sub-paragraph (4) below, to subsist in such part (or in the whole less such part) of the property as produces that amount in that period.

(4) The Treasury may from time to time by order made by statutory instrument prescribe a higher and a lower rate for the purposes of this paragraph; and where tax is chargeable in accordance with sub-paragraph (3) above by reference to the value of the part of a property which produces a specified amount or by reference to the value of the remainder (but not where chargeable transfers are made simultaneously and tax is chargeable by reference to the value of that part as well as by reference to the value of the

remainder) the value of the part producing that specified amount—

(*a*) shall, if tax is chargeable by reference to the value of that part, be taken to be not less than it would be if the property produced income at the higher rate so prescribed; and

(*b*) shall, if tax is chargeable by reference to the value of the remainder, be taken to be not more than it would be if the property produced income at the lower rate so prescribed;

but the value to be taken by virtue of paragraph (*a*) above as the value of part of a property shall not exceed the value of the whole of the property.

(5) Where the person entitled to the interest is not entitled to any income of the property but is entitled, jointly or in common with one or more other persons, to the use and enjoyment of the property, his interest shall be taken to subsist in such part of the property as corresponds to the proportion which the annual value of his interest bears to the aggregate of the annual values of his interest and that or those of the other or others.

(6) Where, under paragraph 1 (3) of this Schedule, a lease of property is to be treated as a settlement, the lessee's interest in the property shall be taken to subsist in the whole of the property less such part of it as corresponds to the proportion which the value of the lessor's interest (as determined under Schedule 10 to this Act) bears to the value of the property.

(7) A statutory instrument made under this paragraph shall be subject to annulment in pursuance of a resolution of the House of Commons.

Termination of interest in possession treated as transfer of value

4.—(1) Where a person beneficially entitled to an interest in possession in any property comprised in a settlement disposes of his interest the disposal—

(*a*) is not a transfer of value; but

(*b*) shall be treated for the purposes of this Schedule as the coming to an end of his interest;

and tax shall be charged accordingly under the following provisions of this paragraph.

(2) Where at any time during the life of a person beneficially entitled to an interest in possession in any property comprised in a settlement his interest comes to an end, tax shall be charged, subject to the following provisions of this paragraph, as if at that time he had made a transfer of value and the value transferred had been equal to the value of the property in which his interest subsisted.

(3) If the person whose interest in the property comes to an end becomes on the same occasion beneficially entitled to the property or to another interest in possession in the property tax shall not be chargeable under this paragraph, except in the case mentioned in sub-paragraph (10) (*b*) below.

(4) If the interest comes to an end by being disposed of by the person beneficially entitled thereto and the disposal is for a consideration in money or money's worth, tax shall be chargeable under this paragraph as if the value of the property in which the interest subsisted were reduced by the amount of the consideration; but in determining that amount the value of a reversionary interest in the property or of any interest in other property comprised in the same settlement shall be left out of account.

(5) If the interest comes to an end during the settlor's life and on the same occasion the property in which the interest subsisted reverts to the settlor, tax shall not be chargeable under this paragraph unless the settlor [or his spouse][1] had acquired a reversionary interest in the property for a consideration in money or money's worth.

(6) If the interest comes to an end and on the same occasion the settlor's spouse becomes beneficially entitled to the settled property, then if—

(*a*) the settlor's spouse is then domiciled in the United Kingdom—[2], and
(*b*) neither the settlor nor the settlor's spouse had acquired a reversionary interest in the property for a consideration in money or money's worth;

tax shall not be chargeable under this paragraph.

[The references in this sub-paragraph to the settlor's spouse include, in a case where the settlor has died less than two years before the interest comes to an end or the interest comes to an end before 1st April 1977, references to the settlor's widow or widower.][3]

(7) Where the person beneficially entitled to the interest is the surviving spouse of a person who has died before 13th November 1974, tax shall not be chargeable under this paragraph if the value of the property in which the interest subsists would, by virtue of section 22 (4) of this Act, have been left out of account in determining the value of his estate had he died immediately before the coming to an end of the interest.

(8) The tax chargeable under this paragraph in a case where—

(*a*) the settlement was made before 27th March 1974; and
(*b*) the interest comes to an end before 10th December 1974;

shall not in any case exceed the tax that would be so chargeable if the values transferred by previous chargeable transfers made by the person beneficially entitled to the interest had been equal to the values (if any) on which tax is chargeable under this paragraph on the earlier termination of an interest in the settled property.

(9) Where a transaction is made between the trustees of the settlement and a person who is, or is connected with,—

(*a*) the person beneficially entitled to an interest in the property; or
(*b*) a person beneficially entitled to any other interest in that property or to any interest in any other property comprised in the settlement; or
(*c*) a person for whose benefit any of the settled property may be applied.

and, as a result of the transaction, the value of the first-mentioned property is less than it would be but for the transaction, a corresponding part of the interest shall be deemed for the purposes of this paragraph to come to an end, unless the transaction is such that, were the trustees beneficially entitled to the settled property, it would not be a transfer of value.

(10) References in this paragraph to any property and to an interest in any property include references to part of any property or interest; and—

(*a*) the tax chargeable under this paragraph on the coming to an end of part of an interest shall be charged as if the value of the property (or part) in which the interest subsisted were a corresponding part of the whole thereof; and
(*b*) if the value of the property (or part) to which or to an interest in which a person becomes entitled as mentioned in sub-paragraph (3) above is less than the value on which tax would be chargeable apart from that sub-paragraph, tax shall be chargeable on a value equal to the difference.

(11) Tax shall not be chargeable under this paragraph if the settled property is excluded property.

[1]Words inserted by FA 1978, s 69 (1), where the acquisition is made after 11 April 1978.
[2]Words repealed by FA 1976, Sched 14, para 13 and Sched 15, Pt V.
[3]Added by FA 1976, s 110 (2) and deemed always to have had effect.

Relief for successive charges on interest in possession

5.—(1) Where the value transferred by a chargeable transfer falls to be determined by reference to the value of any settled property in which there subsists an interest in possession to which the transferor is entitled, and—

(*a*) the value transferred by an earlier chargeable transfer also fell to be determined by reference to the value of that property; and
(*b*) that earlier transfer either was or included the making of the settlement or was made after the making of the settlement;

then, if the period between those transfers is not more than four years, tax shall be charged as if the value of that property were reduced—

(i) by 80 per cent. if that period is one year or less;
(ii) by 60 per cent. if that period is more than one year but not more than two years;
(iii) by 40 per cent. if that period is more than two years but not more than three years; and
(iv) by 20 per cent. if that period is more than three years.

[(2) Where the transferor became entitled to the interest—

(*a*) on a death on which estate duty was payable in respect of the settled property; or
(*b*) in consequence of

(i) a gift inter vivos; or
(ii) a disposition or determination of a beneficial interest in possession in any property comprised in a settlement,

where, by reason of the gift or interest, estate duty or capital transfer tax under section 22 (5) of this Act was payable on a subsequent death in respect of the settled property,

sub-paragraph (1) above shall apply as if the period referred to therein were the period between the death and the chargeable transfer.][1]

[1]Substituted by FA 1976, s 97 (2).

Charge on capital distributions of settled property

6.—(1) Where a distribution payment is made out of property comprised in a settlement and at the time the payment is made no interest in possession subsists in the property or in the part of it out of which the payment is made, the payment is in this Schedule referred to as a capital distribution.

(2) Where a person becomes entitled to an interest in possession in the whole or any part of the property comprised in a settlement at a time when no such interest subsists in the property or that part, a capital distribution shall be treated as being made out of the property or that part of the property; and the

amount of the distribution shall be taken to be equal to the value at that time of the property or, if the interest is in part only of that property, of that part.

[(2A) Where the whole or any part of the property comprised in a settlement ceases to be so comprised in that settlement (otherwise than by virtue of any payment or transfer of assets made by the trustees) at a time when no interest in possession subsists in the property or that part, then if—

(*a*) sub-paragraph (2) above does not apply; but
(*b*) a person at that time becomes entitled to (or immediately thereafter has) an interest in the property or part which would be an interest in possession if held beneficially by an individual,

a capital distribution shall be treated as being made out of the property or that part of the property; and the amount of the distribution shall be taken to be equal to the value at that time of the property or that part of it.][1]

(3) Where, at a time when no interest in possession subsists in property comprised in a settlement or in a part of that property, a transaction is made between the trustees of the settlement and a person who is, or is connected with—

(*a*) a person beneficially entitled to an interest in any of the settled property; or
(*b*) a person for whose benefit any of the settled property may be applied;

and, as a result of the transaction, the value of the property or part is less than it would be but for the transaction, a capital distribution shall be treated as being made out of the property or part of an amount equal to that by which that value is less, unless the transaction is such that, were the trustees beneficially entitled to the settled property, it would not be a transfer of value.

(4) Tax shall be charged on any capital distribution as on the value transferred by a chargeable transfer where—

(*a*) the value transferred less the tax payable on it is equal to the amount of the capital distribution; and
(*b*) the rate applicable is that specified in paragraphs 7 to 9 below;

and in those paragraphs "the sum assumed transferor" means the person who would be the transferor in relation to the chargeable transfer assumed by this sub-paragraph and the appropriate Table for the purposes of those paragraphs (including the calculation of any tax that would have been chargeable as mentioned in paragraph 7 (2) (*a*) below) is the Second Table set out in section 37 (3) of this Act.

(5) The reference in sub-paragraph (4) (*a*) above to the tax payable on a

capital distribution does not include any tax which is payable by a person to whom a distribution payment is made [or, in the case of a capital distribution treated as made under sub-paragraph (2) [or (2A)][1] above or paragraph 15 (3) below, any tax which is payable out of the property whose value is taken as the amount of the capital distribution; and in relation to a capital distribution treated as made under sub-paragraph (3) above or paragraph 12 or 24 (2) below, sub-paragraph (4) (*a*) above shall have effect as if the words "less the tax payable on it" were omitted.][2]

(6) Notwithstanding sub-paragraph (1) above, a distribution payment which is made to the settlor or the settlor's spouse shall not be a capital distribution if the settlor, or as the case may be, the settlor's spouse is domiciled in the United Kingdom at the time the payment is made—[3].

[The references in this sub-paragraph to the settlor's spouse include, in the case of a distribution payment made less than two years after the settlor's death or made before 1st April 1977, references to the settlor's widow or widower.][4]

[(6A) Where the person referred to in sub-paragraph (2) above is the settlor, the settlor's spouse or, if the settlor has died less than two years before the time there referred to, the settlor's widow or widower, and is domiciled in the United Kingdom at that time, that sub-paragraph shall have effect as if the reference in it to a capital distribution were a reference to a distribution payment to the settlor or, as the case may be, the settlor's spouse, widow or widower.][5]

[(6B) Neither sub-paragraph (6) nor sub-paragraph (6A) above applies where, at or before the time when the payment is made to the person concerned or that person becomes entitled to the interest, as the case may be, an interest under the settlement is or has been acquired for a consideration in money or money's worth by—

(*a*) that person; or
(*b*) that person's spouse; or
(*c*) where that person is the settlor's widow or widower, the settlor][6]

(7) . . .[7].

(8) Where a person entitled to an interest in possession in part of the property comprised in a settlement became so entitled as a member of a class, sub-paragraph (2) above shall not apply on his becoming entitled, as such a member, to an interest in possession in another part of that property, if he becomes so entitled on the death under full age of another member of that class.

[1]Inserted by FA 1978, s 70 (1) and (2) which come into force on 11 April 1978.
[2]Words substituted by FA 1976, Sched 14, para 11.
[3]Words repealed by FA 1976, Sched 14, para 12 and Sched 15, Pt V.
[4]Added by FA 1976, s 110 (3) and deemed always to have had effect.
[5]Inserted by FA 1976, Sched 14, para 12 and deemed always to have had effect.
[6]Inserted by FA 1978, s 69 (2) and applicable where the acquisition of the interest is after 11 April 1978.
[7]Repealed by FA 1976, s 105 (1) and Sched 15, Pt V, and deemed always to have been omitted.

Rates of charge on capital distributions following chargeable transfers

7.—(1) This paragraph applies where, at or after the relevant time and before the capital distribution, there has been a transfer of value which satisfies the conditions stated in paragraph 11 (2) below.

(2) So far as the amount on which tax is chargeable, when added to the amount of all previous distribution payments made out of property comprised in the settlement, does not exceed the initial value, the rate chargeable shall be equal to the fraction of which—

(*a*) the numerator is the amount of the tax which would have been charged on the value transferred by the relevant transfer, or such part of that amount as is attributable to the initial value, if the value so transferred had been equal to the aggregate of the initial values of the settlement and any related settlement; and
(*b*) the denominator is the initial value.

(3) So far as the amount on which tax is chargeable, when so added, exceeds the initial value, the rate or rates chargeable shall be the rate or rates that would be applicable if the assumed transferor had made previous chargeable transfers and the aggregate of the values transferred by them were equal to the aggregate of—

(*a*) the values transferred by any chargeable transfers which the person who made the relevant transfer had made before the relevant transfer;
(*b*) the aggregate of the initial values of the settlement and any related settlement; and
(*c*) the amounts of any previous distribution payments out of property comprised in the settlement, so far as the tax (if any) chargeable thereon is chargeable in accordance with this sub-paragraph.

Rate of charge on other capital distributions

8.—(1) This paragraph applies where paragraph 7 above does not apply.

(2) The rate or rates chargeable shall be the rate or rates that would be applicable if the assumed transferor—

(*a*) had made previous chargeable transfers in any case where there had been previous distribution payments made on or after 27th March 1974 out of the settled property; but

(*b*) had made no previous chargeable transfers in any other case;

and, where paragraph (*a*) above applies, the aggregate of the values transferred by the previous chargeable transfers were equal to the aggregate amounts of the previous distribution payment's mentioned therein.

Further property added by settlor

9.—(1) The following provisions of this paragraph apply where, by a transfer of value made by the settlor at any time after the making of the settlement and after 26th March 1974 (in this paragraph referred to as "the subsequent transfer") further property is added to the property comprised in the settlement immediately before the subsequent transfer (in this paragraph referred to as "the previous property").

(2) The subsequent transfer shall be treated for the purposes of paragraphs 6 to 8 above as the making of a separate settlement, and the following provisions of this paragraph shall apply for determining the property out of which any capital distributions made after the subsequent transfer are to be treated as made.

(3) If paragraph 7 above would have applied to a capital distribution made immediately before the subsequent transfer, any capital distribution made after the subsequent transfer shall be treated as made—

(*a*) out of the previous property, if or to the extent that the amount of the distribution, when added to the amount of all previous distribution payments made out of the settled property, does not exceed the previous value defined in sub-paragraph (4) below; and

(*b*) out of the further property in any other case.

(4) For the purposes of sub-paragraph (3) above the previous value is the initial value, increased, if there was an earlier transfer which is a "subsequent transfer" as defined above, by the value, immediately after the earlier transfer, of any property added by it to the settled property.

(5) If paragraph 7 above would not have applied to a capital distribution made immediately before the subsequent transfer, any capital distribution made after the subsequent transfer shall be treated as made—

(*a*) out of the previous property, if or to the extent that the amount of the distribution, when added to the amount of any previous distribution payment made since the subsequent transfer, does not exceed the value of the settled property immediately before the subsequent transfer; and

(*b*) out of the further property in any other case;

and accordingly, where paragraph (*b*) above applies, the rate or rates chargeable shall be determined in accordance with paragraph 7 above (and, where there is a further subsequent transfer, in accordance with sub-paragraphs (3) and (4) above).

Capital distributions after termination of interest of settlor or settlor's spouse

10. Where, after the termination of an interest in possession in a part (in this paragraph referred to as the chargeable part) of any property comprised in a settlement made after 26th March 1974, a capital distribution is made out of the chargeable part, and—

(*a*) the settlor or the settlor's spouse was the person entitled to the interest before its termination, and either the settlor or the settlor's spouse was entitled to an interest in possession in the chargeable part immediately after the making of the settlement; and

(*b*) the making of the settlement either was not a transfer of value or was an exempt transfer or a transfer to the extent of the value of the chargeable part;

paragraphs 6 to 9 above shall apply as if the chargeable part were comprised in a separate settlement made by the person entitled to the first-mentioned interest on its termination and the termination of the interest were the relevant transfer; and as if the subsequent termination of any interest of his in any other part of the settled property were an addition made by him to the property comprised in that separate settlement.

[**10A.** Where a capital distribution is made on the same day and out of property comprised in the same settlement as a distribution payment that is not a capital distribution, the capital distribution shall for the purpose of paragraphs 7 to 9 above be treated as made before the distribution payment.][1]

[1]Para 10A inserted by FA 1976, Sched 14, para 14, in relation to distribution payments made after 15 April 1976.

Interpretation of paragraphs 6 to 10

11.—(1) The following provisions apply for the interpretation of paragraphs 6 to 10 above.

(2) The relevant transfer, in relation to any settlement, is the first transfer of value made at or after the relevant time which satisfies the conditions—

(*a*) that the value of the property comprised in the settlement or of that part of it out of which the capital distributions are made was taken into account in determining the value transferred; and
(*b*) that the transfer was, or would but for paragraph 19 (2) below or paragraphs 2 to 7 of Schedule 6 to this Act [or section 76 of the Finance Act 1976][1] have been, a chargeable transfer; and
(*c*) that, if the settlement was made before 27th March 1974, the transfer was made neither under paragraph 4 above nor or death;

and where it was not a chargeable transfer [(or was a chargeable transfer of some only of the value transferred by it)][3] the reference in paragraph 7 (2) (*a*) above to the tax which would have been charged is a reference to the tax which would have been charged but for paragraph 19 (2) below or paragraphs 2 to 7 of Schedule 6 to this Act [or section 76 of the Finance Act 1976][1].

(3) The relevant time, in relation to any settlement, is, if the settled property became comprised in the settlement on the death of any person, the time immediately before his death, and, in any other case the time when the settlement was made.

(4) Where, by the same disposition, property ceases to be comprised in one settlement and becomes comprised in another settlement, the property shall be treated as remaining comprised in the first settlement.

(5) The amount of any distribution payment which is a capital distribution shall be taken (except for the purposes of paragraph 6 (4) (*a*)) to be the amount on which tax is chargeable in respect of it.

(6) A settlement is related to another if the same transfer of value is the relevant transfer in relation to both; and for this purpose transfers of value made by the same person on the same day shall be treated as one.

(7) "Distribution payment" means, subject to sub-paragraph (8) below, any payment which—

(*a*) is not income of any person for any of the purposes of income tax and would not for any of those purposes be income of a person not resident in the United Kingdom if he were so resident; and
(*b*) is not a payment in respect of costs or expenses;

and "payment" includes the transfer of assets other than money.

(8) The amount of any capital distribution treated as made under paragraph 6 (2), [(2A)][5] or (3) above or paragraph 15 (3) or 24(2) below shall also be deemed to be a distribution payment; but where, after an amount has been taken into account by virtue of this sub-paragraph [or paragraph 6 (6A) above][2] as a distribution payment made out of the whole or part of any property, one or more distribution payments are made (otherwise than under this sub-paragraph [or paragraph 6 (6A) above][2]) out of that property or part, the amount so taken into account shall be treated as reducing the amount of those payments.

(9) "Initial value", in relation to any settlement, means the value, immediately after the relevant transfer, of the property then comprised in the settlement.

(10) "Interest in possession" means an interest in possession to which an individual is beneficially entitled or, if the following conditions are satisfied, an interest in possession to which a company is beneficially entitled, the conditions being—

(*a*) that the business of the company consists wholly or mainly in the acquisition of interests in settled property; and
(*b*) that the company has acquired the interest for full consideration in money or money's worth from an individual who was beneficially entitled to the interest.

[(10A) Where the acquisition mentioned in paragraph (*b*) of sub-paragraph (10) above was before 14th March 1975—

(*a*) the condition mentioned in paragraph (*a*) of that sub-paragraph shall be treated as satisfied if the business of the company was at the time of the acquisition such as is described in that paragraph; and
(*b*) that condition need not be satisfied if the company is authorised to carry on long term business under Part I of the Insurance Companies Act 1974 or Part II of the Insurance Companies (Northern Ireland) Order 1976.][4]

(11) References to settled property shall be construed as referring only to property which is not excluded property.

---

[1]Inserted by FA 1976, Sched 11, para 4.
[2]Inserted by FA 1976, Sched 14, para 12 (2) and deemed always to have had effect.
[3]Inserted by FA 1976, Sched 14, para 16.
[4]Inserted by FA 1977, s 50 with effect from 29 March 1977.

Periodic charge to tax

12.—(1) Where, at a relevant anniversary, no interest in possession subsists in the property comprised in a settlement or in a part of that property, a capital distribution of an amount equal to the value immediately before that anniversary of that property or part shall be treated as made out of that property or part, and tax shall be charged on a capital distribution so treated as made at 30 per cent, of the rate at which it would be chargeable under paragraphs 6 to 10 above on a capital distribution of the same amount made at the same date, but subject to any reduction under sub-paragraph (4) below.

(2) Where the trustees of the settlement are not resident in the United Kingdom a capital distribution of a corresponding amount shall also be treated as made if no interest in possession subsists in the property or in a part thereof at the end of any year in the period of ten years ending with a relevant anniversary, except the last and except any year ending before 1st January 1976; and tax shall be charged on a capital distribution so treated as made at 3 per cent. of the rate at which it would be chargeable under paragraphs 6 to 10 above on a capital distribution of the same amount made at the same date.

(3) Any tax charged by virtue of sub-paragraph (2) above shall be allowed as a credit against the tax chargeable on the [next capital distribution made out of the property or, as the case may be, out of the part concerned, not being a capital distribution treated as made under that sub-paragraph.][1]

(4) Where the whole or part of the value mentioned in sub-paragraph (1) above is attributable to property—

(*a*) which was added by the settlor after the end of the first of the ten years ending with the relevant anniversary; or

(*b*) in which an interest in possession subsisted throughout at least one of those ten years; the rate at which, under sub-paragraph (1) above, tax is chargeable on that value or that part of it shall be reduced by one-tenth for each of those ten years throughout which either the settled property did not include that property, or an interest in possession subsisted in that property.

(5) For the purposes of this paragraph trustees of a settlement shall be regarded as not resident in the United Kingdom unless the general administration of the settlement is ordinarily carried on in the United Kingdom and the trustees or a majority of them (and, where there is more than one class of trustees, a majority of each class) are for the time being resident in the United Kingdom.

(6) For the purposes of this paragraph a relevant anniversary, in relation to a

settlement, is the end of the ten years beginning with the date of the transfer of value which is the relevant transfer in relation to the settlement (or would be the relevant transfer in relation to it if dispositions made or events happening at that date could be chargeable transfers and paragraph (*c*) of paragraph 11 (2) above were omitted) and the end of every subsequent ten years; but no date falling before 1st April 1980 is a relevant anniversary.

[(7) Paragraph 11 above shall apply for the interpretation of this paragraph as it applies for the interpretation of paragraphs 6 to 10, except that paragraph 11 (4) shall be disregarded in determining in relation to any settled property whether the trustees are resident in the United Kingdom.][2]

(8) —[3].

[1]Substituted by FA 1976, Sched 14, para 8 (1).
[2]Substituted by FA 1976, Sched 14, para 17.
[3]Repealed by FA 1976, Sched 15, Pt V.

Tax credit for periodic charge

13.—(1) Subject to sub-paragraph (2) below, where tax is charged at a relevant anniversary on any capital distribution treated by virtue of paragraph 12 (1) above as made out of any property, the effective rate at which that tax is charged (taking into account any reduction under paragraph 12 (4) above) shall reduce the rate at which, apart from this paragraph, tax would be chargeable on any capital distribution made out of that property on or not later than twenty years after that relevant anniversary [not being a capital distribution treated as made under paragraph 12 above].[1]

(2) The amounts by which tax on any capital distribution is reduced under sub-paragraph (1) above by reason of any tax charged under paragraph 12 (1) above shall not together exceed the amount of the tax so charged.

(3) In this paragraph "relevant anniversary" has the same meaning as in paragraph 12 above.

[1]Added by FA 1976, Sched 14, para 8(2).

Transitional relief for settlements made before 27th March 1974

14.—(1) In relation to a settlement made before 27th March 1974 paragraphs 6 to 12 above shall apply with the following modifications.

(2) Subject to sub-paragraphs (3) to (5) below, the rate at which tax is chargeable on any capital distribution made before 1st April 1980 out of property comprised in the settlement (but not on any capital distribution which, under paragraph 9 above, is treated as made out of property comprised in a separate settlement made after 26th March 1974) shall be the following percentage of the rate at which it would be chargeable apart from this paragraph, that is to say—

(*a*) 10 per cent. if the capital distribution is made before 1st April 1976;
(*b*) 12½ per cent. if it is made after 31st March 1976 but before 1st April 1977;
(*c*) 15 per cent. if it is made after 31st March 1977 but before 1st April 1978;
(*d*) 17½ per cent. if it is made after 31st March 1978 but before 1st April 1979; and
(*e*) 20 per cent. if it is made after 31st March 1979

(3) Where any capital distribution made after 31st March 1976 but before 1st April 1977 could not have been made except as the result of some proceedings before a court, this paragraph shall have effect in relation to it as if it had been made before 1st April 1976.

(4) Sub-paragraph (2) above does not apply in relation to a capital distribution treated as made under paragraph 12 (2) above.

(5) Sub-paragraph (2) above does not apply—

(*a*) in relation to a capital distribution treated as made under paragraph 6 (2) above, unless the person becoming entitled as mentioned therein; or
(*b*) in relation to a capital distribution treated as made under paragraph 15 (3) below, unless each of the beneficiaries referred to therein [living at the time of the capital distribution][1]; or
(*c*) in relation to a distribution payment made for the benefit of any person, unless that person;

is an individual who is domiciled in the United Kingdom at the time the capital distribution is made—[2] [and who has not at or before that time acquired an interest under the settlement for a consideration in money or money's worth directly or indirectly from a person not so domiciled][3]

(6) In this paragraph expressions defined for the purposes of paragraphs 6 to 10 above have the same meanings as in those paragraphs.

---

[1]Inserted by FA 1976, s 106 (3).
[2]Words in sub-para (5) repealed by FA 1976, Sched 14, para 13, and Sched 15, Pt V.
[3]Words inserted by FA 1978, s 69 (3) applying to acquisitions after 11 July 1978.

Accumulation and maintenance settlements

15.—(1) This paragraph applies to any settlement where—

(*a*) one or more persons (in this paragraph referred to as beneficiaries) will, on or before attaining a specified age not exceeding twenty-five, become entitled to, or to an interest in possession in, the settled property or part of it; and
(*b*) no interest in posession subsists in the settled property or part and the income from it is to be accumulated so far as not applied for the maintenance, education or benefit of a beneficiary; and
(*c*) either—

[(i) not more than twenty-five years have elapsed since the day on which the settlement was made or, if it was later, since the time (or latest time) when the conditions stated in paragraphs (*a*) and (*b*) above became satisfied with respect to the property or part; or
(ii) all the persons who are or have been beneficiaries are or were either grandchildren of a common grandparent or children, widows or widowers of such grandchildren who were themselves beneficiaries but dies before the time when, had they survived, they would have become entitled as mentioned in paragraph (*a*) above.][1]

(2) Where this paragraph applies to a settlement—

(*a*) a payment made to a beneficiary out of the settled property or part concerned shall not be a capital distribution and a capital distribution shall not be treated as made under paragraph 6 (2) above on a beneficiary's becoming entitled to an interest in the property or part; and
(*b*) no capital distribution shall be treated as made out of the property or part by virtue of paragraph 12 above at any time during the period for which the income is to be accumulated as mentioned in sub-paragraph (1) (*b*) above.

(3) Where no interest in possession subsists in the property comprised in a settlement or some part of that property but the conditions stated in paragraphs (*a*) and (*b*) of sub-paragraph (1) above are not satisfied with respect to the property or part, then, if those conditions become satisfied with respect to the property or any part thereof a capital distribution shall be treated as being made out of the property or part and the amount of the distribution shall be taken to be equal to the value of the property with respect to which those conditions become satisfied.

[(4) Where the conditions stated in paragraphs (*a*) and (*b*) of sub-paragraph (1) above were satisfied on 15th April 1976 with respect to any property comprised in a settlement made before that day, paragraph (*c*) (i) of that sub-paragraph shall have effect with the substitution of a reference to that day for the reference to the day on which the settlement was made, and the condition stated in paragraph (*c*) (ii) shall be treated as satisfied if—

(*a*) it is satisfied in respect of the period beginning with 15th April 1976; or
(*b*) it is satisfied in respect of the period beginning with 1st April 1977 and either there was no beneficiary living on 15th April 1976 or the beneficiaries on 1st April 1977 include a living beneficiary; or
(*c*) there is no power under the terms of the settlement whereby it could have become satisfied in respect of the period beginning with 1st April 1977, and the trusts of the settlement have not been varied at any time after 15th April 1976.

(5) In sub-paragraph (1) above "persons" includes unborn persons; but the conditions stated in paragraphs (*a*) and (*b*) of that sub-paragraph shall be treated as not satisfield unless there is or has been a living beneficiary.

(6) Paragraph 11 above shall apply for the interpretation of this paragraph as it applies for the interpretation of paragraphs 6 to 10; and for the purpose of this paragraph a person's children shall be taken to include his illegitimate children, his adopted children and his step-children.][2]

[1]Added by FA 1976, s 106 (1).
[2]Sub-paras (4), (5) substituted and sub-para (6) added by FA 1976, s 106 (2).

Superannuation schemes

16.—(1) This paragraph applies to any scheme or fund mentioned in subsection (1) or subsection (2) of section 221 of the Taxes Act, to any fund to which section 218 of that Act applies [to any scheme approved under section 226 or 226A of that Act][1], to any exempt approved scheme or statutory scheme as defined in Chapter II of Part II of the Finance Act 1970 and to any other sponsored superannuation scheme as defined in section 226 (11) of the Taxes Act.

(2) An interest in or under a fund or scheme to which this paragraph applies which comes to an end on the death of the person entitled to it shall be left out of account in determining for the purposes of this Part of this Act the value of his estate immediately before his death, if the interest—

(*a*) is, or is a right to, a pension or annuity; and
(*b*) is not an interest resulting (whether by virtue of the instrument

establishing the fund or scheme or otherwise) from the application of any benefit provided under the fund or scheme otherwise than by way of a pension or annuity.

(3) Paragraphs 3 and 4 above shall not apply in relation to an interest satisfying the conditions of paragraphs (*a*) and (*b*) of sub-paragraph (2) above; and where any tax chargeable on a transfer of value is attributable to the value of such an interest, the persons liable for it shall not include the trustees of the scheme or fund but shall, where the transfer is made on the death of the person entitled to the interest, include his personal representatives.

(4) In relation to an interest in or under a fund or scheme to which this paragraph applies, section 23 (2) of this Act shall apply as if the words "other than settled property" were omitted (in both places).

(5) Paragraphs 6 to 12 above shall not apply in relation to any property which is part of or held for the purposes of a fund or scheme to which this pargraph applies.

(6) The reference in sub-paragraph (5) above to property which is part of or held for the purposes of a fund or scheme does not include a reference to a benefit which, having become payable under the fund or scheme, becomes comprised in a settlement; and where in such a case the settlement is made by a person other than the person entitled to the benefit, the settlement shall for the purposes of this Part of this Act be treated as made by the person so entitled.

[1]Inserted by FA 1976, Sched 14, para 18 and deemed always to have had effect.

Trusts for benefit of employees, etc.

17.—(1) Where settled property is held on trusts which, either indefinitely or until the end of a period (whether defined by a date or in some other way) do not permit any of the settled property to be applied otherwise than for the benefit of—

(*a*) persons of a class defined by reference to employment in a particular trade, profession or undertaking or employment by, or office with, a body carrying on a trade, profession or undertaking; or
(*b*) persons of a class defined by reference to marriage or relationship to, or dependence on, persons of a class defined as mentioned in paragraph (*a*) above; or
(*c*) charities;

then, subject to sub-paragraph (2) below, this paragraph applies to that settled property or, as the case may be, applies to it during that period.

(2) Where any such class is defined by reference to employment by or office with a particular body this paragraph applies to the settled property only if the class comprises all or most of the persons employed by or holding office with that body.

(3) Where this paragraph applies to any settled property—

(*a*) the property shall be treated as comprised in one settlement, whether or not it would fall to be so treated apart from this paragraph; and
(*b*) an interest in possession in any part of the settled property shall be disregarded for the purposes of this Schedule if that part is less than 5 per cent. of the whole; and
(*c*) subject to sub-paragraph (4) below, a payment out of the settled property shall not be a capital distribution and shall not be taken into account as a distribution payment; and
(*d*) paragraph 7 above shall not apply to any capital distribution made out of the settled property; and
(*e*) paragraph 12 above shall apply subject to sub-paragraph (5) below, and paragraph 13 above shall not apply.

(4) Sub-paragraph (3) (*c*) above does not apply in relation to any payment made for the benefit of a person who is, or is connected with,—

(*a*) a person who has directly or indirectly provided any of the settled property otherwise than by additions not exceeding in value £1,000 in any one year; or
[(*b*) in a case where the employment in question is employment by a close company, a person who is a participator in relation to that company and either

(i) is beneficially entitled to, or to rights entitling him to acquire, not less than 5% of, or of any class of the shares comprised in, its issued share capital; or
(ii) would, on a winding-up of the company, be entitled to not less than 5% of its assets

but if the trusts are those of a profit sharing scheme approved under the Finance Act 1978, paragraph (*b*) of this sub-paragraph does not preclude the application of sub-paragraph 3(*c*) above in relation to any appropriation of shares in pursuance of the scheme][4]

[(4A) Where any property to which this paragraph applies ceases to be comprised in a settlement and, either immediately or not more than one month later, the whole of it becomes comprised in another settlement, then, if this paragraph again applies to it when it becomes comprised in the second settlement, it shall be treated for all the purposes of this Part of this Act as if it has remained comprised in the first settlement.][1]

(5) Where this paragraph applies to any settled property, tax which would otherwise be chargeable at a relevant anniversary under paragraph 12 (1) above shall be deferred until either a capital distribution is made or this paragraph ceases to apply to the settled property; and when any deferred tax becomes chargeable it shall be charged—

(*a*) at the rate at which it would be chargeable if the relevant anniversary fell on the date on which the tax becomes chargeable; and
(*b*) on an amount determined in accordance with the following provisions of this paragraph.

(6) Where any deferred tax becomes chargeable when this paragraph ceases to apply to the settled property it shall be chargeable on an amount equal to the current value of the settled property [except that if more than one relevant anniversary has passed and, accordingly, more than one deferred tax becomes chargeable—

(*a*) the second deferred tax shall be charged on that value less the amount of the first deferred tax; and
(*b*) the third deferred tax (if any) shall be charged on the amount found under paragraph (*a*) above less the amount of the second deferred tax;

and so on.][2]

(7) Where any of the deferred tax becomes chargeable when a capital distribution is made—

(*a*) it shall be chargeable on an amount determined under sub-paragraph (8) below; and
(*b*) the amount of the tax shall reduce the amount on which tax is chargeable on that capital distribution (and if it exceeds that amount the excess shall reduce the amount on which tax is chargeable on the next capital distribution, and so on).

(8) So far as any tax which would otherwise be chargeable on a relevant anniversary becomes chargeable when a capital distribution is made it shall be charged on an amount (in this sub-paragraph referred to as the first amount) equal to the proper proportion of the current value of the property out of which the capital distribution is made; and where the capital distribution is made after the next relevant anniversary and, accordingly, more than one deferred tax becomes chargeable—

(*a*) the second deferred tax shall be charged on the first amount less the amount of the first deferred tax; and

(*b*) the third deferred tax (if any) shall be charged on the amount found under paragraph (*a*) above less the amount of the second deferred tax;

and so on.

(9) For the purposes of this paragraph—

(*a*) the current value of any property is its value at the time any tax deferred under this paragraph becomes chargeable; and

(*b*) the proper proportion of the current value of any property out of which a capital distribution is made is the proportion which the amount on which tax [would, apart from sub-paragraph (7) (*b*) above, be chargeable][3] on the capital distribution bears to that current value;

and in this paragraph "close company" and "participator" have the same meanings as in section 39 of this Act, "relevant anniversary" has the same meaning as in paragraph 12 above and "year" has the same meaning as in paragraph 2 of Schedule 6 to this Act.

---

[1]Sub-para (4A) inserted by FA 1976, s 107 (2) with effect from 7 April 1976.

[2]Words in sub-para (6) added by FA 1976, s 107 (3) with effect from 7 April 1976.

[3]Words in sub-para 9 (*b*) substituted by s 107 (4) with effect from 7 April 1976.

[4]Words substituted by FA 1978, Sched 11, para 1 (1), applying in relation to any payments out of the settled property made on or after 11 April 1978.

[**17A.**—(1) In relation to property comprised in a settlement to which this paragraph applies, paragraph 17 above shall have effect as if newspaper publishing companies were included among the persons within paragraphs (*a*) to (*c*) of sub-paragraph (1) of that paragraph.

(2) This paragraph applies to a settlement if shares in a newspaper publishing company or a newspaper holding company are the only or principal property comprised in the settlement.

(3) In this paragraph—

"newspaper publishing company" means a company whose business consists wholly or mainly in the publication of newspapers in the United Kingdom; and

"newspaper holding company" means a company which—

(*a*) has as its only or principal asset shares in a newspaper publishing company, and (*b*) has powers of voting on all or most questions affecting the publishing company as a whole which if exercised would yield a majority of the votes capable of being exercised thereon;

and for the purposes of this paragraph shares shall be treated as the principal property comprised in a settlement or the principal asset of a company if the remaining property comprised in the settlement or the remaining assets of the company are such as may be reasonably required to enable the trustees or the company to secure the operation of the newspaper publishing company concerned.][1]

[1]Inserted by FA 1976, s 108 (1) with effect from 7 April 1976.

Protective trusts

18.—(1) This paragraph applies to settled property held on trusts to the like effect as those specified in section 33 (1) of the Trustee Act 1925; and in this paragraph "the principal beneficiary" and "the trust period" have the same meanings as in that section.

[(2) For the purposes of capital transfer tax—

(*a*) there shall be disregarded the failure or determination before the end of the trust period, of trusts to the like effect as those specified in paragraph (i) of the said section 33(1); and

(*b*) the principal beneficiary shall be treated as beneficially entitled to an interest in possession in any property which is for the time being held on trusts to the like effect as those specified in paragraph (ii) of the said section 33 (1)][1]

[1]Substituted by FA 1978, s 71 (1) and deemed to have come into force on 11 April 1978 and applies if the failure or determination is after that date; but no capital distribution shall be treated as made by virtue of Sched 5, para 15 (3) by reason only of the coming into force of this provision (FA 1978, s 71 (2)).

Trusts for the benefit of mentally disabled persons

19.—(1) This paragraph applies to settled property held on trusts under which during the life of a mentally disabled person [or of a person in receipt of an attendance allowance][1]; no interest in possession in the settled property subsists and which secure that any of the settled property which is applied during his life is applied only or mainly for his benefit.

(2) Where this paragraph applies to any settled property, then—

(*a*) if [the person mentioned in sub-paragraph (1) above][2] is the settlor, neither the making of the settlement nor any addition made by him to the settled property shall be a chargeable transfer; and
(*b*) a distribution payment made out of the settled property for the benefit of the mentally disabled person [or, as the case may be, for the care or maintenance of the person in receipt of the attendance allowance][3] shall not be a capital distribution.

(3) Sub-paragraphs (5) to (9) of paragraph 17 above shall apply where this paragraph applies to any settled property as if the references to that paragraph were references to this paragraph and references to that paragraph ceasing to apply to the settled property included references to the death of [the person mentioned in sub-paragraph (1) above][2].

(4) In this paragraph "mentally disabled person" means a person who by reason of mental disorder within the meaning of the Mental Health Act 1959 is incapable of administering his property or managing his affairs [and "attendance allowance" means an allowance under section 35 of the Social Security Act 1975 or the Social Security (Northern Ireland) Act 1975][4].

---

[1]Inserted by FA 1977, s 51 (1), (2), with effect from 29 July 1977.
[2]Substituted by FA 1977, s 51 (1), (3), with effect from 29 July 1977.
[3]Inserted by FA 1977, s 51 (1), (4), with effect from 29 July 1977.
[4]Added by FA 1977, s 51 (1), (5), with effect from 29 July 1977.

[*Trustees' annuities etc.*

19A. Where under the terms of a settlement a person is entitled by way of remuneration for his services as a trustee to an interest in possession in property comprised in the settlement, then, except to the extent that the interest represents more than a reasonable amount of remuneration—

(*a*) the interest shall be left out of account in determining for the purposes of this Part of this Act the value of his estate immediately before his death, and
(*b*) tax shall not be charged under paragraph 4 (2) above when the interest comes to an end.][1]

---

[1]Inserted by FA 1976, s 109

Charitable trusts

20. Paragraphs 6 to 12 above do not apply in relation to settled property held for charitable purposes only.

Compensation funds

21. Paragraphs 6 to 12 above do not apply in relation to any fund which is maintained or administered by a representative association of persons carrying on a trade or profession and the only or main objects of which are compensation for or relief of losses or hardship incurred or likely to be incurred through the default or alleged default of persons carrying on the trade or profession or of their agents or servants.

Administration period

22.—(1) Where a person would have been entitled to any interest in possession in the whole or part of the residue of the estate of a deceased person had the administration of that estate been completed, the same consequences shall follow under this Schedule as if he had become entitled to an interest in possession in the unadministered estate and in the property (if any) representing ascertained residue, or in a corresponding part of it, on the date as from which the whole or part of the income of the residue would have been attributable to his interest had the residue been ascertained immediately after the death of the deceased person.

(2) In this paragraph—

(*a*) "unadministered estate" means all the property for the time being held by personal representatives as such, excluding property devolving on them otherwise than as assets for the payment of debts and excluding property that is the subject of a specific disposition, and making due allowance for outstanding charges on residue and for any adjustments between capital and income remaining to be made in due course of administration;
(*b*) "ascertained residue" means property which, having ceased to be held by the personal representatives as such, is held as part of the residue;
(*c*) "charges on residue", and "specific disposition" have the same meanings as in Part XV of the Taxes Act and the reference to the completion of the administration of an estate shall be construed as if contained in that Part.

[*Survivorship clauses*

22A.—(1) Where under the terms of a will or otherwise property is held for any person on condition that he survives another for a specified period of not more than six months, this Part of this Act shall apply as if the disposition taking effect at the end of the period or, if he does not survive until then, on his death (including any such disposition which has effect by operation of law or is a separate disposition of the income from the property) had had effect from the beginning of the period.

(2) Sub-paragraph (1) above does not affect the application of this Part of this Act in relation to any distribution or application of property occurring before the dispositions there mentioned take effect.

(3) Where the death with which the period mentioned in sub-paragraph (1) above begins occurred before 13th March 1975, that sub-paragraph shall not apply in relation to any property if or to the extent that, by virtue of section 121 (1) (*c*) of the Finance Act 1972 (relief for property given to a surviving spouse), the value attributable to it was disregarded for the purposes of estate duty chargeable on that death.][1]

[1]Inserted by FA 1976, s 105 (1) and deemed always to have had.

Sales and mortgages of reversionary interests

23.—(1) Where a reversionary interest in settled property was before 27th March 1974 sold or mortgaged for full consideration in money or money's worth, no greater amount of tax shall be payable by the purchaser or mortgagee when the interest falls into possession than the amounts of estate duty that would have been payable by him if none of the provisions of this Act had been passed; and any tax which, by virtue of this paragraph, is not payable by the mortgagee but which is payable by the mortgagor shall rank as a charge subsequent to that of the mortgagee.

(2) Where the interest was sold or mortgaged to a close company in relation to which the person entitled to the interest was a participator, sub-paragraph (1) above applies only to the extent that other persons had rights and interests in the company.

(3) Sub-paragraph (2) shall be construed as if contained in section 39 of this Act.

Close companies

24.—(1) In relation to a person who is a participator in his capacity as trustee of a settlement, subsection (1) of section 39 of this Act shall not apply; and

(*a*) the references in that section to subsection (1) thereof shall have effect as references to sub-paragraph (2) below; and

(*b*) in relation to tax chargeable by virtue of sub-paragraph (2) below, [subsections (4) and (8D)][1] of that section shall apply with the necessary modifications.

(2) Where any part of the value transferred by a close company is apportioned to a trustee of a settlement under section 39 of this Act, then—

(*a*) if an interest in possession subsists in the settled property a part of that interest corresponding to such part of the property as is of a value equal to the part so apportioned less the amount specified in sub-paragraph (3) below shall be treated for the purposes of this Schedule as having come to an end on the making of the transfer; and

(*b*) if no interest in possession subsists in the settled property, the part of the value so apportioned less the amount specified in sub-paragraph (3) below shall be treated as a capital distribution made at the time of the transfer;

and where an interest in possession subsists in part only of the settled property paragraphs (*a*) and (*b*) above shall apply with the necessary adjustments of the values and amounts referred to therein.

(3) The amount referred to in paragraphs (*a*) and (*b*) of sub-paragraph (2) above is the amount (if any) by which the value of the settled property is more than it would be apart from the company's transfer, leaving out of account the value of any rights or interests in the company.

(4) Nothing in subsection (4) of section 39 of this Act shall be taken to prevent a transfer of value assumed to have been made by a person falling under sub-section (3) (*a*) of that section from being a relevant transfer as defined in paragraph 11 above.

(5) Where a close company is entitled to an interest in possession in settled property the persons who are participators in relation to the company shall be treated for the purposes of this Schedule as being the persons beneficially entitled to that interest according to their respective rights and interests in the company.

(6) In this paragraph expressions defined in section 39 of this Act have the same meanings as in that section.

[1]Substituted by FA 1976, s 118 (5) in relation to transfers of value or dispositions made after 15 April 1976.

CAPITAL GAINS TAX

The principal sections are ss25 and 42 of the FA 1965, s42 dealing only with foreign trusts. Other important provisions are s22(5) of the Act which deals with the definition of a settlement for capital gains tax purposes, and Sched 7, para 13, which deals with interests under trusts.

The FA 1978 (not reproduced here) contains the reliefs and exemptions for small gains (Sched 7, paras 5 and 6) and the 'held over' relief for the disposal of business assets (Sched 8, para 2).

FINANCE ACT 1965

PART III

22. Disposal of Assets and Computation of Gain

(5) In relation to assets held by a person as nominee for another person, or as trustee for another person absolutely entitled as against the trustee, or for any person who would be so entitled but for being an infant or other person under disability (or for two or more persons who are or would be jointly so entitled), this Part of this Act shall apply as if the property were vested in, and the acts of the nominee or trustee in relation to the assets were the acts of the person or persons for whom he is the nominee or trustee (acquisitions from or disposals to him by that person or persons being disregarded accordingly).

25. Settled property

(1) In relation to settled property, the trustees of the settlement shall for the purposes of this Part of this Act be treated as being a single and continuing body of persons (distinct from the persons who may from time to time be the trustees), and that body shall be treated as being resident and ordinarily resident in the United Kingdom unless the general administration of the trusts is ordinarily carried on outside the United Kingdom and the trustees or a majority of them for the time being are not resident or not ordinarily resident in the United Kingdom:

Provided that a person carrying on a business which consists of or includes the management of trusts, and acting as trustees of a trust in the course of that business, shall be treated in relation to that trust as not resident in the United Kingdom if the whole of the settled property conists of or derives from property provided by a person not at the time (or, in the case of a trust arising under a testamentary disposition or on an intestacy or partial intestacy, at his death) domiciled, resident or ordinarily resident in the United Kingdom [and if in such a case the trustees or a majority of them are or are treated in relation to that trust as not resident in the United Kingdom the general administration of the trust shall be treated as ordinarily carried on outside the United Kingdom][2].

(2) A gift in settlement, whether revocable or irrevocable, is a disposal of the entire property thereby becoming settled property notwithstanding that the donor has some interest as a beneficiary under the settlement and notwithstanding that he is a trustee, or the sole trustee, of the settlement.

(3) On the occasion when a person becomes absolutely entitled to any settled property as against the trustee all the assets forming part of the settled property to which he becomes so entitled shall be deemed to have been disposed of by the trustee, and immediately reacquired by him in his capacity as a trustee within section 22 (5) of this Act, for a consideration equal to their market value.

(4) On the termination at any time after 6th April 1965 of a life interest in possession in all or any part of settled property, [the whole or a corresponding part of each of the assets forming part of the settled property and not ceasing at that time to be settled property][3], shall be deemed for the purposes of this Part of this Act at that time to be disposed of and immediately reacquired by the trustee for a consideration equal to [the whole or a corresponding part of the market value of the asset].[3]

[For the purposes of this subsection a life interest which is a right to part of the income of settled property shall be treated as a life interest in a corresponding part of the settled property.][2]

(4A)—[8]

(5), (5A)—[4].

(6)—[5].

(7)—[6].

(8) On the occasion when a person becomes absolutely entitled to any settled property as against the trustee, any allowable loss which has accrued to the trustee in respect of propety which is, or is represented by, the property to which that person so becomes entitled (including any allowable loss carried forward to the year of assessment in which that occasion falls), being a loss which cannot be deducted from chargeable gains accruing to the trustee in that year, but before that occasion, shall be treated as if it were an allowable loss accruing at that time to the person becoming so entitled, instead of to the trustee.

(9) If tax assessed on the trustees, or any one trustee, of a settlement in respect of a chargeable gain accruing to the trustees is not paid within six months from the date when it becomes payable by the trustees or trustee, and before or after the expiration of that period of six months the asset in respect of which the chargeable gain accrued, or any part of the proceeds of sale of that asset, is transferred by the trustees to a person who as against the trustees is absolutely entitled to it, that person may at any time within two years from the time when the tax became payable be assessed and charged (in the name of the trustees) to an amount of capital gains tax not exceeding tax chargeable on an amount equal to the amount of the chargeable gain and, where part only of the asset or of the proceeds was transferred, not exceeding a proportionate part of that amount.

(10) In this section "life interest" in relation to a settlement—

(*a*) includes a right under the settlement to the income of, or the use or occupation of, settled property [for the life of a person other than the person entitled to the right, or for lives][1],
(*b*) does not include any right which is contingent on the exercise of the discretion of the trustee or the discretion of some other person, and
(*c*) does not include an annuity, notwithstanding that the annuity is payable out of or charged on settled property or the income of settled property

(11) For the purposes of this section, where part of the property comprised in a settlement is vested in one trustee or set of trustees and part in another (and in particular where settled land within the meaning of the Settled Land Act 1925 is vested in the tenant for life and investments representing capital money are vested in the trustees of the settlement), they shall be treated as together constituting and, in so far as they act separately, as acting on behalf of a single body of trustees.

(12) If there is a life interest in a part of the settled property and, where that is a life interest in income, there is no right of recourse to, or to the income of, the remainder of the settled property, the part of the settled property in which the life interest subsists shall while it subsists be treated for the purposes of subsections (4),[7] of this section as being settled property under a separate settlement.

(13)[5].

---

[1]Words substituted by FA 1966, Sched 10, para 1 (3).

[2]Words at the end of the proviso to subs (1) added by FA 1969, Sched 19, para 8 (3), (4).

[3]Words substituted, and the last paragraph inserted, by FA 1971, Sched 12, paras 7, 8, in relation to a death occurring, or an interest terminating, after 30 March 1971.

[4]Repealed by FA 1971, Sched 14, Pt V, in relation to a death occurring after 30 March 1971.

[5]Repealed by FA 1971, Sched 14, Pt V.

[6]Repealed by FA 1971, s 59 (2) and Sched 14, Pt V.

[7]Repealed by virtue of FA 1971, Sched 14, Pt V.

[8]Subs (4A) (which was inserted by FA 1971, Sched 12, para 12, in relation to a death occurring after 30 March 1971) repealed by FA 1975, Sched 13, Pt I, in relation to a death occurring on or after 13 March 1975.

---

42. Non-resident trust

(1) This section applies as respects chargeable gains accruing to the trustees of a settlement if the trustees are not resident and not ordinarily resident in the United Kingdom, and if the settlor, or one of the settlors, is domiciled and either resident or ordinarily resident in the United Kingdom, or was domiciled and either resident or ordinarily resident in the United Kingdom when he made his settlement.

(2) Any beneficiary under the settlement who is domiciled and either resident or ordinarily resident in the United Kingdom during any year of assessment shall be treated for the purposes of this Part of this Act as if an apportioned part of the amount, if any, on which the trustees would have been chargeable to capital gains tax under section 20 (4) of this Act, if domiciled and either resident or ordinarily resident in the United Kingdom in that year of assessment, had been chargeable gains accruing to the beneficiary in that year of assessment; and for the purposes of this section any such amount shall be apportioned in such manner as is just and reasonable between persons having interests in the settled property, whether the interest be a life interest or an interest in reversion, and so that the chargeable gain is apportioned, as near as may be, according to the respective values of those interests, disregarding in the case of a defeasible interest the possibility of defeasance.

(3) For the purposes of this section—

(*a*) if in any of the three years ending with that in which the chargeable gain accrues a person has received a payment or payments out of the income of the settled property made in exercise of a discretion he shall be regarded, in relation to that chargeable gain, as having an interest in the settled property of a value equal to that of an annuity of a yearly amount equal to one-third of the total of the payments so received by him in the said three years, and

(*b*) if a person receives at any time after the chargeable gain accrues a capital payment made out of the settled property in exercise of a discretion, being a payment which represents the chargeable gain in whole or part then, except so far as any part of the gain has been attributed under this section to some other person who is domiciled and resident or ordinarily resident in the United Kingdom, that person shall, if domiciled and resident or ordinarily resident in the United Kingdom, be treated as if the chargeable gain, or as the case may be the part of the chargeable gain represented by the capital payment, had accrued to him at the time when he received the capital payment.

(4) In the case of a settlement made before 6th April 1965—

(*a*) subsection (2) of this section shall not apply to a beneficiary whose interest is solely in the income of the settled property, and who cannot, by means of the exercise of any power of appointment or power of revocation or otherwise, obtain for himself, whether with or without the consent of any other person, any part of the capital represented by the settled property, and

(*b*) payment of capital gains tax chargeable on a gain apportioned to a beneficiary in respect of an interest in reversion in any part of the capital represented by the settled property may be postponed until that person becomes absolutely entitled to that part of the settled property, or disposes of the whole or any part of his interest, unless he can, by any means described in paragraph (*a*) above, obtain for himself any of it at any earlier time,

and for the purposes of this subsection, property added to a settlement after the settlement is made shall be regarded as property under a separate settlement made at the time when the property is so added.

(5) In any case in which the amount of any capital gains tax payable by a beneficiary under a settlement in accordance with the provisions of this section is paid by the trustees of the settlement such amount shall not for the purposes of taxation be regarded as a payment to such beneficiary.

(6) This section shall not apply in relation to a loss accruing to the trustees of the settlement.

(7) In this section "settlement" and "settlor" have [the meanings given by section 454 (3) of the Income and Corporation Taxes Act 1970][1] and "settled property" shall be construed accordingly.

SCHEDULE 7

Paragraph 13 Debts and Interests in Settled Property

(1) No chargeable gain shall accrue on the disposal of an interest created by or arising under a settlement (including, in particular, an annuity or life interest, and the reversion to an annuity or life interest) by the person for whose benefit the interest was created by the terms of the settlement or by any other person except one who acquired, or derives his title from one who acquired, the interest for a consideration in money or money's worth, other than consideration consisting of another interest under the settlement.

(2) Subject to sub-paragraph (1) of this paragraph, where a person who has acquired an interest in settled property (including in particular the reversion to an annuity or life interest) becomes, as the holder of that interest, absolutely entitled as against the trustee to any settled property, he shall be treated as disposing of the interest in consideration of obtaining that settled property (but without prejudice to any gain accruing to the trustee on the disposal of that property deemed be effected by him under section 25 (3) of this Act).

DEVELOPMENT LAND TAX

The principal provisions are s28, 29 and 30 of the DLTA 1976.

28. Property held on a bare trust

(1) At any time when an interest in land is held on trust—

(*a*) for a person absolutely entitled as against the trustees, or
(*b*) for a person who would be so entitled but for being an infant or other person under disability,

this Act shall apply as if the interest were vested in, and the acts of the trustees in relation to the interest were the acts of, the person referred to in paragraph (*a*) or paragraph (*b*) above (acquisitions from or disposals to the trustees by that person being disregarded accordingly).

(2) If at any time—

(*a*) an interest in land becomes held on trust as mentioned in subsection (1) above, and
(*b*) immediately before it came to be so held the interest in land was settled property,

then, for the purpose of this Act, the interest shall at that time be deemed to have been disposed of by the trustees as settled property and immediately reacquired by them as an interest held on trust as mentioned in subsection (1) above; and for those purposes the disposal and reacquisition by the trustees shall be assumed to have been made for no consideration (so that section 10 above applies).

(3) For the purposes of this section, an interest in land is held on trust for a person absolutely entitled as against the trustees where that person has the exclusive right, subject only to satisfying any outstanding charge, lieu or other right of the trustees to resort to the interest for payment of duty, taxes, costs or other outgoings, to direct how that inerest shall be dealt with.

In the application of this subsection to Scotland, the words from "subject" to "outgoings" shall be omitted.

(4) Any reference in this section to a person absolutely entitled as against the trustees or to a person who would be so entitled but for being an infant or other person under disability includes a reference to two or more persons who are or would be so entitled jointly; and in this subsection the expression "entitled jointly",—

(*a*) except in the application of this subsection to Scotland, means entitled as joint tenants, tenants in common or as coparceners; and
(*b*) in the application of this subsection to Scotland, means entitled as joint owners or owners in common.

(5) In this Act—

(*a*) an interest in land which is held on trust as mentioned in subsection (1) above is referred to as being held on a bare trust; and
(*b*) in relation to an interest so held, any reference to the beneficiary or the beneficiaries is a reference to the person or persons for whom the interest is for the time being so held; and
(*c*) in relation to an interest in land (in Northern Ireland) which is settled land for the purposes of the Settled Land Act 1882 by virtue of section 59 of that Act (infant absolutely entitled to be as tenant for life) any reference to the trustees includes a reference to any person entitled to exercise the powers of a tenant for life by virtue of an order under section 60 of that Act (powers of infant tenant for life to be exercised by trustees of the settlement or persons ordered by the court).

(6) If, immediately before a project of material development is begun on any land, an interest in that land which is held on a bare trust is a major interest, the interest of a beneficiary in that land is not a major interest for the purposes of this Act.

29. Disposal of beneficial interests under bare trusts

(1) The provisions of this section apply if, where an interest in land is held on a bare trust, the beneficiary or one of the beneficiaries disposes of his interest in the property held on trust.

(2) For the purposes of this Act, in any case where the interest in land held on a bare trust forms part only of the property which is held on trust as mentioned in subsection (1) of section 28 above,—

(*a*) the interest of a beneficiary in that property shall be treated as an interest in land only; and
(*b*) any consideration for the disposal of that interest shall be treated as reduced to such amounts as appears to the Board or, on an appeal, to the Commissioners concerned to be just and reasonable, having regard to the value of that portion of the trust property which consists of property other than an interest in land.

(3) In the following provisions of this section the interest in land held on a bare trust is referred to as "the legal interest" and the interest disposed of as mentioned in subsection (1) above is referred to as "the beneficial interest".

(4) Without prejudice to section 28 (1) above, if there is only one beneficiary for whom the legal interest is held on trust, then, for the purposes of this Act,—

(*a*) the disposal by the beneficiary of the beneficial interest shall be treated as a corresponding disposal by him of the legal interest; and
(*b*) the interest acquired by the person to whom the disposal is made shall be treated as legal interest or, in the case of a part disposal, as the interest which would be the granted interest in relation to that corresponding disposal of the legal interest.

(5) Subject to subsections (6) and (7) below, where there is more than one beneficiary for whom the legal interest is held on trust then, in the application of the provisions of this Act in relation to the disposal of the beneficial interest,—

(*a*) the cost of acquisition, the market value and the current use value of the beneficial interest at any time, and
(*b*) the expenditure on improvements or on relevant improvements, in relation to the beneficial interest,

shall (before taking account, where the disposal is a part disposal, of any provision of this Act applicable to part disposals) be taken to be the relevant fraction of the amounts which would be that cost, value or expenditure in relation to a disposal (not being a part disposal) of the legal interest occurring at the same time as the disposal of the beneficial interest.

(6) The relevant fraction referred to in subsection (5) above is that of which the numerator is the market value of the beneficial interest at the time of the disposal and the denominator is the aggregate of that market value and the market value at that time of the interest or interests of the other beneficiaries; and subsection (5) above shall not have effect to determine the market value of any interest for the purposes of this subsection.

(7) In any case where the beneficiary acquired the whole or any part of the beneficial interest from a person who was a beneficiary at the time of the acquisiton, subsection (5) above shall not apply to determine the cost of acquisition of the beneficial interest or, as the case may be, the part so acquired; and for the purposes of this subsection any reference to a part of the beneficial interest is a reference to an interest which, in relation to the disposal of the beneficial interest, is such a part for the purposes of Part I of Schedule 2 to this Act.

(8) In any case where—

(*a*) there is a disposal of an interest in land held on a bare trust (in this subsection referred to as "the relevant interest"), and
(*b*) one of the beneficiaries acquired the whole or part of his interest in the land as mentioned in subsection (7) above, and
(*c*) that beneficiary makes a claim in that behalf,

then, for the purposes of determining the amount of realised development value which accrues on the disposal and the liability of each beneficiary in respect of that realised development value, the disposal (but not the acquisition) of the relevant interest shall be treated as a contemporaneous disposal of each of the beneficial interests and the consideration for the disposal shall be apportioned accordingly; but nothing in this subsection shall affect the operation of section 12 of this Act in relation to the disposal.

30. Settled property

(1) Subject to subsection (8) below, in this Act "settled property" means an interest in land which is held on trust for any person or persons in such circumstances that it is not held on a bare trust, and, subject to the following provisions of this section, in relation to settled property, the trustees of the settlement shall for the purposes of this Act be treated as a single and continuing body of persons, distinct from the persons who may from time to time be the trustees.

(2) In relation to settled property which, in England and Wales or in Northern Ireland, is settled land,—

(*a*) the tenant for life or statutory owner for the time being, and
(*b*) the trustees of the settlement (so far as not comprised in the expression "statutory owner"),

shall be treated for the purposes of this Act as constituting and, in so far as they act separately, as acting on behalf of a single and continuing body of trustees distinct from the persons of whom that body is for the time being composed.

(8) In subsection (2) above—

(*a*) in its application in England and Wales, "settled land" and other expressions to which a meaning is assigned by the Settled Land Act 1925 have the same meaning as in that Act; and
(*b*) in its application in Northern Ireland "settled land" and other expressions to which a meaning is assigned by the Settled Land Act 1882 have the same meaning as in that Act and references to a statutory owner shall be construed as references to any person having under section 58 of that Act the powers of a tenant for life.

(4) For the purposes of this Act, in any case where land in Northern Ireland is settled land within the meaning of the Settled Land Act 1882 but, under the settlement, any estate or interest in land stands for the time being limited to any persons by way of succession without the interposition of any trust (and, accordingly, without being settled property, within the meaning of this Act),—

(*a*) the tenant for life and the trustees of the settlement (if any) shall nevertheless be treated as constituting a single and continuing body of trustees; and
(*b*) any disposal of an interest in land which is effect in exercise of the powers conferred by that Act or of any such additional or larger powers as are referred to in section 57 of that Act or which is otherwise effected by the tenant for life and could have been effected in exercise of those powers shall be treated as a disposal of settled property by that body of trustees; and
(*c*) any realised development value which accrues on such a disposal shall be treated as accruing to that body of trustees;

and expressions used in this subsection to which a meaning is assigned by section 2 of the Settled Land Act 1882 have the same meaning in this subsection as in that Act.

(5) In the case of a settlement falling within subsection (4) above, the settled

property which is treated as being the subject of a disposal falling within paragraph (*b*) of that subsection shall be deemed for the purposes of this Act to be the legal estate in fee simple or other interest which, by virtue of the settlement referred to in that subsection, stands limited to any persons by way of succession.

(6) Subject to subsection (7) below, if and so long as any land in Northern Ireland remains settled land, within the meaning of the Settled Land Act 1882, and subject to a settlement falling within subsection (4) above, neither—

(*a*) the beneficial interest of the tenant for life referred to in subsection (4) above, nor
(*b*) any estate or interest in reversion or remainder which is comprised in the subject of the settlement for the purposes of that Act, nor
(*c*) any other interest arising under the settlement,

shall be treated for the purposes of this Act as an interest in land.

(7) In any case where, by virtue of the disposal to him of one or more interests falling within subsection (6) above and not by virtue of a disposal effected under the powers conferred by the Settled Land Act 1882, a person becomes entitled on an interest in land (in this subsection referred to as "the relevant interest") which, in his hands, is not settled and, within the meaning of the Settled Land Act 1882, then,—

(*a*) if he acquired the relevant interest or any part of it otherwise than for value, he shall be treated for the purposes of this Act as having so acquired the interest or part from the settlor by the disposal of an interest in land; and
(*b*) if he acquired the whole or any part of the relevant interest for value, the disposal by virtue of which he acquired that interest or part shall be treated for the purposes of this Act as the disposal of an interest in land, notwithstanding that, immediately before the disposal, the interest disposed of was an interest falling within subsection (6) above;

and for the purposes of this subsection a part of the relevant interest means an interest which, disregarding the provisions of subsection (6) above, would be such a part for the purposes of the application of Part I of Schedule 2 to this Act to a disposal of the relevant interest.

(8) In this Act "settled property" does not include an interest in land held by a person as trustee or assignee in bankruptcy or under a deed of arrangement or, as respects Scotland, as trustee on a sequestrated estate or as a judicial factor who has powers or duties corresponding to those possessed by such a trustee, or as trustee for behoof of creditors.

(9) Subsections (2) and (3) above do not extend to Scotland and subsections (4) to (7) above extend to Northern Ireland only.

STAMP DUTY

The main provisions dealing with trusts are contained in the Stamp Act 1891, Sched 1 (some of the main headings are set out below and these incorporate subsequent amendments to the schedule) and the F (1909–10) A 1910, s74.

STAMP ACT 1891—FIRST SCHEDULE

Appointment of a new trustee, and **appointment** in execution of a power of any property, or of any use, share or interest in any property, by any instrument not being a will (see s62).	50*p*
Conveyance or **transfer** on sale, or any property (see ss54–61).	(ad valorem)
Conveyance *or* **transfer** of any kind not hereinbefore described (see s62).	50*p*
Declaration of any use or trust of or concerning any property by any writing, not being a will, or an instrument chargeable with ad valorem duty as a [unit trust instrument] (words in square brackets added by FA 1962, s30(1))	50*p*
[**Policy of life insurance**	
Where the amount insured exceeds £50 but does not exceed £1,000	5*p* for every £100 or part of £100 of the amount insured
Where the amount insured exceeds £1,000	50*p* for every £1000 or part of £1000 of the amount insured
(see s91, 98, and 100)] (this heading in square brackets was substituted by FA 1970, s32 and Sched 7, para 17(1)).	
Surrender of any kind whatsoever not chargeable with duty as a conveyance on sale (this original heading was amended so as to read as above by FA 1949, s52(10) and Sched 11, Pt V and FA 1971, s69 and Sched 14 Pt VI).	50*p*

FINANCE (1909–10) ACT 1910
PART V—STAMPS

74. Stamp duty on gifts inter vivos

(1) Any conveyance or transfer operating as a voluntary disposition *inter vivos* shall be chargeable with the like stamp duty as if it were a conveyance or transfer on sale, with the substitution in each case of the value of the property conveyed or transferred for the amount or value of the consideration for the sale:

Provided that this section shall not apply to a conveyance or transfer operating as a voluntary disposition of property to a body of persons incorporated by a special Act, if that body is by its Act precluded from dividing any profit among its members and the property conveyed is to be held for the purposes of an open space or for the purposes of its preservation for the benefit of the nation.

(2) Notwithstanding anything in section twelve of the principal Act, the Commissioners may be required to express their opinion under that section on any conveyance or transfer operating as a voluntary disposition *inter vivos*, and no such conveyance or transfer shall be deemed to be duly stamped unless the Commissioners have expressed their opinion thereon in accordance with that section.

(3) Subsection (2) of section fifteen of the principal Act, which enables certain instruments to be stamped after execution, shall apply to conveyances or transfers operating as voluntary dispositions *inter vivos* as if those conveyances or transfers were specified in the first column of the table in paragraph (*d*) of that subsection, and the grantor or transferor were specified in the second column of that table.

(4)[3].

(5) Any conveyance or transfer (not being a disposition made in favour of a purchaser or incumbrancer or other person in good faith and for valuable consideration) shall, for the purposes of this section, be deemed to be a conveyance or transfer operating as a voluntary disposition *inter vivos*, and (except where marriage is the consideration) the consideration for any conveyance or transfer shall not for this purpose be deemed to be valuable consideration where the Commissioners are of opinion that by reason of the inadequacy of the sum paid as consideration or other circumstances the conveyance or transfer confers a substantial benefit on the person to whom the property is conveyed or transferred.

(6) [The foregoing provisions of this section shall not apply to][1] A conveyance

or transfer made for nominal consideration for the purpose of securing the repayment of an advance or loan or made for effectuating the appointment of a new trustee or the retirment of a trustee, whether the trust is expressed or implied, or under which no beneficial interest passes in the property conveyed or transferred, or made to a beneficiary by a trustee or other person in a fiduciary capacity under any trust, whether expressed or implied, or a disentailing assurance not limiting any new estate other than an estate in fee simple in the person disentailing the property . . .[2] and this subsection shall have effect notwithstanding that the circumstances exempting the conveyance or transfer from charge under this section are not set forth in the conveyance or transfer.

[1]Words added by FA 1942, s 44.
[2]Words repealed by FA 1942 s 44.
[3]Repealed by FA 1962, s 34(4), (7) and Sched 11, Pt V.

INDEX